Soul On Fire

"Whoever is near me is near to the Fire,
Whoever is far from me is far from the Kingdom of God."

The Gospel according to Thomas.

Soul On Fire
A Guide To The Journey Beyond Anxiety

S.C. Papenfus PhD

PRISM · UNITY

Published in Great Britain in 1998 by
PRISM PRESS
The Thatched Cottage
Partway Lane
Hazelbury Bryan
Sturminster Newton
Dorset DT10 2DP

Published in Australia by
UNITY PRESS
P.O. Box 532
Woollahra
NSW 2025

Distributed in the USA by
ASSOCIATED PUBLISHERS GROUP
Nashville
TN 37218

ISBN   1 85327 103 9

Printed by The Guernsey Press Company Ltd,
The Channel Islands

Contents

Section One

Beyond Us, Ourselves

1   The Fire/Tao/Logos of Our Being

"All things are an equal exchange for Fire and Fire for all things."

Heraclitus

I have written this book in the hope that it might help us all to realise our essential being and personal destiny. It is written out of love for the deep process that we share. In this process, we are one. Come, experience yourself in Heraclitus's Fire. You are, indeed, meant to be a 'soul on Fire'.

You are the Fire. I am the Fire. It doesn't belong to me any more than it does to you. Nor does it belong to you more than it belongs to anyone else. No-one above us, no-one below us. We are in the fire together. We are what the Fire is.

Don't ask God for the fire; He has given it to you, already. You are His Fire. And He is yours. The Fire is outside you and it is inside you.

There is no need to envy anyone else's Fire. You are only envying yourself. You are your neighbour's Fire.

Exclude your neighbour from the Fire and you exclude yourself. Protect your neighbour from the Fire and you cease to feel it yourself. It's madness, I hear you say. Yes, it is.

Madness is purification by Fire. Know yourself to be the Fire or it will burn you up. Become the Fire through training of the self and all life as you know it will be transformed.

3

And all that you are will be fulfilled by this transformation.

WHAT IS THE FIRE?

The Fire is a healing, transforming experience. It is the power of universal love that mediates between our awareness and our being. Becoming consciously one with our Fire means making a quantum leap in self-understanding, enabling us to relate ancient mystical knowledge to a free, loving and creative way of being in the world.

THE WAY AHEAD

I have tried to organise these writings in such a way that they are able to function as a complete guide to mastering anxiety. In the training that I invite you to undertake, it is my belief that you will be able to enter a direct experience of your Fire - a direct experience of the essential depth and aliveness of your being. This is where we discover who we really are, who we can be and what makes it all possible. Complete liberation from the grip of extreme states necessarily includes discovery of the Fire that fuels our creative freedom and transforms our life in the world.

If you are not suffering from anxiety, you can still benefit from using this book to discover how the process of growing beyond this state illustrates the potential inherent in our Fire - the Tao or Logos of our being - to *force* us into extreme states that can successfully be overcome only through entering the depth of our being. This is where we realise the fullness of our creative potential. Creative freedom, in the service of universal love, *is* our calling and our destiny. In one way or another, it claims us and beckons to us.

4

Through discovering, in depth, 'the being that I *am*', we come to ourselves with new self-understanding. The conscious awareness 'under' which we 'stand' is renewed. A new kind of knowledge enables us to live as we always felt, deep down, we could. The Fire is our inherent, God-given potential - the Tao or Logos of our being - coming to know itself in us.

VITAL QUESTIONS

When the Fire of our being comes to know itself in us, we know who we really are - in a universal, cosmic sense. We are filled with an all-pervading sense of peace and a deep recognition of our essential unity with the whole of life. This realisation enables us to answer, for ourselves, the following questions:

- On what does our creative freedom depend?
- How is it possible for us to lose our creative freedom?
- How can we recover our creative freedom?
- What is the relationship between creative freedom and the depth of our being?
- What is the price of creative freedom?
- How can we pay this price?
- What will it cost us if we refuse to pay it?

These are vital existential questions. The whole quality of our life depends on the answers that we give to them. In another sense, however, the questions themselves seem to be transcended when we realise our Fire, experiencing it as the integrating essence of all being! Nonetheless, we come to recognise that we exist not only in a universal, cosmic sense, but also in a personal, historical sense. The Fire transcends the historical-personal stream of our becoming, but we do not. We live not only in a universal cosmic realm of being, but also in a personal historical

5

realm.

This double thread of being brings us to a way of truly answering the vital existential questions that we need to ask. It also enables us truly to live out the answers that we give to them. To live out the meaning and the fullness of the Fire, in our historical-personal existence, becomes both the aim and the fulfilment of our life.

THEMATIC EXPLORATIONS

As you read the following text, I invite you to relate what you already understand about yourself to explorations that point to and participate in the full potential of your being.

The Fire invites us to know it and to serve it with our whole self. In fact, it invites us to know it and serve it *AS* our whole self. If we accept this invitation we become the Fire of universal love, thereby renewing the inner life of our mind and transforming our way of being in the world.[1]

Working with the Fire relates our personal-historical existence to universal dimensions of being. These, in turn, act as a touchstone for our evaluation of the quality of the energy and information that is flowing in our various perceptual channels. By relating to this energy and information as "my way of personally embodying the universal Fire", we come to know and understand ourselves in the mutually interpenetrating realms of our existence.

In this chapter certain 'themes' are used to facilitate the kind of understanding that we need in order fully to know and live from the Fire of universal love, discovered within.[2] In our exploration we look not only at the nature of our everyday thinking, feeling, deciding and doing, but also at the maze of our unaware condition. Both of these processes, taken together, place us in a unique relationship to the Fire.

THE POWER OF AWARENESS

It is important to understand that the universal Fire/Tao/Logos of our being itself remains unconditioned by the experiences that we undergo, in our personal life.

Through our experience of the unconditioned Fire that is able to know itself in us, we become able to understand the deep meaning of what moves within our consciousness. The unconditioned Fire of our being remains constant, even as we, ourselves, change.

Here is another consideration. Whenever we alter the focus of our awareness, the content of our consciousness changes. We can, if we choose, relate these changes to one another. In this way, we become able to take account of what is occurring within us, and to remain mysteriously aware of the continuity of what we call 'ourselves', even in the process of change.

We are both the Fire of our being and the awareness that it gives us to evaluate, in depth, transformations taking place in our lives.

If we regard 'information' as that which tells us where we are in relation to where we wish to go - or how we are in relation to how we wish to be - then we are able to see that what renews and transforms our self-understanding are differences that make a difference to us, because they let us know where we are in relation to where we intend to go, or how we are in relation to how we intend to be.[3]

Our awareness enables us to appreciate both 'what is happening' in our personal-historical existence and 'what is possible'. It enables us to use our memory and imagination to compare and contrast similarities and differences, to understand what is leading to what and to act in the light of what we understand.[4]

Our awareness thus enables us not only to see what is happening, but also to see how we see it. It enables us to explore our perspective and to experiment with alternative ways of looking at things. Thus our awareness enables us not only to see what we see and how we see it, but it also enables us to alter our way of seeing, our way of responding and our way of living. All in all, our awareness empowers us to govern our way of being in the world.[5] When we discover how to use our awareness to transform our way of being in the world, we realise the self-transforming power of inherent creative freedom.

EXPLORING OUR CREATIVE POTENTIAL

To the extent that we use our conscious understanding to engage in cycles of action and reflection, we are able to see what is leading to what and to become aware, also, of what we might prefer, instead.[6] This, in turn, raises the question of what we can do in order for the fullness of our creative potential to realise itself in us.[7]

We can illustrate the self-governing process of our becoming by drawing a circle, representing cycles of reflection and action, some of whose effects we selectively focus upon us as they feed information into our consciousness, so enabling us to change and/or refine our future actions and reflections.

As self-governing beings, we are able to evaluate the quality of our life not only by observing cycles of information and energy that constitute our primary awareness but also by relating these to secondary processes taking place in us - processes of which we are not immediately aware. It is through this expanded (yet still selective) change in the focus of our awareness that we become able to evaluate the mutually interdependent self and circumstances that we create, sustain and/or transform, by the way we think, feel and act.

We can learn to go beyond the edges of a 'merely practical' focus of awareness and intent, thus entering into new dimensions of creative freedom. We can represent this process by drawing two arrows entering and leaving the cycle of actions and reflections that constitute our primary awareness. These two arrows represent our ability to explore aspects of life that lie outside the narrow band of our merely practical, end-gaining intentions. We may even choose to focus our awareness on the self-governing processes that are present in our body, just as they are present in the whole of Nature. This, in turn, enables us to relate the dynamic Fire that sustains all life to the intentions that we are pursuing, in our particular circumstances.

THE LIVING GROUND OF OUR BEING

It is in letting go of our limited end-gaining intentions that we become able to enter into what the mystics call the 'Tao' or 'Logos' or 'Fire' of our being. In essence, this means that we become able to participate in a mysteriously self-balancing 'totality of being' that not only keeps us in balance with ourselves, but also keeps the whole realm of nature in balance with itself. This living Ground of all existence can be thought of as sustaining each and every being in its integral relationship to the whole.

The self-balancing Tao/Logos/Fire of our being is not only the dynamic Ground of the whole realm of nature, but it also has special significance for those aspects of nature that are able to become consciously self-reflective of their own existence, namely beings like ourselves. The special significance of our 'Fire' for what we call our 'personal life' lies in the fact that we can use our Fire-centred awareness both to maintain our inner

9

balance and to promote our creative freedom. By becoming aware of how the universal Fire functions in us, we can, in fact, learn from It what It requires of us, so that we can purposefully and powerfully embody It and serve It.

This kind of understanding becomes especially helpful to us when we lose our sense of balance and need to restore it. By learning to selectively focus our attention upon processes taking place in us, outside of our conscious intentions, we learn to centre ourselves within the self-balancing power of the Tao/Logos/Fire that sustains us even as it promotes our creative freedom in the service of universal love.

Fire-centring practices enable us to evaluate the quality of the self and circumstances that we are creating. When the consequences of our particular way of thinking and acting feed back into our Fire-centred awareness we become able to see, in great depth and extent, the difference between what is, what is possible and what is desirable. In all of this, we discover that our capacity for centring our conscious awareness in non-purposive mind-body attunement is what enables us to realise a standard against which to evaluate alternative possibilities of purposive thinking, doing and becoming.

As we let go of our purposive intending, we deepen our awareness of essential processes taking place within us. These are processes that we do not intend, and yet we depend upon them as a fish depends upon the water in which it swims. These processes point to and participate in the self-balancing essence of 'Brahman' - the 'Tao', the 'Logos', the 'Fire' of our being - that, through mind-body attunement and meditation, we discover to be non-different to our 'atman' - our 'self', our 'soul'.

Whereas the self-reflective awareness that we have of our own existence constitutes each one of us *as* a 'self', a 'person', a 'psyche', a 'soul', it is through deepening our awareness, in particular ways, that we come to appreciate the nature of that larger, deeper process that is able to become aware of itself in us. Such is the psyche that is able to reflect on its own Logos and identify with it. Such is our 'soul on Fire'!

We can represent our psyche as a circle whose selective focus (enabling us to act and reflect) creates a boundary - an interface, an edge - to our awareness. This is our primary awareness. It either separates off the sense that we have of our own existence from the deeper ground of our being or it relates us to that deeper ground. It all depends on the focus of our awareness.

It is the self-reflective awareness that we have of ourselves, as we pursue our aims and intentions, that creates the boundary which, in turn, contains us. The boundary that we create may well limit our self-reflective awareness to the merely practical, end-gaining pursuit of self-limiting goals. On the other hand, we can learn to use our conscious intent to enter into an awareness of the self-governing depth of our being. In this way, we transform the nature of the boundary that previously contained us. Over time, we become able to transform our life in the world.

IDENTITY, SEPARATION AND RELATION

Whatever we do, the boundary created by the selective focus of our awareness separates out primary from secondary information processes. Primary processes are those that, at any one time, carry information within our immediate conscious awareness. Secondary processes, by contrast, are those that are further away from our immediate conscious awareness. We generally identify ourselves with the content of our primary awareness, but we may well be a whole lot more and other than we consciously know ourselves to be. We are also the Tao, the Fire, the Logos of our being and the potential that it

11

holds out for our personal growth and development.

We are able to enter the Tao/Logos of our being, losing ourselves in it, yet also finding ourselves in it. The boundary created by our primary awareness can be so let go that we discover ourselves to be an integral part of what lies beyond it. Later, we become able to use this experience to relate ourselves to our Fire, even as the I that says 'I' of itself is able to relate to all that it is, in the life that it is living.

LOSING AND REGAINING OUR CREATIVE FREEDOM

We recognise the Logos - the Tao, the Fire - as That which serves to maintain all being in a state of integral balance. It can also be thought of as That which enables us to integrate our life in an aware and freely creative, value-realising way.

And yet we can lose our creative freedom.

When this happens, we lose our ability to retain the kind of perspective on our own existence that enables us to unify our life and to live within the unity that we create.

And yet we can not cease to be self-reflectively aware of how we are in our own existence. Therefore we are bound to suffer when we lose our way, for we cannot return to a state of unawareness.

In learning to engage in a practice that is able to integrate our personal perspective, we become able to return to self-governing balance, even when such balance seems to be lost. With the reintegration of our perspective, we come to see that a life which is truly free and creative is mediated by meaning and ordered by value, reflected upon in the essential depth of our being.

Looking back, we can therefore see how it was that our loss of creative freedom involved losing touch with the essential self-balancing depth of our being. As a result, we lost our capacity to discern what was ultimately of value and what was not.

On further reflection, we found that we were bound to conclude that a life which is truly meaningful and value-realising rides on beliefs, expectations, attitudes and aims that co-ordinate our actions and reflections with one another, at a deep level of self-sustaining inner balance.

To recover from extreme states of imbalance, we need to let go of the kind of anxious projecting and reacting that undermines the intrinsic order of the Tao in us.[8] We need to let go of security traps, unhealthy relationship traps, power traps and all forms of emotion-backed demands that things turn out exactly as we want them to . . . or else!

By engaging in a practice that allows the Tao freely to return us to a state of inner balance, we become able to explore and overcome the self-conflict, divisions and obstacles that previously prevented us from thinking, feeling and acting of one accord. This can only happen if we enter into a value-realising communion with the depth of our being.

MYTHICAL REPRESENTATIONS

The process of overcoming doubts, fears, inner contending and all manner of inner division is mirrored in Greek mythology by the story of Theseus, who is placed in a labyrinth and must either find his way out or be devoured by the Minotaur. The labyrinth is an image of our self-division; the Minotaur, the beast of our anxiety-based reactive bondage. Unless we learn to stop reacting to what we fear might happen to us, in emotionally driven ways - ways that negate our inner balance - we will not be able to regain our creative freedom. What we need, therefore, is a way to take responsibility for what we are doing so that we can break the vicious cycle that maintains the extreme state in which we find ourselves.

Theseus is able to find his way out of the labyrinth with the aid of Ariadne's thread. This is a thread of awareness and memory. It enables him to escape the destruction and death that would otherwise be his fate.

And so it is also with us. If we learn to use our understanding and awareness to follow what is leading to what in us - and where it is leading us - we have a good chance of being able to escape from the trap of our unaware conditioning. But our awareness itself first needs to be sufficiently accepting, stable and open to allow us to monitor what keeps us the way that we are, without the monitoring process itself emotionally overwhelming our awareness. Monitor, Minotaur! Through learning to stay attuned to our self-governing essence - the Tao or Logos or Fire of our being - we discover a freedom to know and do what liberates us from reactive bondage. In this way, we become able to re-enter the God-given realm of our creative freedom.

LOGOCENTRIC AWARENESS

Learning to attune our awareness to the self-integrating power of the Logos can be likened to the Logos becoming conscious of itself in us. In much the same way, St Paul was able to say, "It is no longer I who live, but Christ who lives in me."[9] In other words, he found that his whole personality had become re-organised, in such a way that its centre of gravity had shifted from an 'I', with which he no longer identified himself, to a self-integrating depth of being that enabled him to transform his life in a universally meaningful and value-realising way.

As with St Paul, so with ourselves. In one way or another we are all ultimately governed by the Logos.

Either we freely and purposefully use our awareness to realise integral balance and value-realising direction, or we find ourselves driven to seek a way to overcome the resulting pressures of psychological imbalance, illness or fate.

Whenever a particular way of life takes root in us - a way of life that governs our being outside the process that maintains the integral balance of nature in us - we necessarily undergo certain patterned experiences. These patterned experiences, properly appreciated, serve to return us to a self-integrating alignment with the Tao or Logos of our being. Arnold Mindell formulated this process in terms of a general principle that he calls the 'Awareness Principle'. This he states as follows: "The processes that we perceive, our focus, channel changes, edges, problems and illnesses are organised in such a way as to make us aware, as quickly as possible, how our secondary process conflicts with our primary one."[10]

The terms 'primary process' and 'secondary process', as Mindell uses them, refer, as I have previously explained, to information-bearing events that are, respectively, closer to our conscious awareness and further away from it. The Awareness Principle points to an inherent organisation that governs our experiences in such a way that we become aware 'as soon as possible' of conflicts that exist between our secondary and primary processes. This inherent organising principle is what we have already identified as the self-balancing Tao or Logos or Fire of our being.

The reason why our 'primary processes' are closer to our conscious awareness is because we use the information that they contain to consciously and purposefully realise our aims. If we say that 'information' is what tells us where we are in relation to where we are going, then it becomes clear that the reason we are less aware of information contained in our so-called 'secondary processes' is because these processes either do not give us information relevant to our aims, or because they operate in us in a way that confirms the value of our primary processes and facilitates the realising of our conscious aims.

Secondary processes - uncontrolled, unintended - usually take place in us outside of the framework established by the primary processes that we use to pursue our intentions. Normally, we find that we can afford to ignore secondary processes. This applies, for example, to the way that we breathe, the way our heart beats or the way that we hold ourselves or move. Ordinarily, we may not even think of attending to these processes. It is only when what we intend ultimately interferes with them that they fail to sustain us in our aims. We become aware of this, of course, almost immediately, or, as Mindell puts it, 'as soon as possible'.

If we say that it is the self-integrating power of the Tao or Logos or Fire of our being that ultimately grounds the organisation of our experiences, we can say also that it is the process inherent in this power that we need somehow to know and serve, when we seek to unify our life and to live within the unity that we create. St Paul identified the process that enabled him to reconcile all the contradictions present in his life with the person of Christ. In the life and teaching of Jesus Christ and in the self-reflective awareness that he had of his own existence, St Paul felt that he had discovered the supreme saving knowledge that had been hidden from humankind since the beginning of time. Thus he was fit to declare that it was Christ himself - his person, his life and his teaching - that had become the saving power that integrated his conscious being in the world. Through his own experience of this power he saw fit to declare also that this was the saving power that was meant to redeem the entire human race.

In much the same way, we find St John, in his Gospel, referring to Christ as 'the Logos' (usually translated as 'the Word'). He, too, saw in Jesus Christ the embodiment of that self-integrating order of being that is able to return everything to the meaning and balance that it was somehow always meant to have.

ARCHETYPES OF THE LOGOS

In personalising the Logos or Tao or Brahman, through viewing it as exemplified in or embodied by a particular person - Jesus Christ, Gautama Buddha or Krishna, say - this enables us to identify ourselves with the person, the life and the teaching of this individual and, in this way, to enter the Logos or Tao or Brahman that enables us to create for ourselves the kind of life to which this identification delivers us.[11]

Following Carl Jung, we may refer to all such personal embodiments of the self-integrating essence of our being as 'archetypes'. Likewise, we may use this term to refer to personal types that exemplify a certain kind of deviation from the Logos or Tao. If we adopt this way of thinking, we can use the term 'archetype' to refer to all symbolic embodiments of exemplary processes that enable us to awaken to the meaning of conflicts that exist between our primary and secondary processes.

ATTUNEMENT TO THE TAO

Every way of life that governs our being must necessarily thread itself through the Tao also. If we appreciate what is happening and act according to our insights, we are able to become individuated, saved, enlightened, liberated, Self-realised. If we fail to appreciate what is happening, this failure is bound to exert a toll upon our physical and mental state. "If you bring forth what is within you, what you bring forth will save you," says the Gospel of Thomas, "If you do not bring forth what is within you, what you do not bring forth will destroy

17

you."(12)

A mind that seeks attunement with the Tao - the Logos, the Fire - of its origin cannot at the same time seek to compete with, rival or replace this self-integrating source of our being. "We cannot be like God without God" is how Thomas Merton put it.(13) The myth of Oedipus provides us with an archetype of the rivalling, competing, replacing tendency, where Oedipus unwittingly kills his father and sexually violates his mother. He thus becomes a rival of the very source and substance of his own being, or, to put it another way, he seeks, through his own ignorance and false consciousness to take possession of the self-integrating source and substance of his being. But this source and substance is not his to possess, dominate and control. It is his. But it is not his to control and manipulate. He can only seek to know it and serve it. It works freely for him, yet he does not know this.

The Biblical account of the Fall of Adam and Eve likewise represents a tendency, archetypically present in all of us, to seek to determine what is good and what is evil, outside of the created balance that is already inherently present in the whole of nature. According to the story, God told Adam and Eve that it was good for them to taste and eat the fruit of every tree in the Garden of Eden. All, except for one tree. It was also right for them to use their creative freedom to name every creature in the garden and hence to know every creature by the name that they had given to it. What was forbidden to them however, was to eat the fruit of the tree of knowledge of good and evil. Eating this fruit meant abrogating the right to decide for themselves what was good and what was evil, outside of the self-integrating realm of nature itself. By eating the fruit of the forbidden tree, Adam and Even cut themselves off from an integral awareness of the goodness contained in the natural balance of things. Knowledge of this realm is what we are meant to realise and experience, so realising our creative potential. On the other hand, eating the fruit of the forbidden tree leads us to a false consciousness of our being in the world. Such false consciousness is necessarily full of self-conflict and inner divisiveness. To regain our inner peace and integrity we need to return to the inherent Logos of being. By ceasing to identify ourselves with our false consciousness - that is, to die to our egocentric ego - we become instead spiritually transformed in the self-integrating order of the Logos. We become what Don Juan would call "luminous beings", no longer indulging our historically determined 'personality', formed by our unaware conditioning.[14]

THE DARK SIDE OF GOD

Emergence of what Jung calls the "Shadow" represents the development, in consciousness, of a symbolic representation of the imbalance that afflicts us. At best, the Shadow serves to make us aware of what will return us to a self-integrating way of life. The Shadow thus represents to us what the mystics call "the dark side of God", an *awareness* of the inner divisions and imbalance present within us. Awakening to such an awareness serves to return us to a state of wholeness, a 'Logocentric' awareness, a purposeful self-integrating sense of the Fire of our being.

A BEGINNER'S MIND

To be able to enter into a process of spiritual rebirth, we need somehow to open ourselves to an unconditional acceptance of the way we are - a choiceless awareness of what is happening to us (and in us) - and, at the same time, to place our trust in a process that is able to liberate us from the way we are. Shunryu Suzuki refers to such a state as "having a beginner's mind".[15] It not only enables us to re-enter the self-sustaining balance of our essential nature, but it also generates in us the kind of discernment of what is happening in the present moment that transforms our life. In short, we discover our capacity for creative freedom and what we create transforms us.

Through what is called his "great renunciation" the Buddha vowed to cease striving for any other goal than to consciously realise the essence of his own being. This was, however, only the first stage of his great renunciation. The second stage involved his renouncing his enjoyment of the unending bliss of his enlightenment, so that he might lead others out of the blind suffering of their illusions into the same realisation that he had attained.

Whatever practice we employ to realise the essence of our being, this practice needs to attune us to processes that lead us to experience our self-integrating essence in some or other exemplary form.

"I live now, not with my own life, but with the life of Christ who lives in me", is how St Paul expressed his own experience of salvation.[16] He had discovered an awareness of his own depth that enabled him to integrate his life in a completely fulfilling self-integrating way.

None of us can return to what we might imagine to be 'the unreflective consciousness of an animal' without becoming monstrous in a way that animals are not. The monster, the Minotaur! We cannot return to a state of unawareness and still remain a human being, a person. Hence, anyone who advises us to try to 'forget about the past' and 'just live for the future' must be viewed as giving us very bad advice indeed. We carry the past with us and we need to use both our memories and our present awareness to enable us to live better. Why else would we have a memory? In fact, we need to re-experience our past in a different way. We need to feel our Fire in it, if we are not to be burnt up by our memories of what happened to us and by our felt need to protect ourselves from being hurt again. Only by doing so can we learn to avoid repeating the past and continuing to be both hurt by and divided against our creative Fire.

Through achieving a new awareness of what led to what - and what is now leading to what - in us and around us - we become able to choose how to think and act in a more valuable, life-enhancing way.[17]

The loving, open awareness that we can acquire of our own existence not only gives us soul, but actually sets our soul on Fire. In a mysterious way, the inexpressible source and substance of all being discovers itself in us. On the other hand, when the self-reflective awareness of our 'I' seeks to block awareness of its own feelings - and the memories associated with these feelings - then, all manner of self-division and inner contending results. We become incapable of thinking, feeling and acting of one accord and our sense of wholeness and creative freedom disappears. [18] This state of affairs makes it imperative for us to re-enter the wholeness of our being, so that we can live out this wholeness in free and whole relationships, in a free and whole community, all of which if they do not exist in our experience, nonetheless pre-exist in the Fire of our being - the Fire of all being.[19]

THE SOURCE OF OUR CREATIVE FREEDOM

"That which is one is one, that which is not one is also one", say the Hindu mystics. Whatever is subjective and voluntary in us is built upon inherent self-integrating processes that take place in us, of their own accord. We do not need to intend them to be so. Our body ordinarily functions according to processes that maintain its essential balance and equilibrium. It is through our reliance on this balance and equilibrium that we become able to present certain possibilities to ourselves, to evaluate which we prefer and to decide what we are prepared to do and, if necessary, to suffer, in order to realise them. Such thinking, imagining, comparing, contrasting, evaluating, choosing and acting all contribute to the process of unifying our life in a wholehearted, value-realising way. What comes from the Source, returns to the Source. Our undivided inner unity is a unity that serves universal love, the Fire that upholds and integrates all being.

As we have seen, our body not only functions in accordance with inherently self-balancing processes but it also functions according to the way we think. If, therefore, our experiences are such that we find ourselves thinking in ways that lead us both to anticipate and to resist 'bad' experiences (that we would not like to repeat) we become aware of a conflict between what we would not like to happen and what we anticipate might well happen again. Thus, unless we are able to discern what to do, instead of repeating past mistakes, we are likely to do the very thing that we fear, the very thing that we hope we will not do again. We are likely to repeat the very past mistakes that we wish to avoid. This is equivalent to our going round and round in the labyrinth of our unaware conditioning and negative inner rehearsal.

Whatever we imagine, we inwardly rehearse. Our body prepares us to meet whatever we are thinking about. On the other hand, if we choose not to think about the situation that we wish to avoid, we will have no alternative but to repeat, willy-nilly, what we did last time.

Because fear is one of our strongest emotions, whatever we fear strongly causes us to feel convinced that we will not be able to cope. This is called 'being bluffed by our feelings'. We *can* learn to do better, but only if we cease fearing our fear itself. We need to accept our fear, examine what we do and imaginally construct an alternative way of dealing with the situation that we fear. Only variety can replace variety. We can only replace one process with another. We cannot replace a cycle of reactive bondage with nothing. We can only replace it with a cycle of creative freedom.

Resisting what we do not wish to happen only serves to intensify our fears and perpetuate the cycle of fear and worry that we have unwittingly created. To be able to escape from this cycle, we need Ariadne's thread.

To learn to accept our feelings means learning to re-enter the source of our creative freedom. By so doing, we become better able to focus our observations on what is leading to what in us. This, in turn, means learning to refine our understanding and our awareness, so that we can break out of the vicious cycle in which we have become trapped. To accept our feelings is to cease resisting them. This means, in some way, 'dying' to our fearful, experience-resisting 'I'. It means ceasing to identify ourselves with resistance to our fears and forebodings. Such acceptance is total. It is unconditional. When we learn how to thread an unconditionally accepting, non-resisting awareness through memories of what has led to what, we are able to develop a value-realising appreciation of what we ultimately want, and, by so doing, we come to know how to think and act in the service of the Fire of our being. Such is the unconscious goal of all life - and the conscious goal of the mystical genius!

"That which is one is one, that which is not one is also one." As we enter deeper levels of non-purposive awareness, we become more and more conscious of how it is that all processes occurring within us and around us derive from and serve the essential source of our creative freedom, the essential unity that life is.

ACHIEVING A SELF-INTEGRATING PERSPECTIVE

Because we actually maintain our self-divisive perspective through the way that we talk to ourselves, we need to learn how to replace all misguided self-talk with practices that serve, as Castaneda's don Juan put it, "to erase our personal history" - by which he meant erasing the effects of past conditioning on present experience. This means, in effect, learning how to think, feel and act in ways that do not involve, as don Juan puts it, "explaining everything to ourselves, while at the same time wanting to maintain a freshness and a newness in everything we do."[20] These two processes are mutually exclusive. We cannot, at one and the same time, retain a 'beginner's mind' and also maintain hope in an established (virtually closed) perspective - especially one that causes us to worry about what fits in and what does not.

Don Juan's advice to Carlos Castaneda about erasing his personal history is aimed at enabling him to cease being trapped in a closed and defensive way of viewing his life, and himself in it. At one time he suggests that Castaneda act as if what he was doing were his last act on earth. If we act this way, it has the effect of bringing the continuity of our personal history to an end. By "letting death become our advisor" we sense the ultimate importance of what we are doing, in the present moment.

Whatever practice we employ to experience life with 'a beginner's mind', this practice needs to enable us to stop worrying and fretting. "You indulge", don Juan warns Castaneda, advising him that such indulging in his doubts and fears does not in any way make him into a sensitive man, as he might imagine. He suggests to him that this is only "a pretence". It would be far better for him "to accept in humbleness what he is", as befits a "spiritual warrior".[21]

In the practice of looking straight ahead of him as he walks, not focusing his eyes on any particular object, but rather taking in the entire 180 degrees that are available to his unfocused vision, Castaneda would be able so to fill his conscious awareness in an unfocused way that no room would be left for him to pre-occupy himself with one-to-one relationships between elements of visual focus and their mental and emotional associations. This would, in turn, serve to enable him to stop talking to himself and thus to enter a deep silence within himself, where he could appreciate, with untrammeled awareness, the unconditioned inner peace and inherent wholeness of the essential ground of his being.[22]

Whatever feature of experience it is that we habitually focus upon, this feature tends to pre-occupy our awareness in such a way as to cause all else in our life to turn around it - and so determine our life's meaning. Hence, for example, if all else turns around our self-pity, or, conversely, our felt need to stay in control of situations, then such a feature, in turn, serves to establish the overall perspective that determines the way we live. It also serves to establish who we are, as people among people.

To study our perspective - and the predominating feature that it turns upon - raises the level of our awareness to one in which we perceive our own perspective. In this way, we become aware also of the manner in which this feature influences our expectations and attitudes in ways that we do not consciously intend, and now, being aware of this process, would certainly prefer to avoid.

In one of Castaneda's books he discusses the awareness-expanding task of studying our weaknesses. He asks la Gorda, a fellow apprentice, how it would be possible to "stalk one's weaknesses". She replies, "The same way that you stalk prey. You figure out all your

25

routines until you know all the doings of your weaknesses and then you come upon them and pick them up, like rabbits in a cage."[23]

A FIRE-CENTRED JOURNEY

Appreciating the processes of our awareness enables us to embark on a liberating journey of training and transformation in the Fire of our being. Some particular sections in this book are set out to enable people who are trapped in cycles of reactive bondage to escape from such cycles and to enter, instead, into cycles of creative freedom. These sections focus upon how certain features can dominate our perspective in vicious self-feeding cycles, making it difficult for us to escape the inner division and emotional drivenness that results. Getting out of the maze in which such cycles place us may seem like a daunting task, but the way to escape is systematically put forward in manageable steps and stags. It *can* be done. *You* can do it. Following the practices as set out will enable you to master the art of self-discovery in depth of being and creative becoming.

2   *Being, Knowing, Loving the Fire*

"The Kingdom of God is inside you and it is outside you. When you come to know yourselves, you will then be known and you will realise that you are sons of the living Father. But if you do not know yourselves, then you will dwell in poverty and it is you who are that poverty."

The Gospel according to Thomas [1]

We are value-realising beings capable of living in the world with a high degree of self-awareness, creative freedom and responsibility. Becoming creatively free involves both inner work and outer work. It involves the cultivation of a new kind of awareness, one that enables us not only to act as we intend but also to intend what is worthwhile.

In the process of cultivating this awareness it is important that we develop a spiritual relationship with reality as we know it, a relationship that represents our way of embodying the Fire/Tao/Logos that integrates and balances all being in its essence.[2] We can really only answer the vital questions that life puts to us out of the depth of our being, where we make contact with the universal Fire of our being, discovering there the true touchstone and compass of our existence. If we are not to find ourselves trapped and bound by anxious projections and reactions, unawarely conditioned into us, we need to make access to a deeper self-integrating order, discovered within. It is to this order that we need to trust ourselves, actually abandoning ourselves to it, allowing it to guide us and transform our life in the world.

THE PROMISE AND THE PERILS OF THE PROCESS

At best, our understanding of ourselves is the fruit of a slow yet steady accumulation of small insights - insights into issues and choices, actions and outcomes - all of which are ultimately measured and evaluated against the self-integrating Fire, experienced in the depth of our being. This is where we come to know and experience our 'self' as the one who is attuned to the meaning and value of what really constitutes a worthwhile life.

As our actions transform existing situations, further insights are able to dawn upon us. Our awareness thereby achieves greater attunement to the deep core of value, discovered within. We become more skilled in taking action that accords with and confirms what the Fire requires of us. In this way, the Tao/Fire/Logos of our being comes to realise itself in our particular embodiment of it. In this way, too, our particular being-in-the-world becomes inclusive of all that is, in the essential order and vitality of universal being.

At worst, we despair of our ability to understand ourselves and our circumstances. We may even try to close ourselves off from the self-reflective awareness that brings us not so much to insight and understanding as to anxiety, pain and humiliation. We become increasingly less able to act in aware, creative ways and we become, instead, prey to increasingly more irrational and degrading fears and anxieties.

Whenever secondary processes - unintended, uncontrolled and seemingly uncontrollable - capture our full attention, despite what we intend, we can think of this as placing us in an 'extreme state', that is to say, in a state of extreme imbalance and instability. So long as we resist what seems to be happening to us, in this state, we remain unable to monitor and transform the self-feeding cycle that maintains our extreme imbalance and instability.

At best, in this worst of all possible states, asking ourselves the question "How can balance be restored when all sense of balance has been lost?" brings us to a point of radically reassessing how we are the way we are. Given that our assessment is correct, we become able to realise what is happening, what is possible, and what is desirable. And so, in the depths of our torment, we discover also the depth of our self-transforming creative Fire.

And what is possible? Not only me as I am, but also me as I could be. Not only the actual relationships that I have to myself and my circumstances, but also possible relationships that I could have. Not only the world as it is, but also the world as it could be.

Because we are able to use words and images - as well as other symbols such as music and rhythm - to relate to actual and possible reality, feelings generated in our body enable us to line up 'what is' and 'what is possible' with what really is desirable.

In all of this, we use our body as an instrument to feel and evaluate what is good and what is less good, what is desirable and what is undesirable, what is of value and what is not.

SOLIDARITY

Whenever we enter into the spiritual struggle of other human beings, we develop empathy with them. They, in turn, identify with us and they experience our taking upon ourselves some of the weight of their anxiety, pain and humiliation. This, in turn, enables them to think about their difficulties and dilemmas, in a more expansive and integrated way. And so, we become an integral part of their personal growth and development.

Our ability to control the state that we are in is a measure of our ability somehow to abandon ourselves to the flow of powerful emotions in us - and yet not to be overwhelmed by them. We need spiritual training to let go of our felt need to try either to control or to get rid of such emotions, rather than finding a way to accept them and work with them.

A METACOMMUNICATOR

Developing an awareness of what is, what is possible and what we can do to realise what is ultimately desirable, is what Arnold Mindell calls "developing a metacommunicator".[3] A metacommunicator is what enables us to work with extreme states of consciousness, without our becoming trapped in them, finding ourselves unable to escape from them, becoming overwhelmed by them. This is equivalent to Theseus using Ariadne's thread to discover his way out of the Labyrinth. It can also be compared with "Maxwell's demon", a concept developed in quantum physics in which an aware humanlike being, by virtue of its awareness and understanding, is able to regulate what is happening in an otherwise closed system, thereby saving the system as a whole from destroying itself.

Self-discovery beyond anxiety, beyond depression and beyond chemical dependence are all possible, given our ability to develop and use a 'metacommunicator' of our own.

When psychological problems and difficulties take over our thinking, feeling and reacting, outside the range of our voluntary control, our ability to work with our body's involuntary processes becomes critical. Anxiety states cannot be overcome in any other way. This is why it is so important for us to be able to give one another the kind of nurturing support that can enable those of us trapped in extreme emotional states to learn how to work with them, rather than simply remaining trapped in them.

All in all, we need to learn how to accept the state in which we find ourselves, so that we can see and understand, in a clear and helpful way, what we are already aware of but only in an obscure and unhelpful way.

Working with our Fire involves staying with, monitoring and facilitating dynamic wholeness in the flow of all our processes. To do this, we need to learn how to accept and trust the totality of what is occurring in us, even when we find ourselves trapped in extreme states. This acceptance and trust constitute a *Basic Attitude* that allows the Fire of our being to realise itself in us, so returning us to a state of clear awareness and self-governing freedom.

"How, after all, shall we understand madness and how shall we distinguish it from sanity, except that we place ourselves outside both one and the other, which is for us impossible?" asked the Spanish philosopher, Miguel de Unamuno.[4] Arnold Mindell, as if in answer to this question, indicates that to engage in process work with extreme states requires that we be both outside the extreme state itself and outside its polar opposite. Through exploring how our extreme state is maintained, we use our second attention to become sufficiently free to accept the way that we are, so that we can learn to transform the way that we are.

Using our freedom to accept what is beyond our voluntary control enables us to use our second attention to regain control at a deeper level of trust and awareness.[5]

When we realise how our metacommunicative awareness enables us to resolve conflicts between our primary and secondary processes, we gain insight into how it is possible for us to regain control of our thoughts and actions, even in extreme states. As a result, we no longer fear being 'labelled', in superficial and personally disempowering ways. Such labelling becomes irrelevant to us. Instead, we find ourselves in possession of a 'saving awareness' that enables us to overcome the vicious cycle of being overwhelmed and dominated by secondary processes that seem to take possession of our whole being - even as we struggle against this process - and this possession of our being always seems to be destructive and personally devastating.

A SINGLE PROCESS

If we try to control extreme states, outside of the organic unity to which they belong, they tend to work against us. For example, if we try to control the anxiety that accompanies all inner contending and/or inner conflict, without using our awareness to explore the underlying bases of such anxiety, we miss the mark. If, on the other hand, we use our second attention to experience, express and explore the nature of the conflict within us, this allows our awareness to flow back and forth between our primary and secondary processes, until the two extremes of our inner conflict find a way to integrate at a new level, so delivering us to a new unity of being. It is with the meaning and value that we discover in this new unity that we are now able to identify ourselves.

As we work with our own lack of inner unity - or, for that matter, with the inner disunity of others - we need to do so with the conviction that the basic unity of the Tao/Logos/Fire underlying our existence - and hence our potential awareness also - is our best guide. Such a basic attitude, once we are able to adopt it and go along with it, is able to become our 'metacommunicator' - 'Ariadne's thread', 'Maxwell's Demon' - saving us from egocentric confusion and reactive bondage. Such a basic attitude enables the conflict between our primary and secondary processes to enter our primary process, in a valuable and helpful way. This is how new integrated states of self-discovery are able to realise themselves in us.

The trapped, defensive, egocentric ego is largely unaware of the pattern of its own functioning. It does not appreciate its own perspective. This tends to make it defensive of itself. Instead of being able to let go, at some level, so that it can trust and observe the process in which it is caught, it clings to itself and seeks to defend itself against all odds.

The egocentric ego should not be condemned for the way it is. It should, rather, be encouraged to accept itself *as it is*, so that it can begin to look at and understand the pattern of its functioning. In this undertaking, it may well become aware of the fact that it *has* a perspective, thereby becoming aware also of the possibility of its realising an *alternative* perspective. With any luck, the egocentric ego might even become able to enter a second awareness of itself, thereby becoming able to let go of its self-limiting and uncreative way of being, in favour of an expansive, self-transforming open-ness to new possibilities.

In all of this, we come to look upon the inner disunity and conflict that take us into extreme states not simply as 'afflictions' from which we suffer, but rather as processes that are capable of evolving towards inner coherence and unity.[6] What blocks this evolution is usually our failure to accept the implicit order of our being, an order that is able to deliver us to a new kind of self-integrating balance. This, in turn, we recognise to be the very way of awareness and being that enables us to be compassionate, worthwhile human beings, in our own right. Our desire to disclose to others the secret of the Tao, the Logos, the Fire, the Brahman of our being becomes, for us, at this stage, an integral part of our life.

We are indeed souls on Fire!

REALISING OUR HUMAN POTENTIAL

Through consciously identifying the secondary processes taking place in us with the living Ground of our being, we become able, firstly, to identify our being as a whole with a living process that operates, by and large, outside of our conscious control, and thereafter to choose to work with this process in a more conscious way. This kind of identification and understanding take us beyond merely working to 'master' or 'overcome' extreme states. It takes us into a process of self-discovery, in which we find out who we really are and who we can be.

In later chapters, we focus upon the practice of Hatha Yoga and related bodyminding disciplines, upon the art of meditation, upon the discipline of journalling and upon the practice of focused speaking-and-listening. As we become more and more skilled in these practices, we enter into more and more fulfilling experiences of self-discovery in depth of being and creative freedom.

Who am I? Where do I come from? Where am I going?

Our Self is both actual and potential. Between 'what is' and 'what can be' our Fire builds a bridge that embodies the dynamic of our becoming in a way that is itself balanced and integrated. So long as we are able to observe and monitor the state that we are in, we can use our awareness to overcome our fear of extreme states and, instead, work with them to realise the Fire of our creative freedom.

All in all, we need to practice using our second attention to become aware of what is and what is possible, so that we can realise what is good for all of us to be and do.

Being able to accept, in some way, our body's 'extreme', 'out of control' states enables us to use our body's potential to integrate, harmonise and balance our actions and reflections in a value-realising way. We see what is worthwhile and what is not. Our new presence of mind enables us to use our imagination to scan a plenitude of possibilities, choose those that are desirable and, if they mutually support one another, plan to realise them in manageable steps and stages.

How beautiful it is, to be a soul on Fire!

EDGES

Primary and secondary processes are divided from one another by 'boundaries' or 'edges'. These usually prevent us from becoming aware of information that might reach us but does not.

An edge splits off information contained in primary processes from potential information contained in secondary processes. It splits off signals of which we are not aware from signals that we are primarily aware of.

Because an edge serves the function of enabling us to define ourselves in a consistent way - enabling us to think, feel and act within one and the same framework of value-realising intent - this enables us to discern where we are heading. If we consider the value of any goal to lie in the further goals that realising it enables us to pursue, we can see how it is that value orders our priorities and our intentions. In all, information processing that serves our conscious aims excludes what does not fit into the perspective that our intending creates.

Our edges enable us consistently to align ourselves with beliefs, values and aims that integrate our conscious intent. Together, these beliefs, values and aims point to and participate in a whole way of life with which we identify ourselves, even if such identification is, to a large extent, based on unconscious conditioning. Such unconscious conditioning may even add up to what R.D. Laing called "the obvious"[7] - a kind of blind awareness, based on our ability to fit into consensus reality, in an unreflective way.

Hence, we may say that edges protect our conscious awareness from signals whose meaning might otherwise threaten to destabilize our identity or interfere with our pursuit of chosen aims.

This is the function that probably *is* served by our edges, until we become able to envisage and experience, in a positive way, what it is like to pay attention to secondary signals, messages and modes of perception that currently lie beyond our capacity to embrace them and be embraced by them.

WORKING WITH FIRE

Certain kinds of Fire-centred work involve using our awareness to identify perceptual channels in which secondary signals are flowing and then to follow these signals, see what they mean, evaluate alternative ways of thinking, acting and intending, and commit ourselves to the value-realising intent that emerges. In all of this, the "I AM" of our being is recognised as existing both in the processes of our perception, in the value-realising intent that emerges and in our potential to commit ourselves to new forms of being in the world.

Information-bearing signals undergo a special kind of change when we observe them. Firstly, we become more deeply aware of what these signals are and what they mean. Secondly, we become able to re-evaluate our own intentions in terms of what we feel and understand.

When we come to an edge in our awareness, we recognise that our identity is being challenged by the meaning of some of the information that we are receiving. In Fire-centred work, we use our awareness, in different ways, to see how the information that we are receiving conflicts with and challenges the beliefs, values, expectations, attitudes and aims that serve to co-ordinate our self-reflective being in the world.

Here are some of the aims that can be pursued in Fire-centred work:

1. Mastering skills that enable us to stalk and control the state of our awareness and being.
2. Mastering skills that enable us to transform the state of our awareness, understanding and being.
3. Achieving a Fire-centred awareness of self and others.
4. Engaging in Fire-centred disciplines that promote our personal growth and development.
5. Improving the quality of our relationships with others.
6. Teaching the skills of Fire-centred awareness to others.
7. Developing deep democracy within ourselves and in the world around us.
8. Realising the Tao - the Logos, Brahman, God - as the ultimate subject of our being.
9. Promoting a Fire-centred revolution in world work and world consciousness.

STEP BY STEP

All so-called 'symptoms' of psychological and physical disturbance can be seen to constitute manifestations of the Fire/Tao/Logos of our being. Recognising this constitutes an important first step for anyone who wants to work with their symptoms in a Fire-centred way, thereby learning both to overcome their ego-centricity and to escape from their reactive bondage into a realm of creative freedom.

By using our awareness to bring our body into harmony with its inherent, self-balancing Fire and by accepting the way that it functions, when it seems to be trapped in what feel like 'extreme' reactions, we become able to regain our conscious equilibrium and actually regain control of the state we are in.

The inherent self-integrating balance of our body's own functioning, relative to our purposive being-in-the-world, translates itself into symbols and images that represent this relationship to us and enable us to work with it, independently of actual self-other, self-circumstance exchanges. In other words, the images that evolve create, in us, an 'inner life' or 'inner world'. This is the life and world of what Sogyal Rimpoche and Arnold Mindell call 'the dreambody'.[8,9]

The experience that we acquire through working with our dreambody is also an experience of what is called 'wu-wei' - effortless effort. Such work develops a deeply spiritual attitude in us, rooting our whole intent within the practice and the experience of wu-wei itself. This state is able to become, thereafter, a standard whereby all else may be judged and evaluated. The ground of our being - the Tao, Logos, Fire of our being - becomes, thus, the core of our identity, recognised as the very source and substance of our being-in-the-world.

I explore the process and the experience of meditation, as a way to realise the ground of our being, in *Meditation Training and Transformation*. I also explore the effects of meditation on our everyday life. Meditation, we discover, is an exemplary form of what the Taoists call wu-wei - effortless effort - and what don Juan Matus would call 'not doing'.

"There must be a renewal in the inner life of your mind," St Paul tells us.[10] Through the practice of meditation, we learn that the dreambody - our soul on Fire - has laws of its own. In all practices that aim at an integration of our psyche with its Logos - our soul with its Fire - that which lies beyond our limited primary awareness is able to enter only when we consciously let our dreambody follow its own processes and obey its own laws. When this happens, a renewing of our inner life takes place. In the practice of journalling, set out in *Journal Training and Transformation*, I show how we can use the tensions and tones of our body to liberate ourselves from cycles of reactive bondage and engage in a continuously liberating process of Fire-centred personal growth and development.

Controlling extreme reactions through the relaxation response is a good start, but insufficient to enable us to find fulfilment in that larger realm in which we "live and move and have our being".[11] Once we are able to free ourselves from our compulsive 'doing', we need to work, thereafter, with our 'not-doing', our 'being'. This involves becoming aware of our feelings and what they lead us to imagine, so long as we do not act them out but, instead, allow their energy to work through our conscious awareness in psychologically integrating ways.

Every time we let go of our 'doing' in favour of becoming aware of the processes of our 'being', we let go of differences and distinctions that belong to what Chuang Tzu called "the merely practical".[12,13] Thus, in meditation and in journalling, the ego becomes a willing servant of a more profound level of awareness. In this process, the ego is surrendered but it is not annihilated. Instead, the ego is transformed and it carries a new consciousness of self and circumstances into the realm of everyday possibilities. Religiously speaking, we may say that the ego 'dies' so that it may ' rise again' and live in a new form.

As in the discipline of life journalling, so also in the practice of speaking-and-listening. We learn to follow and observe the flow of our inner processes, until at last we arrive at a profound inner silence. Both of these practices lead us to a profound meditative awareness of our own being. I explore the theory and practice of speaking-and-listening in *Training and Transformation in the Speaking-and-Listening Process.*

Creative freedom evolves as we surrender our claims to an isolated independence and enter instead into a new kind of life, where everything is accepted as being mutually interdependent. The isolated defensive ego needs to repress its awareness of many things in order to maintain its limited and self-limiting view. And yet, like "a light shining in the darkness that cannot overwhelm it"[14] we come to realise that there is something else in us - the Tao, the Logos, the essential process of our being - that seeks us out in order to make us whole and free.

"Being your total self in the world is an important and difficult task", states Mindell.[15] The less consciously integrated our life, the more we experience its unconscious processes as external forces impinging upon us and disturbing us. The unconscious processes that belong to our larger Self - our Fire/Logos - move us towards the realisation of a certain kind of experience. This experience itself is balancing and harmonizing to our life. Not realising this, we may resist the experience towards which we are unconsciously moving, thus intensifying the very disturbances, bodily symptoms, compulsions, panic attacks, depression or increasing chemical dependence that we so badly want to escape. False solutions need to be abandoned so that we can learn, instead, how to embrace, embody and live out the Logos of love. I elaborate on this theme in the section entitled *The Anxiety Process and How to Master it.*

Letting go of our compulsive, impulsive or otherwise unskilled 'doing', to which our inner conflicts give rise, and engaging instead in a process that Mindell calls "amplification" and Weinberg[16] calls "magnification", enables our inner conflicts to reveal and heal themselves. We find that this process creates the necessary changes in attitude and outlook that 'save' us from our reactive bondage and 'deliver' us to creative freedom.

The goal of Yoga and related mind-body disciplines is the kind of balanced mind-body attunement, flow and functioning that results in 'effortless effort', the Buddhist wu-wei, which occurs when the spontaneous action of freely available energy lifts us to a sense of timelessness, a sense of 'the fullness of time' and a largesse of being. I cover all of this in *Bodymind Training and Transformation*.

The different practices, mentioned above, can be put into practice in any order you wish. Please feel free to engage in the practices set out in whatever section most appeals to you, regardless of the order in which I present them. On the other hand, if you find yourself suffering from anxiety, it may be best for you to follow the course of self-discovery that is systematically set out in this book, along with the specific criteria of attainment that apply to this course.

Section Two

The Courage to Be

3   *Stalking and Mastering the Ways of Anxiety*

*"The Self is the dearest of all things, and only through Self
is anything else dear."*

Upanishads

States of reactive bondage often trap us in highly
predictable patterns of flip-flop reactions. We are likely to
remain trapped in these patterns, so long as they remain
unconscious and unarticulated. The I AM, the Fire, the
Logos, the Tao of our being is, paradoxically, both the
course of our reactive bondage and the door to our
creative freedom.[1]

THE NATURE OF THE ANXIETY TRAP

People who suffer from anxiety states are more
concerned about the way they feel than any other
problem. Working with processes that constitute extreme
emotional states enables us to observe and understand
how we feel the way we do, rather than being
overwhelmed by our feelings.

Emotion is what sets us in motion. It moves us
into action. The extreme emotional state that constitutes
'the anxiety trap' results from our body preparing us to
fight or to run, even though there is nothing to run from
and nowhere to run to. It is the very thought of being
anxious and not being able to control the way we feel that
causes our emotions themselves to escalate out of control,

45

in a spiral of self-feeding panic. When we come to fear being trapped in this state, we bring it on, just by thinking about it. It is the thought of what will ultimately become of us, because we are so emotionally out of control, that fuels the state we are in, bringing us to the terrifying conclusion that we will never ever be able to control the way that we feel. And this is what further sensitises us to the thoughts and feelings of panic, resulting in our body becoming more and more tense and anxious - as it continues to prepare us, uselessly, to fight or to run. And so on and on and on . . .

ARIADNE'S THREAD

To escape from the trap of our anxiety and panic - rather than being 'consumed' by it - what we need is Ariadne's thread, a metacommunicator, a Maxwellian demon. Because we are both confused and bewildered by what is happening to us, discovering that we are in a labyrinth - one that has a certain definite design, from which we can escape, if we take the necessary steps - may be the first bit of relief that we experience. If we are, at least, sufficiently able to learn to appreciate the process, we can begin to control it.

We have nothing to lose but our fear of fear itself. Masihambe! Let's go for it.

SOLIDARITY

Others have been where we are now. They know the score. Realising that we are not alone in our struggle is a great help. Let us, at least, settle ourselves enough to pay attention to our metacommunicator. Panic we may, yet we are willing to pay this price for the sake of gaining our liberty. Maxwell's demon is entering the maze of our own body and mind! And yet, he is our surest ally. Let us follow him around, so that we can learn to control the process that is unconsciously in control of us. Until we consciously appreciate what is going on, we will not be able to understand what we can do - or cease from doing - to prevent our whole system from destroying itself.

OUR PSYCHE IN THE LOGOS

The actual physiological containment of our extreme, seemingly out of control state, exemplifies the inherent balance of the Fire - the Logos, the Tao, the course of nature - in our body and in our life. Following its manifestations reveal the set and limited nature of the 'fight or flight' response, giving us a process to observe, accept and work with.[2] Instead of trying merely to resist the process, as if it were somehow a threat to us, we can resign ourselves to monitor and modify aspects of the total system to which the fight or flight response belongs. In this way, we become able to defuse the strength of its demand that we 'either fight or run'! This, as we have already realised, is no solution at all. Since neither of these reactions is appropriate, we need to use our conscious awareness - our psyche, our very own little Maxwellian demon - to transform the system, of which we are a part, instead of allowing it to control and dominate us, in this demoralising and humiliating way.

And so we learn, first and foremost, that our psyche *can* work within its Logos. Our psyche arises from its Logos. It belongs to it. And it is actually *meant* to learn how to co-operate with it so that it can subtly embrace the way that the Logos functions in us. In this way, we learn also to control and enhance the way that we live in the world.

Soul enters Fire. Soul embraces Fire as its own source and ground. Soul and Fire, Psyche and Logos, achieve conscious union, vitally alive and together, in undivided creative freedom.

STUDYING THE DESIGN OF THE LABYRINTH

Learning to understand something of the structure and function of the so-called 'autonomic nervous system' is a great help. As its name implies, this network of nerve structures, connected to various organs and muscles, is considered to function more or less autonomously, that is to say, 'in its own right' or 'in its own name' - rather than in our name! It is presumed to function outside of our own conscious control or, to put it another way, outside of our conscious desires and intentions. Nonetheless, the presumed 'autonomy' of our autonomic nervous system can be shown to be - at least to some extent - responsive to the way that we think. Like the accelerator of a car, it controls the speed of our engine - our energy supply - even though it is not meant to play any part in deciding where we want to go or what we are going to do.

In one sense, then, we can say that our autonomic nervous system sustains the underlying energy level of our being-in-the-world. It responds to the way that we think and it prepares us to act upon what we decide to do. On the other hand, the strength of our feelings - our accelerator force - can take our thinking and reacting outside of our conscious control!

And yet . . . by becoming aware of what is happening and how it is happening, we can learn to adopt a *Basic Attitude* to our own feelings, thereby steadying our thinking to the degree that is necessary to 'take our foot off the accelerator', so to speak.[3]

The understanding and skills that I would like you to develop are aimed at giving you a capacity not only to master your anxiety state but also to enable you to help others do the same. This is why we are going to get to know, very well, the design of the maze that can so severely and unremittingly trap us and apparently torture us. As Alan Watts once put it, "To be human is precisely to have that extra circuit of consciousness which enables us to know that we know and thus to take an attitude towards all that we experience."(4)

For this to be possible, and for what we know to become a 'saving knowledge', we need to practise bringing the processes of our autonomic nervous system under our conscious control. And to do this, we need to practise what don Juan calls a 'not doing'. This requires that we enter, as soon as possible, into the practices of mind-body attunement, relaxation and meditation.

EXPLORING THE MAZE

In these practices - mind-body attunement, relaxation and meditation - we learn both to notice what enters our mind and also to let go of all those thoughts and feelings that draw the focus of our attention away from the self-regulating processes that are able to take place, in us, freely and spontaneously, of their own accord. In this way, we practise entering the Fire - the Tao, the Logos of our being - that which, of itself, is able to govern the state of our being. This we learn to do by letting go of our 'doing' and entering, instead, into an unconditioned state of 'not doing'.

The state that we enter, in our practice of relaxation and meditation, is one that is entirely unconditioned by previous experience. It is an inborn potential for high level self-integration, just waiting for us to enter it, experience it and be it. It also happens to be a highly satisfying state that establishes, in us and for us, a standard of unconditional self-acceptance.(5)

We need to know that this state is available to us and that it can be re-entered time and time again.(6)

Once we become adept at entering this state, we can, thereafter, use the 'letting go' that it requires of us, to let go of the thoughts and tensions that maintain our anxiety states. Through using our routine - our developing skill - for engaging in the so-called 'relaxation response', we can then use these skills to stay relaxed in 'imaginal' practice of entering and mastering situations that previously would have thrown us into a panic. And, after this, we can engage in 'actual' practice, step by step, enabling us to enter situations which we would previously have avoided, due to our fear of panicking.[7]

We become able to enter these situations, now, because we are able to *face* them the right way, *accept* the way that we feel, let go of all tension in our body, and *flow* through panic with sufficient presence of mind to cease fuelling our thoughts with anxious misgivings. We are also able to *let time pass,* as our anxiety leaves us, at its own natural pace. Such is the Fire-centred practice that enables us to master anxiety states.

By exploring the maze - the labyrinth that previously trapped us in our anxiety - we discover our way out. We learn how to govern the organisation of our energy - or, rather, we learn how to let the organisation of our energy govern itself. This involves more than simply learning to control the state that we are in. It may also involve our reviewing and changing many of the beliefs, expectations, attitudes and aims that previously prevented us from entering our Fire.

Because of what you discover about yourself and your potential, you find that you are able to change many false, limiting and destructive *beliefs* that you previously held about yourself and your world, exchanging them for more positive and constructive beliefs - ones that are confirmed by what you find yourself able to do - and the way in which you are able to do it.

You become able to change your *expectations,* especially those that make it possible for you to escape from the worry-tension-anxiety-worry cycle. Instead, you transform the expectations that formerly trapped you in this cycle, so that they come to be more in line with the

Fire/Tao/Logos-centred reality from which you now prefer to live.

You become able to change your *attitudes*, especially those tendencies to think and act in anxiety-fuelling ways, learning instead to think and act in a manner that is relaxed, aware and attuned to the universal essence of your own self-realised nature.

Finally, you become able to change your *aims* - particularly the aim of seeking to 'get rid of' or 'escape from' anxiety. Instead, you now find yourself able to accept the processes involved in your anxiety state, understand the function that they serve and work with them in a free, creative and confident way.

ANXIETY CONDITIONING AND CREATIVE FREEDOM

Whatever we do when we are overwhelmed by panic creates a pattern that establishes what our future reactions are most likely to be. These reactions, because they are so intimately tied to your anxiety state itself are, by the same token, unlikely to be easily accessible to calm, conscious review. Because they are unconsciously conditioned into us, when we think about them they tend automatically to fill us with anxiety. Hence it seems best to us that we simply avoid thinking about them. However, next time we become anxious, this usually means that we act in much the same way, again. In essence, this is what it means to be 'conditioned'. And this is how we know that we *are* conditioned. What we do does not spring from our awareness and personal choice. Something else chooses for us what to do - our unconscious conditioning

Anxiety-dominated reactions present us with a dual task. Firstly, we need to look at what we do when we are in the grip of anxiety. Secondly, we need to replace what we are doing either with an alternative 'doing' or with a specific form of 'not doing'.

Our precept here must be "Only variety can replace variety". All in all, we need to appreciate and unlearn our 'wrong reaction readiness' by replacing it with 'right action readiness' or 'right response readiness'.(9)

Conscious appreciation clears the way for the work that needs to be done, yet such appreciation cannot be attained while we are being overwhelmed by panic. Inner balance needs to be restored, before we can consciously appreciate the way ahead.

THERAPEUTIC PARTNERSHIPS

It may be that it falls to the lot of a therapist to enable you to achieve the kind of inner balance that will enable you to begin the process of mastering your anxiety state. On the other hand, it may be your task, at some later time, to work with someone who is suffering from anxiety. In either case, you will find the following steps a useful guide to beginning the praxis of anxiety mastery.

1. A safe context (refuge, haven) is created, one in which the client is able to feel at home and at ease.
2. Trust and confidence is established between client and counsellor.
3. A sense of hopefulness is engendered in the client through clear and full identification of all the components of the anxiety state.
4. Interest in learning about the components of anxiety is extended to an awareness of their function and how this function - and the processes that sustain it - can be transformed.
5. The sense of hopefulness initially felt by the client is extended to a willingness to practise procedures that

lead to a capacity to relax routinely, and, by extension, to use of this routine to defuse anxiety.

6. The client's understanding is developed so that easy-to-learn steps and stages in moving from one level of anxiety mastery to the next may be engaged in.

7. Co-intentionality is established between client and counsellor through an agreement to engage in an overall plan of mastering anxiety and, if possible, a further plan of self-discovery beyond anxiety is embarked upon - to both facilitate and consolidate progress.

In summary, we can say that it is in the systematic co-ordination of thinking and responding, over time, that the basis of a therapeutic partnership lies. The process of self-discovery beyond anxiety uses anxiety mastery as its starting point. Through turning this subjective experience - that we did not initially understand - into an awareness of processes (that we consciously empower to control themselves) that we enter into a wider realm of self-discovery. We enter this realm, now, not because we are desperate to escape from the state in which we find ourselves but rather because the depth of our being that we have experienced and the promise that it contains enthralls us and draws us toward the realisation of higher states of being.

THE FIRST INTERVIEW

One of the aims of a first interview with someone who is suffering from an anxiety state is to enable them to enter into a state of stress-free mind-body attunement. This, in itself, serves as a demonstration of how conscious release of muscular tension is able to defuse anxiety, by replacing the 'fight or flight' response with what is sometimes called the 'relaxation response'.

The attainment of this state can now be employed to illustrate how the client has unconsciously been using similar relaxation procedures to recover from panic and regain composure. It is then pointed out to clients that they already know how to relax and regain presence of mind - yet only in certain circumstances, those in which they feel 'safe'.

An enactment of the process enables the client to recognise what they do and to understand how they do it. The counsellor demonstrates the experience of being in a panic and calming down, as follows:

> Tighten jaw muscles
> Pull mouth down at sides
> Raise shoulders
> Extend arms and fingers
> Dart eyes about, anxiously
> Tense whole body
> Breathe in fully
> Try to breathe on top of already full lungs
> Say such things as:
>> "I can't breathe"
>> "I've got to get out of here"
>> "I'll make a fool of myself in front of all
>>   these people"
>> "I feel faint"
>> "O God! What'll I do? What'll I do?"
>> "I've got to get out of here"

The counsellor then walks across the room, pretends that he is now out of the enclosed crowded place, leans against something, totally relaxes all tightly held muscles, breathes out fully and, with long in and out breaths says, "Oh, thank goodness I'm out of there", "I'll be alright, now", "I can calm down alright, now that I'm out of there", and so on.

After this demonstration, the counsellor turns to the client and says something like:

"Does that look familiar?"

"Can you identify with what I was going through there?"

"Does anything like that ever happen to you?"

Having secured the client's identification with all the feelings and actions involved, three specific components are focused upon. It is emphasised to the client that it is these three components that are particularly significant in the mastery of panic states:

(a) All tension is released from the body
(b) All tightly held breath is released completely
(c) All frightening thoughts and anticipations are let go, in favour of a deeply felt and trusted conviction that everything will soon be OK.

Once the counsellor is sure that the client has identified these three component processes, s/he is assured that if they were to do the same thing in actual situations of panic, they would have no need to leave the scene.

Usual responses to such a declaration generally include the following:

"I wish it was that easy"

"That's easier said than done"

"Maybe so, but I wouldn't like to have to try it"

and so on.

On the other hand, if such responses are not forthcoming and the client says nothing, verbalisation of the thoughts s/he might be thinking but not expressing are put to him/her, thus:

"You're probably thinking to yourself that it's not as easy as it looks"

"Easier said than done, says you"

In either event, the client is asked, at this stage, to recall how s/he felt when they first entered the room and how, through being directed to focus their attention on the tensions and tones of their body, they were able to attain a deep state of relaxation. Releasing their breath, being able to breathe freely and easily, did they not feel completely relaxed, calm and at ease.

When the process of relaxation and the experience of deep calm and tension-free ease has been recalled, the client is reassured that mastering anxiety and panic is all a matter of learning what panic is and what it involves, learning what to do and what to cease doing, rehearsing these processes and putting them into practice in previous 'panic situations'.

> "And when you are able to relax whenever you want to, because you now have a practiced routine for doing this, all you need to do is to extend this practice to situations where mild degrees of anxiety are felt, gradually becoming more and more skilled and adept, so that you begin to be able to face more and more situations with confidence and relaxed ease."

It may be useful, at this stage - if you have not done so already - to outline all the component processes involved in the stress response, also known as the 'fight or flight response' or the 'sympathetic response', at the same time, explaining their functions:

1. Our heart beats fast: this ensures that blood circulates well throughout the whole body, supplying the muscles with fresh blood and oxygen, taking away the waste products of exertion, such as carbon dioxide.
2. We breathe shallowly and rapidly: this ensures that carbon dioxide is released and blood is re-

oxygenated, supplying oxygen to the muscles for rapid release of energy.

3. Blood vessels in the gut and skin contract, raising blood pressure. The skin looks pale and drawn. This paleness is caused by lack of blood in the skin. The skin also looks drawn, because the muscles beneath it are tense. All blood now courses directly through the major muscle groups of the body. The blood flowing through these muscles supplies them with energy.

4. Our skin sweats to enable it to cool down, on account of the vigorous physical exercise that our body has prepared us to undertake. Because there is so little blood in the skin it feels cold when we sweat. This is commonly known as 'breaking out in a cold sweat'.

5. Our muscles tense up, in preparation for immediate vigorous physical action.

"All in all", we explain, "Our body prepares us to fight or run. This is a natural, built in, primitive response to danger. In itself, the fight or flight response is not dangerous. It is not life-threatening. It certainly does not mean that we are going mad, although it may feel that way because our reactions are out of our control."

Further reassurances are given, if it seems appropriate, that this state is not abnormal or life-threatening. Other 'symptoms' of the fight or flight response can now be explored, especially if the client looks puzzled, possibly asking himself, "Is what I am going through supposed to be normal?" Suggest, "There may be other things that you experience too. Shall we look at other common symptoms that anxiety sufferers experience?"

Identifying and explaining now begins in deeper earnest.

"Diarrhoea?" - when adrenaline is released its action is not specific. It speeds up all bodily functions, including

those of the muscles of the gut. Diarrhoea is a common experience.

"Dizziness? A feeling of being about to faint?" - this often occurs when we breathe too fast or too rapidly. It may also result from a shortage of sugar in the blood stream.

"Jelly legs?" - tension held in muscles over a long period of time leads to exhaustion. Muscles just begin to give way, due to the prolonged strain.

"Tingling sensations in the hands and face?" - this is due to overbreathing; too much oxygen in the blood.

"Blurred vision? Buzzing in the ears?" - these are common experiences, yet everyone does not necessarily experience them.

"A lump in the throat? Difficulty in swallowing?" - this is due to tension being held in the muscles of the throat.

"A dry mouth?" - as I said, the blood vessels in the gut and skin constrict. This goes for blood vessels in the mouth as well. Not only is your mouth dry, but your whole gut stops secreting digestive juices.

"Butterflies in the stomach?" - a common experience; this or a knot in the stomach.

"Difficulty in breathing?" - you have probably breathed all the way in and are unconsciously holding your breath, instead of breathing out. When you have difficulty in breathing, it is probably because you are trying to breathe on top of lungs that are already full of air. Yet you do not realise this, so you struggle to breathe and panic even more.

"Feeling rooted to the spot, unable to move?" - this is due to the tension that you are holding in your muscles.

For some patients much of their anxiety is allayed once the symptoms of their anxiety have been pinpointed and explained. Seeing the way that they all fit together to prepare the body for immediate vigorous physical action often prepares the client to accept the way that he or she feels. Such acceptance is a necessary part of their recovery. It may be useful to say to the client, "Unless we learn to accept the way we feel, we will not be able to work with the processes that underlie the way we feel. Unless we accept the way we feel, we will not have the basic material available for us to work on."

The following explanation often proves to be beneficial: "If there were some real external danger that we could fight or run away from, we would be able to deal with it and then calm down. As you know, the body prepares us to fight or run. On the other hand, if fighting or running away is not appropriate, we end up, instead, lumbered with a state of pent-up tension. Only if we are able to release some of that tension will we have a chance to calm down. This is how we release ourselves from the fight or flight response. We also need, however, to release the breath, as well as releasing our mind from frightening thoughts."

The idea of *sensitisation* can now be introduced. "We become sensitised to our own nervous reactions. As a result, we listen in with alarm to feel if any of the symptoms of anxiety or panic are present or on their way. And what we look for, we find. We trigger the anxiety response simply by checking up on whether or not it is present. In fact, we stimulate fear simply through our investigating the presence or absence of 'fear symptoms'. This is how we sensitise ourselves. In the end we have only to think fear to feel fear. Anything that reminds us of fear and loss of control brings on the dreaded fight or flight response."

It is explained to the client that although this is a most unfortunate state of affairs from the point of view of his unconscious, anxiety-based conditioning, it can nonetheless be consciously reversed. Such reversal, called *'desensitisation'*, involves the following steps and stages:

    (a) learning what the anxiety response involves

    (b) ceasing to be afraid of it

    (c) learning to relax, routinely

    (d) using the relaxation response to defuse anxiety, by facing anxiety evoking situations with relaxed acceptance of the way we feel and resolute patience, as we wait until our anxiety symptoms pass away of their own accord.

THE TAO IN ANXIETY MASTERY

Because we are able to become aware of the vicious-cycle-runaway involved in anxiety states, we can work on reversing the processes involved. The straightforward factuality of the approach outlined above does not, because of its factual nature, detract from the symbolic nature of the understanding and control to which it also lends itself. Other approaches, using symbolic fantasy encoding of anxiety symptoms - and using such encoding to transform images that, in turn, induce the parasympathetic (relaxation) response - can be very powerful. The basic principle remains the same. However, for the sake of simplicity, I do not intend to cover this area in this book.

In all such approaches, however, we will still be working with the essential Ground - the Fire - of our being. Letting go of all attempts to exert tight control and manipulation over this dynamic Ground of our experience involves practising what is called 'effortless effort' - in Chinese, 'wu-wei'. This results in a state of stress-free inner balance and harmony reasserting itself, of its own accord, which, in turn, confers clear presence of mind upon us, so leaving us creative and free, in the everyday realm of our existence.

SELF-DISCOVERY BEYOND ANXIETY

There follows, now, a systematic outline of this self-discovery course, calling to your attention Fire-centred practices, expected outcomes and criteria of attainment whereby you can measure the progress that you are making. These criteria are not meant to rob you of your own creative freedom in evaluating procedures and outcomes in your own way. Rather, they are meant simply to serve as a guide to what is possible.

4 Letting Go

"The quality of consciousness changes as the subject performs different operations."[1]

Persons suffering from anxiety states are prone to be more concerned about the state they are in than with any other problem. They feel that their most pressing need is for some kind of immediate relief from the state they are in. They often claim that they would be prepared to go to any lengths to obtain relief from the thoughts and feelings that are characteristic of this state: tension, anxious thoughts and anticipations, and distressing physical reactions, such as:

- a pounding heart
- a churning stomach
- difficulty in breathing
- choking sensations
- legs that feel like jelly
- sweating
- dizziness
- nausea

Such persons often feel that their anxiety is so devastating that they refuse to go anywhere where they fear panic may strike. In addition they may only need to imagine panic for the distressing feelings of anxiety to be upon them in full force.

The basic problem with anxiety states lies in the sufferer's fear of being overwhelmed by fear itself and of being rendered helpless and defenceless as a result.

'Fear of fear itself' is a phrase that describes the anxiety state very well. This dilemma has also been called 'agoraphobia' or 'anxiety neurosis'. The problems confronting the sufferer increase as he or she becomes more and more afraid of going to more and more places - anywhere, in fact, where he or she anticipates or imagines that panic may strike.

Common fears often complained of include:
- travelling away from home
- crowded places
- standing in a queue
- isolated places
- fear of collapsing, panicking, fainting
- becoming paralysed, rooted to the spot, unable to move
- giddiness
- entering shops
- going anywhere where panic may strike, and the sufferer feels unable to make a quick escape to a place where they feel they can calm down and allow their anxiety to leave them.

Other fears also complained of include:
- heights
- death
- physical injury
- physical illness
- going mad
- feelings of unreality
- persistent frightening thoughts
- losing a loved one

- blushing
- insecurity
- harming others - especially a child
- inability to cope with work
- loneliness
- general anxiety with no specific cause

Anxiety states usually have their origin in some very frightening experience or experiences, or in continual stress of one sort or another, such as domestic stress, stress in childhood, or stress at work. The stress need not necessarily be unpleasant, although, of course, unpleasant stress can exact a high toll, especially unhappy childhood stress from which the child has neither escape nor recourse to understanding. A domineering parent or parents, a parent who suffered from depression or anxiety, an unhappy parent or parents, or an alcoholic parent, can cause a child to feel continually under a threat that he or she does not understand, and in relation to which he or she feels constantly 'on guard'. On the other hand, a person may, without any of these preliminary experiences, simply find themselves subject to frightening symptoms of anxiety when they are out and about somewhere. They may, for example, be subject to unexpected and hitherto unexperienced symptoms of anxiety such as palpitations, giddiness, difficulty in taking a deep breath and choking sensations. Because so often no adequate explanation is to hand, the unfortunate 'victim' of panic becomes alarmed and worried. He dwells upon the nature of his experiences and becomes concerned that they might occur again. Because of this preoccupation the sufferer sensitises himself or herself to the slightest indication of approaching anxiety. He or she learns, thus, to listen in with alarm to any of the physical signs that indicate that panic is on its way and may strike again soon. This sensitisation increases the likelihood of panic developing 'out of' increased heartbeat, a feeling of tension or a feeling of unease.

These sensations are met with fear and alarm, bringing on all the intense physical reactions that the sufferer finds so distressing:

- pounding heart
- churning stomach
- sweating
- jelly legs
- inability to take a deep breath, and so on.

Lack of understanding as to what is happening and how to control it brings on a sense of bewilderment, which adds to the already present strain. At this stage, you may well begin to fear for the worst. "I'm going to die", "I'm going to have a heart attack", "I'm going crazy". These frightening thoughts make the situation even worse.

By becoming *sensitised* to the physical signs of anxiety, the sufferer learns to anticipate and to expect an anxiety attack, whenever they feel the signs of anxiety in their body. "You tense up against the coming onslaught, expect the worst and . . . sure enough, it comes." This is a common experience. The anxiety state comes in waves of hair-raising panic, each mounting in intensity over the last.

In addition to the symptoms already mentioned, the intensely sensitised person may also complain of any of the following:

- missed heart-beats
- pain in the region of the heart
- a feeling of fullness and burning in the face
- agitation
- extreme irritability
- tightness across the chest
- headaches
- a lump in the throat

- diarrhoea
- easily induced weakness
- blurred vision
- aching muscles

In many cases sufferers complain of flashes of almost devastating panic.

It may help you to know that despite the severity of these symptoms their pattern is nonetheless set and limited. Nerves under stress, or sensitised, to anxious thoughts always release the same chemicals to act on the same muscles and organs, always producing the same results. These results are known as the 'sympathetic response' because they are the result of the action of our so-called 'sympathetic nervous system'. They are also known collectively as the 'flight or fight response' - a primitive inborn physiological response to stress brought about by the sympathetic nervous system in response to danger, whether real or imagined.

The 'fight or flight' response prepares the body to take immediate physical action whenever we 'feel' under threat. Our heart starts beating faster to get a good circulation of blood going. We breathe faster to increase our oxygen supply. Our blood pressure increases so as to ensure a good overall blood distribution. Blood drains from the skin and the organs of digestion to serve the muscles of voluntary movement. Our muscles tense up in preparation for immediate physical action.

In a primitive jungle-type situation, fighting or running away would probably be appropriate action for us to take. However, in most situations that we are likely to meet, or be in, fighting or running away would create more problems than it would solve. So we stand our ground instead. As a result, so long as we do not consciously release tension from our bodies, this tension is likely to keep our anxiety going in a vicious cycle-spiral of increasing tension, panic and fearful anticipation.

If we were in a jungle-type situation and effectively attacked or ran away from danger, our muscles would, thereafter, automatically relax and this would signal to our nervous system to switch off the sympathetic response. As a result, our heart would slow down, our breathing rate would decrease, our blood pressure would be lowered, blood would flow back into our skin and into our organs of digestion, and so on. We would, at the same time, calm down and regain our sense of peace and presence of mind. These processes are known collectively as the 'parasympathetic response', because they are controlled by the parasympathetic nervous system.

What we usually do not realise is this: even if we do not run or attack we *still* have a *chance* of calming down and releasing ourselves from the grip of panic, by:

- consciously letting go of tension, and
- ceasing to fuel our anxiety with fearful thoughts and anticipations.

Release of muscular tension signals to the sympathetic nervous system to switch off all the distressing feelings of the 'fight or flight' response, giving us a chance to calm down and collect our thoughts once again, as the 'parasympathetic response' takes over.

Letting go of tension, accepting the feelings in our bodies, and letting them pass as we 'do nothing', is the most effective strategy for coming to terms with anxiety and panic. It makes use of a built-in counter-anxiety process known as the 'parasympathetic response', or, if you prefer the term, the 'relaxation response'.

To sum up: we become anxious and we panic because we anticipate frightening things happening to us. Such thoughts cause our sympathetic nervous system to react with the 'fight or flight' response, producing all the distressing feelings of panic in us. Our usual reaction is to tense up in reaction to these feelings and continue to add further frightening thoughts, further anticipations of the thing that 'could' happen to us. In this way, we gear ourselves into an even greater anxiety state. Our panic escalates. A sense of powerlessness over anxiety and panic develops in us, making us veritable prisoners of our own fear. To release ourselves from the grip of panic, the grip of the fight or flight response, we need to make use of a process that reverses the inner causes of our panic. This we can do by making use of the 'relaxation response', namely letting go of all tension that we are holding in our bodies and ceasing to fuel our fears with frightening anticipations.

There are, of course, other alternatives to the use of the relaxation response. These come under the heading of 'props', using this term in the sense of 'propping up an unworkable system'. If we are not going to get to the basis of the problem and learn to make use of a built-in effective process of self-regulation, we have little alternative than to try to dampen down the undesirable consequences of our refusal to accept due responsibility for ourselves. Instead we can use alcohol or tranquilizers to:

- try to dampen down our 'fight or flight' responses, and
- try to artificially change our consciousness.

We can choose to depend on 'understanding friends' to help us to do everyday normal things. We can restrict our movements, by not going to places where we feel that panic may strike. We can go out only under certain conditions in which we have not learned to panic yet - 'only in the dark' or 'only when it rains'.

These props - alcohol, tranquilizers, understanding friends, restriction of travelling, going out only in the dark or rain - all have a nasty habit of giving way. We begin to demand 'too much' from our 'understanding friends', wearing down their understanding, tolerance and patience. We eventually become trapped in our own homes, unable to go out of the front door. These props do not get to the basis of the anxiety state itself, namely our own habit of sensitising our nervous system to anxious thoughts and anticipations. An overdependence upon props does not give us the opportunity we need to learn how to govern our own anxiety. In fact, if we place too much dependence on them we weaken our faith in ourselves and we actually begin to interfere with our self-regulating potential. It is not that our ability to become self-regulating is destroyed, it is ignored. So long as it is ignored, discouraging memories build up inside us. This is why all props, especially when they are relied upon exclusively and with undeserved faith and dependence, must prove to be ultimately unreliable.

Going to the root cause of anxiety in our ongoing moment-to-moment living is the only effective way to deal with it. After all, the fight or flight response is a purely natural and sometimes useful response to real danger. The problem is not the response itself, but our habit of evoking it when it is uncalled for and our inability to control its effects.

Using the procedures outlined in this book can enable anyone who correctly applies them to master anxiety and re-enter the mainstream of living. If there is a little voice inside you, right now, saying 'others can do it, but not me', understand that this is nothing other than your habit of fearfully anticipating failure. Simply let go of the idea, do not dwell upon it or follow it in your thoughts to wherever it may lead you. This is known technically as 'negative inner rehearsal'. It can be safely left aside, without any ill effect.

Our nervous system cannot tell the difference between actually threatening situations and those vividly imagined or anxiously dwelt upon. In all cases, our nervous system reacts with the 'fight or flight' response, which, in turn, is responsible for producing in us all the distressing sensations which we experience as panic. The powerful emotions that we feel trick us into believing that, because they are so powerful, something very serious must be happening to us. In fact, this is not the case. On the other hand, by 'worrying' that it is - that is, by fearfully imagining and anticipating our future anxiety and panic - we are actually *rehearsing* our feared 'loss of control'. This increases its likelihood and intensifies the swiftness and power of our nervous reactions. So we learn to associate this fear with more and more situations, and our anxiety thus extends itself, until we find ourselves trapped in small pockets of as-yet safe, secure areas, where, by contrast, we have not 'rehearsed' our panic states but have instead practised letting go, calming down and feeling safe.

When we are in a state of panic what we normally do is to try to leave the place we are in, as quickly as possible, so that we can find a safe place where we are able to let out a big sigh of relief, collapse in a heap, cease frightening ourselves by anticipating further anxious experiences of panic - and . . . calm down, instead.

Yes, *we do know how to calm down*. We do it very well in certain places. Why, then, do we not extend this same strategy to other places and other times as well?

The reason, of course, is not difficult to understand. We do not really know what we are doing *in order* to calm down. We do not understand *how* we are doing it. We do not realise that what we are doing is something that we can *routinely* put into practice in panic situations, and not only at those times and in those places which we have learned to associate with 'safety'.

To engage in an effective programme of mastery of anxiety and panic we need to understand, clearly, that

these states continue to be reproduced in us by two
things and two things only:

    (i) anxious thoughts, and

    (ii) tension held in our muscles.

To be able to release tension from our muscles whenever
we wish to do so requires regular routine practice of
relaxation. In fact, unless we practise relaxing at times
other than those when we are tense and anxious,
relaxation itself is going to become associated with
anxiety and vulnerability and, in the end, we are not
going to be able to relax at all. Regular routine practice of
relaxation is a must. I recommend my own "Relaxation &
Meditation" tape to facilitate relaxation practice,
although, of course, it is not essential and any effective
relaxation procedure will suffice.

    Because tension builds up in our muscles largely
unconsciously, it is not, at the same time, going to be
released unconsciously. Instead, we need to practise
conscious release of tension, so that, when we need to use
it, we will have a practical routine available to allow us to
do so.

    Relaxation can, for us, become a normal routine so
that, like the routine of dressing or driving a car, it can be
carried out without our having to work it all out from the
start each time.

    A simple phrase, associated with relaxation and
meditation, can be used to evoke a calm, relaxed state
and a positive frame of mind.

    You may well find, especially if you are making
use of two of my tapes, "Mastering Panic" and
"Relaxation & Meditation", that the following phrases are
useful:

        Let go and let God.
        Sigh, sink and sag.
        This too shall pass.
        Easy does it.

Face, accept, float and let time pass.
Practise, don't test.
100 per cent acceptance not 99 per cent.
I am open to receive the Power within.

When we are assailed by anxiety and panic our normal reaction is to tense up. This tension is part and parcel of our anxiety itself, and it serves to perpetuate a vicious cycle of reactive bondage to fear. To release ourselves from this cycle we need to let go of as much tension as possible. Note the words 'let go', because relaxation is always a question of 'passively releasing', rather than 'actively doing'. We should not *try* to relax. Any effort involved in relaxing only works against the process. When we release tension we find that our panic may rise to a peak and then gradually die down. This process of peaking and gradually subsiding is completely assured, so long as we ourselves do not get in the way of it by tensing up or thinking anxious thoughts. Instead, we should be ready to give ourselves quiet, confident instructions as we, first, enter into a stage of relaxed 'doing nothing', and then get quietly on with everyday living.

The change of physical and mental set involved in moving from 'tension-filled panic' to 'tension-free confidence' means moving through an in-between stage, or 'middle ground'. It is in this 'middle ground' that we come around. While in this 'middle ground' there is nothing we can do and 'doing nothing' is exactly what we need to do. When we have come around, in our own good time, in the 'middle ground', we shall be ready to go calmly, quietly and confidently on with our everyday affairs.

The 'middle ground' that we enter into when we release ourselves from the grip of tension (by 'letting go' and by ceasing to add fearful thoughts) can usefully be considered as a 'separator state' - a state of mind that allows our body to readjust to normal living by a process of inner reorganisation and self-regulation. In this 'separator state' we cease to unwittingly go along with harmful and destructive processes, and engage instead in a process of self-abandonment to our own inner powers. This allows us to calm down and start afresh, with a new outlook and a self-stabilising response set.

Three stages are involved in the mastery of a panic state. These are as follows:

(i) The panic state.

(ii) The separator state.

(iii) The self-regulating state.

It is useful to know which state we are in as we engage in freeing ourselves from the grip of panic.

To enter into the 'separator state' means to release oneself from the grip of physical tension and anxious thoughts. People often find it useful to associate the process of letting go with the phrase "Let go and let God". This marks the end of tension and an entry into the 'middle ground'. In this middle ground, which functions in us as a 'separator state', all the symptoms of anxiety need to be accepted, one hundred per cent, for as long as they last. In the middle ground itself all of these symptoms - pounding heart, jelly legs, churning stomach, sweating and so on - do us no harm whatsoever! As long as we do not tense ourselves up against them, and as long as we do not stoke our fears with frightening thoughts, these symptoms will continue for a while and then gradually subside. While in the middle ground state - the separator state - the phrase "Sigh, sink and sag" is useful to repeat. Going along with the actual physical processes of sighing, sinking and sagging, as we repeat the phrase, calmly and slowly, enables us to enter more fully into our 'not doing'. While in this state we trust ourselves to the inner power of our parasympathetic response to return us to our presence of mind. We can say to ourselves, if we wish, "This too shall pass", for indeed, given time, it will pass.

When our anxiety state has left us - as if 'bored' with our lack of attention to its fears and tensions - it is a good idea to mark our moving into the next stage - the self-regulating state - with the phrase "Easy does it", so as to set the tone for the way in which we are going to re-engage in active life and let ourselves 'get on with' ordinary living.

A long-term programme of mastering panic gains in ease of practice and power of mastery every time we use it. Panic and anxiety *can* only come in a wave, and must subside again, if only we consciously release tension from our muscles and cease to add fearful thoughts and imaginings. If we remain seated (if seated), or if walking, sag and slow down, sighing and sinking to encourage relaxation and 'not doing', and are prepared to accept the symptoms of the 'fight or flight' response for as long as they last - harmlessly 'doing their worst' - panic will pass, as surely as night passes into day. *There will be no mounting panic.* Of this you can be absolutely assured.

What you have just read are a set of instructions. Just reading these instructions may be reassuring, but do not let it stop there. You need to put these instructions into practice so that you gain the benefits of direct experience of the principles involved, and acquire thereby an intelligent commitment to your own health and wellbeing.

Until you understand the principles involved, you are bewildered. When you see them, put them into practice or else you will miss the mark and simply continue to believe yourself a 'victim' of 'this thing', as panic states are so often referred to. Abstract knowledge only becomes committed understanding with practice. If possible, join a local self-help group in your area or start one of your own with the help of a local psychologist, a doctor, a social worker, a community nurse, or simply with some committed fellow sufferers, who could be contacted through advertising in your local newspaper.

Sitting back is no way to capitalise upon your understanding! It is no way to regain your self-confidence and 'repressed responsibility'! 'Responsibility' means 'the ability to respond'. This responsibility is only developed through practice. Only if you are going somewhere - a place to go to, friends to meet, something to do - will you be able to remain balanced and self-regulating, just as only when a person is going forward on a bicycle can he remain balanced and steer it.

Constant acceptance of the symptoms of the fight or flight response, until their coming no longer meets with tense resistance, fear and bewilderment, is the road to mastery of anxiety and panic. Constant acceptance is, of course, not easy at first. On the other hand, a long period of recovery means that we have ample opportunity for practice. Our learning experience can become all the more thorough and complete as a result. It means that we will have had repeated practice in coping with panic the right way until the right response - the 'relaxation response' - becomes routine.

'Right response readiness' can be practised at home in the form of 'visualising' what we need to do before we actually go out and do it.

To practise 'right response readiness' at home, sit in a chair in a relaxed posture and visualise yourself entering into and meeting previously 'anxious situations', in a relaxed and confident way. Visualise everything in detail, step by step, and continue to remain relaxed and positive in your outlook. If, at any time, you feel anxiety and panic coming upon you - although this is certainly not a necessary requirement of the practice - you should simply switch to visualising yourself going

into the relaxation routine. You should put what you are
going to do in words. For example, say to yourself:

> *Let go and let God.*
> *Sigh, sink and sag.*
> *This too shall pass.*
> *Easy does it.*
> *Face, accept, float and let time pass.*

Since we sensitise ourselves, through worry, to react to
our thoughts (of being in certain situations) with panic,
an effective antidote to the worry process is 'positive
visualisation' practice.

Whenever we worry, we present to our minds
some image or idea of what we do not want. As a result,
we trigger off within ourselves feelings of unease and
concern. The sensitised person reacts to these feelings
with tension and escalating panic. In order to reverse this
process, positive visualisation is recommended.

When we worry, we present fearful and
undesirable ideas, images and expectations to ourselves
in a fearful and driven way. The same thoughts, fears
and anticipations keep occurring to us in the same way,
over and over again. Worry is the opposite of thinking in
a positive and creative way. We start off with some
picture of an undesirable state or outcome in our minds.
We keep dwelling on this as a possibility. As a result, we
gear ourselves emotionally to meet it. Appropriate
emotions are generated: fear, anxiety, frustration, anger,
resentment and so on. These emotions, in turn, keep the
worry going. If we physically relax and change the
nature of the outcome or state we are visualising in a
positive way - that is to say, if we change our 'goal
picture' - worry can be replaced by positive thoughts,
feelings and subsequent actions. To cease worrying, we
need to visualise *what we want*, not *what we do not want*.
Worrying is always a useless and self-defeating process.
On no account should we condone it or attempt to justify

it in ourselves, at any time. If, for the rest of our lives, we never worried again, no harm whatsoever would result. This is an important principle to grasp and understand.

Applying positive visualisation to the issue of anxiety and panic works in this way. Suppose that a certain situation (for example, waiting to board a bus) makes you tense and anxious, visualising yourself as tense and anxious in such a situation merely intensifies this tendency in you, much in the way of a self-fulfilling prophecy. On the other hand, were you to spend short periods of time visualising yourself as calm, confident and relaxed in all situations (e.g. all situations related to a bus journey) you would begin to see yourself as a more confident and easy-going person, in such situations. Eventually - sometimes immediately - you would experience the necessary confidence that would allow you to enter into and meet just such a situation.

Emile Coue's 'Law of Reversed Effort' applies here. This law states: "The less effort required to visualise successful action and outcome, the easier the actual practice will be."

When visualising, start with something you feel fairly positive about already, before moving to more difficult areas. Sit in a chair and relax, using your relaxation routine. When you feel completely relaxed, visualise things the way you would like them to be; for example, visualise yourself as free of all anxiety, calm and confident, or at least greatly improved. Imagine yourself in the situation, able to cope with everything just the way you want to. Use any and all details that will make the visualisation experience more real for you. Let yourself feel confident and powerful with it. It should be an invigorating and enjoyable experience.

Keeping the visualised experience in mind, make some positive affirming statements about yourself, such as:

"I feel calm and relaxed in all situations."

"God is the power in which I trust."
"I am open to receive the power within."

Visualising yourself mastering panic and anxiety should be done in a similar way. By imagining yourself letting go and accepting the 'fight or flight' response in you, 'doing nothing', and calming down until you are ready to let yourself carry on with everyday life. Again, practise using the appropriate affirmations and commands, in a calm and confident way:

> *Let go and let God.*
> *Sigh, sink and sag.*
> *This too shall pass.*
> *Easy does it.*
> *Face, accept, float and let time pass.*
> *Practice, don't test.*
> *100 per cent acceptance not 99 per cent.*
> *God is the strength in which I trust.*
> *I am open to receive the Power within.*

The basic method of creative visualisation is relatively simple, yet its effects are deep and profound, as you will surely discover for yourself.

Dr Claire Weekes,[2] who might well be considered 'the Patron Saint of Agoraphobics', makes some very important points about mastering panic states.

"When we panic," she says, "It is essential to recognise not one fear but two separate fears; a first fear and a second fear." The first fear, she explains, is made up of all the components of the fight or flight response: beating heart, churning stomach, a dry mouth, sweating, shaking and tension. The second fear, on the other hand, is the fear that we add ourselves when we begin to imagine all the terrible things that might happen next. We should, she suggests, accept all the symptoms of the 'first fear', while at the same time releasing ourselves from all excess tension. We should also cease to add any 'second fear'. She sums up her advice as to what to do when panic strikes in four words: "Face, accept, float and let time pass." We should *face* and understand the symptoms we feel, instead of trying to ignore them or run away from them. We should *accept* all the symptoms of the fight or flight response, instead of vainly trying to 'get rid of them'. We should *float* with our feelings, not tensing up against them, but letting go of all tension as if we were a row of corks on a fisherman's net, gently bobbing up and down on calm water. Finally, we should *let time pass*, not being impatient for the panic feelings to leave us, not speeding up our movements, as any hurry only increases our tension and second fear. 'Letting time pass' means waiting confidently in a tension-free state for the symptoms of the fight or flight response to die down, and for calm and presence of mind to return.

Dr Weekes recommends that we do not test ourselves to see if the improvements we have made are sustained. For example, if we went well on a walk around the block last week, we should not see if we can do as well this week and perhaps be disappointed if we fail. The idea of *testing* means the added pressure of suspense and the question of failure or loss of ability, whereas practising holds no urgent demands. When testing ourselves, not applying the programme too well means failure: when practising, it only means an opportunity to see what we have neglected to do, and to practise again.

Whatever we accomplish in a practising session, we should not be tempted to treat almost as failure, saying "I did it, but . . . " and adding "I wasn't as good as I used to be" or "It wasn't as good as I hoped or expected." Etta Jennings, co-ordinator of the Northern Ireland Agoraphobia Society, encourages members to quickly spot any tendency to put themselves down. "No 'buts' please," she insists, "Say instead 'I did it, great', and give yourself a golden crown. You deserve it. Only you know what you have come through. Every time you practise take down your crown and give it a polish."

It may be a good idea to visualise our mind being divided into two parts: one part that suffers and another part that looks on, almost as an over-seer, guiding operations and patiently waiting for full presence of mind to return. If this strategy works well for you, go ahead and use it. If not, it does not matter. Simply let go of it, and practise what works best for you.

A word about Set-backs

Sooner or later, during or after recovery, a set-back is bound to occur. Memory alone will bring it. During the set-back we often feel as if our problem is as bad as ever it was, for all the upsetting symptoms of the sympathetic response seem to have returned as strongly and as distressingly as ever. Remember, however, that the symptoms of a set-back are no more than the symptoms of stress - the symptoms of the fight or flight response. No matter how severe a set-back may seem, it is no cause for alarm. If you treat it in the same way as you would any other panic attack, you will immediately be back on the road to recovery again. A set-back will take its own head. It will take its own time to go.

Most upsetting, perhaps, for the sufferer is the fact that a set-back may occur just before full recovery is attained. As such it should simply be accepted as an extra opportunity - even a bonus - to continue practising until full mastery of anxiety and panic is attained.

I wish you every success in your practice and visualisation. With a full understanding of these principles, full and detailed positive visualisation and constant practice, a vast improvement in your condition is assured. With continual practice full recovery is well within your powers.

God bless you.

5   *We, Ourselves*

*"Man must discover mind. He has to sort out and detach from
one another feeling and doing, knowing and deciding."*[1]

Psychological management of anxiety states can perhaps
best be undertaken in a self-help group, whose members
seek to ensure that its processes invest it with the
following characteristics:

(i) They focus attention clearly and
unambiguously upon relevant issues.

(ii) They confront all the issues involved.

(iii) They boldly urge understanding and
commitment based on what has been found to
be practically effective.

(iv) They intend only what is best in a spirit of
unconditional love.

(v) They have faith in one another, bearing
patiently with one another's difficulties.

The understanding and commitment that an effectively
working group attains will ultimately align itself with a
set of guiding principles. In the process of achieving this
alignment, however, there will be group members who
have attained a confident understanding and those who
are as yet full of uncertainty, doubts and misgivings.
Open dialogue between such persons helps both parties.
It opens up new meanings, possibilities and choices for
'newcomers', and it helps to consolidate the
understanding of 'old hands'. The most effective way of

engaging the understanding and commitment of new members is through the personal testimony of people who have entered the group with similar difficulties, and who have acquired some mastery in overcoming these difficulties through following the programme recommended. When experienced group members give full and accurate witness to their presenting difficulties and their initial faltering attempts to master anxiety and panic, their growing confidence in their ability to apply relevant strategies enables new members to identify themselves with the overall programme. An initial restricted understanding of the issues and principles involved will not prevent new members from emotionally investing their interest and hope in a story that is being told and relived in front of them. Later on they will learn how to articulate the steps and stages, aims and processes, operations and principles involved. In the beginning, however, all that is needed is an identification of the new member with someone who once felt as he is feeling and who now has made some progress. Such identification carries the new member through a sequence of experiences that leads him or her to feel some hope in the beliefs, expectations, attitudes and aims adopted. In this way, experienced members will, by their own testimony, be able to encourage newcomers who have problems akin to their own. A kind of vicarious experience of anxiety mastery takes place whenever identification occurs, including some 'inner rehearsal' of the strategies undertaken and beliefs adopted. A sense of shared identity emerges both in the vicarious experience and in the ensuing dialogue. Courage, hope and faith in the programme of anxiety management develops.

An effectively working group will be on the lookout for false and limiting beliefs, expectations, attitudes and aims. The group as a whole will attempt to understand how inexperienced or misguided members have come to accept false, harmful, limiting beliefs and aims. Persistent efforts will be made to correct the credulity, the carelessness and the bias that led anxiety sufferers to mistake the false for the true, the worthless for the valuable and the destructive for the constructive. Group members learn thus to see what others need to see. They also learn to understand how to encourage others to commit themselves to the sort of understanding and commitment that is essential for the mastery of their psychological difficulties.

In self-help groups, we learn to understand the nature of the false beliefs that are keeping an anxiety sufferer locked into vicious cycles of projection and reaction - projecting harmful and limiting beliefs and expectations onto various situations and reacting to these projections. We need to be able to explain the differences involved in helpful and harmful ways of coping with anxiety so that sufferers can be encouraged to understand and adopt what is helpful and discard what is unhelpful.

The first step in this process is always taken by those who understand, rather than by persons who are beset by anxiety and bewilderment. The group looks for mistaken beliefs and unhelpful reactions. It looks for self-justifications, rationalisations and a minimising of problems. It helps new members to see connecting links between limiting and harmful beliefs, defensive attitudes, fearful expectations and misguided aims. It seeks to demonstrate and clarify how these unhelpful factors co-ordinate, adding up to confusion, bewilderment and continuing panic.

In order to facilitate the development of an effectively working self-help group, it is useful to pay attention to pertinent questions that need to be answered in a clear and unambiguous way. Certain questions act as 'pointers' which focus attention upon what is useful and important, so helping anxiety sufferers to 'get their bearings'. Using such pointers, the group can enable its members to reorder their priorities, to discard misguided and harmful beliefs and aims, and to become increasingly more attentive, insightful and better able to master their anxiety. All this involves two-way dialogue. Irrelevant and misleading talk should therefore be avoided or swiftly checked by a person in the group who adopts the role of leader. An alternative to this is to have a circle or hoop on the table or floor in the middle of the group, where group members can place 'markers' (coins or pebbles) to indicate that they consider dialogue to be degenerating into irrelevant or misleading talk. Group members quickly get the message and the markers are removed when constructive dialogue is restored. In this way dialogue progresses from a consideration of problems and issues to the establishment of helpful projects and strategies. Thus irrelevant argument, rationalisation and inner conflict are replaced by understanding and purposeful commitment. What is only apparently useful is replaced by what is actually useful.

The group as a whole works to attain "insight into insight and insight into oversight".[2] This is the key to its practical effectiveness. It provides an antidote to flights from understanding and problem avoidance which form the basis of those oversights which are often systematically inter-related. Insights into 'what is leading to what' provide the basis of prescriptions regarding 'what to do' and 'what not to do'. Such prescriptions, when understood and received as practical tasks, give rise to further insights and further practical tasks.

The following 101 'pointers' set out in question-and-answer form what is essential for anxiety sufferers to understand and to put to good effect. There is a certain sequence and order in the presentation of these pointers which corresponds more or less to the requirements of group members' growing understanding, commitment and progress. The pointers listed below are answered in the same sequence in the text which follows:

One Hundred and One Pointers

1. What does the term 'agoraphobia' mean?
2. What are the common complaints of persons suffering from agoraphobia?
3. Why are agoraphobics reluctant to go where they fear panic may strike?
4. What are common places that agoraphobics tend to avoid?
5. What conditions give rise to agoraphobia?
6. Is agoraphobia a learned reaction?
7. Will avoidance reactions disappear of their own accord?
8. What is the difference between agoraphobia and ordinary fear?
9. How does treatment of agoraphobia differ from treatment of a physical disease?
10. How does bewilderment increase the problem of anxiety management?
11. What is the way out of the vicious cycle of anxiety and bewilderment?
12. What is the 'fight or flight' response?
13. What are the 'symptoms' of the fight or flight response?
14. What is the 'wrong reaction readiness'?
15. What is the relaxation response?
16. What is the difference between reaction and action?
17. What is 'right action readiness'?
18. What is a 'separator state'?
19. What keeps our panic going?
20. What is the basis of tension?
21. How can we use the relaxation response to master panic?
22. What is the first rule for mastering agoraphobia?

23. How do expectations affect our psychological state?
24. What is 'second fear'?
25. What is creative visualisation?
26. What is worry?
27. How can we use creative visualisation to master agoraphobia?
28. What does it mean to 'practice' and 'not to test'?
29. How do beliefs affect our psychological state?
30. What false and harmful beliefs do agoraphobic persons need to overcome?
31. Why do we have difficulty in breathing?
32. What is that lump in the throat?
33. Will our heart burst?
34. Will we have heart failure?
35. Why do we have jelly legs?
36. Why do we have dizzy spells?
37. Why do we have feelings of unreality?
38. How do attitudes affect our psychological state?
39. What attitudes do we need to change?
40. What aims do we need to change?
41. What is sensitisation?
42. What does a sensitised person do?
43. How can we desensitise our nervous reactions?
44. How does panic mount?
45. How can mounting panic be controlled?
46. What is the difference between mastering agoraphobia and putting up with anxiety?
47. What kind of props do agoraphobics use?
48. What is the problem with props?
49. What are the four concepts for mastering agoraphobia?
50. What does 'facing' mean?
51. What does 'accepting' mean?
52. What does 'floating' mean?
53. What does 'letting time pass' mean?
54. What is imaginal practice?
55. What is the law of inner rehearsal?

56. How does practising anxiety management fail?
57. What is the Law of Reversed Effort?
58. What is the Alexander Principle?
59. Why is it important to walk tall and breathe freely?
60. Why should we regularly practise relaxing?
61. What is the first thing to do when panic strikes?
62. What are the 'terrible twins' of agoraphobia?
63. What will happen if we stop worrying?
64. How can we reframe a worrying thought?
65. How can we be bluffed by our feelings?
66. How can we avoid being bluffed by our feelings?
67. Is self-talk important?
68. What is a mental diet?
69. How can we go on a mental diet?
70. What can we expect from going on a mental diet?
71. What are negative emotions?
72. What are common examples of negative emotions?
73. How can depression grow out of agoraphobia?
74. How can affirmations of positive belief help us?
75. What are common examples of negative and harmful beliefs?
76. What constructive and positive beliefs can be affirmed to replace harmful and destructive ones?
77. Why is it useful to draw up a list of avoidance situations in order of anxiety?
78. What is an anxiety ladder?
79. How can we construct an anxiety ladder?
80. How can we convert an anxiety ladder into a progress ladder?
81. How specific should our progress ladder be?
82. Why are target criteria important?
83. If we succeed in completing a practical task, what should we do next?
84. If we succeed in a practical task what should we *not* do?
85. What does 'bridging the gap' mean?
86. How should we practise facing feared situations?

87. Should we use tranquilisers?
88. What happens if we panic and forget what to do?
89. What happens when we have a set-back?
90. What are the symptoms of a set-back?
91. What should we do when we have a set-back?
92. Is keeping a Personal Life Book important?
93. Why does trying to forget not work?
94. When does practising anxiety management fail?
95. How important is the food we eat?
96. Is exercise important?
97. What is the Law of Requisite Variety?
98. Should we take up new and varied interests now or wait until we have recovered first?
99. Why is it important for us to tell others about our anxieties and our progress in mastering them?
100. Why is it important to let others talk out their anxieties?
101. Why should we learn to understand and ask and answer these questions?

Answers to the questions are written out in full to assist participants in the running of self-help groups. It is a good idea to divide groups into three parts:

(a) Discussing difficulties, progress reports, accomplishment of practical tasks, personal testimonies and the setting of new practical tasks. (40 mins.)
(b) Reading, testing of knowledge, the setting of learning tasks where appropriate and objective discussion. (40 mins.)
(c) Resumed discussion of difficulties, progress reports and the setting of new practical tasks. (40 mins.)

In the second part of the group session, a reading of relevant literature takes place, and/or there is a testing of knowledge regarding questions and answers set from the previous week, and/or objective discussion of issues and understanding (not personal difficulties). This section facilitates an objective and impersonal understanding of issues and prevents understanding of psychological difficulties from degenerating into purely a 'personal problem'.

It may be a good idea to start and end the session with some bio-energetic exercises done to music. Bob Marley's "Don't worry about a thing" and "One Love" make good starting and ending tunes. Bio-energetic exercises can include hip-rotation, stretching up (grape picking), and arms loose swing-around. After the session it is a good idea to have some tea and to socialise and chat in an inconsequential way.

The substance of our pursuit of anxiety mastery is outlined in the following answers to the 101 questions set out above:

1. What does the term 'agoraphobia' mean?
Agoraphobic means, literally, 'fear of the market place'; in other words, fear of crowded places. More generally, it is used to include any state of high anxiety in which our concern to relieve ourselves from this state interferes with our ability to lead a normal life.

2. What are common complaints of persons suffering from agoraphobia?
Common complaints include a thumping, rapidly beating heart, missed heartbeats, pain in the region of the heart, extreme irritability, constant tiredness, giddiness, sweating, tingling sensations in the fingers, agitation, tightness across the chest, noises in the ears, a lump in the throat, difficulty in taking a deep breath, a feeling of fullness and burning in the face, easily induced weakness, blurred vision, aching muscles and, most common of all, flashes of incapacitating panic and a desire to escape to a place where one can calm down.

3. Why are agoraphobics reluctant to go where panic may strike?

This reluctance is due to their fear that they will lose control of their own reactions, panicking, running away, vomiting, passing out, or 'something worse'.

4. What are common places that agoraphobics avoid?

Common places that agoraphobics avoid include crowded places, isolated places, travelling away from home, standing in a queue, entering shops, going to church, going into a café, in fact going to any place where they fear that panic may strike and they will be unable to make a quick escape should their fears, as they anticipate, overwhelm them.

5. What conditions give rise to agoraphobia?

Conditions or situations associated with the development of agoraphobia include accidents, operations, difficult confinements, problem marriages, an upbringing with unhappy or neurotic parents, alcoholic parents, or any situation of continuous stress. The stress itself need not be harrowing or unpleasant. Agoraphobia may also arise without any apparent associated condition or situation of stress. In such cases, panic suddenly erupts for no apparent reason.

6. Is agoraphobia a learnt reaction?

Yes, it is. It is not always easy to identify what leads to our initial sensitivity and panic proneness. Some situation triggers off a fearful thought to which our body reacts and we become alarmed at this reaction, which we associate as the place where we panicked or 'that kind of place'. In this way, automatic fear learning takes place. We usually end up trying to avoid such places or we try to make quick escape from them whenever we feel a subsequent onset of panic. Fear learning is an automatic, unconscious process. Obviously we do not set out to learn how to feel anxious. Although becoming agoraphobic is an unconscious process, we can only 'unlearn' our agoraphobia by *consciously* understanding it and taking steps to reverse the unconscious learning that has taken place.

7. Will avoidance reactions disappear of their own accord?

No they will not. We need to practise facing feared situations with a relaxed and confident attitude so that our anxiety can spend itself and calm, confident control can return.

8. What is the difference between agoraphobia and ordinary fear?

Agoraphobia differs from ordinary fear only in relation to the situations that give rise to it. In agoraphobia, people are not afraid of some actual menacing situation, person, animal or object. Instead they are afraid of being overwhelmed by their own anxiety reactions in situations where there is no real external threat or danger.

9. How does anxiety management differ from treatment of a physical disease?

The difference lies in the changes required. Physical diseases involve pathological changes *in the body* that need to be controlled or eradicated. In agoraphobia our fear reactions do not involve a morbid change of tissues, organs or biochemicals in the body. Instead, anxiety states involve fearful thoughts (about what might happen to us), avoidance reactions and continuing anxiety states, associated with certain places. Anxiety management involves a change in thinking and behaving in order to bring anxious feelings and panic reactions under control.

10. **How does bewilderment increase the problem of anxiety management?**

Bewilderment increases the problem of anxiety management by placing the anxiety sufferer in the situation of continually asking 'What is happening to me?', and 'Why is this happening to me?'. In the absence of a clear and helpful understanding of what is involved, an anxiety sufferer is bound to fear for the worst, thus adding more frightening thoughts to his panic reactions. In this way he makes the original problem worse than it was before.

11. **What is the way out of the vicious cycle of anxiety and bewilderment?**

The way out of this distressing vicious cycle is, firstly, to understand the overall condition of agoraphobia, and secondly, to take remedial action in accordance with this understanding.

12. **What is the 'fight or flight' response?**

The fight or flight response is a primitive automatic reflex action that occurs in the body whenever we confront danger. This danger need not be an actual external threat. It can be a danger that we imagine to be present and project out into our circumstances, or it can simply be a danger that we dwell upon 'in our mind's eye'. Whether the danger is real or imagined, our body reacts to it by preparing us to take immediate vigorous physical actions, such as fighting or running away, whenever we feel under threat.

13. **What are the symptoms of the fight or flight response?**

The symptoms of the fight or flight response are the effects of adrenaline, a chemical which is released into our bloodstream by our so-called 'sympathetic nervous system' whenever we feel threatened or under stress.

Our sympathetic nervous system automatically prepares us to fight or run away. The psychological effects or 'symptoms' of the fight or flight response (also known as the sympathetic response) are in accordance with these preparations:

(a) increased heart-rate, to increase the flow of blood to our lungs and muscles
(b) increased breathing rate, to increase oxygen supply to our muscles
(c) increased sweating, to cool our body down
(d) increased blood pressure, to ensure a good distribution of blood to the muscles of movement
(e) increased muscular tension in preparation for vigorous physical activity

14. What is 'wrong reaction readiness'?

Wrong reaction readiness is a state of readiness for fighting or running away, in a situation where such reactions are inappropriate and will, in fact, cause more problems than they solve.

15. What is the relaxation response?

The relaxation response is a process of releasing tension from our body in order to defuse and counteract the fight or flight response. Release of tension from our muscles signals to the sympathetic nervous system to switch itself off because vigorous physical activity is not needed. The relaxation response is therefore a natural countermeasure to the anxiety state. It signals to what is called 'the parasympathetic nervous system' to restore our bodily functions to their normal equilibrium. Hence, it does the following things:

(a) it slows down our heart rate
(b) it allows blood to flow from the muscles of movement back to the skin and the stomach
(c) it reduces blood pressure.

All in all, it facilitates calm self-possession and relaxed ease. The 'relaxation response' is also known as the 'parasympathetic response'.

16. What is the difference between reaction and action?
The difference between reaction and action is that reactions are usually automatic and unregulated, whereas action is consciously co-ordinated and regulated with respect to the attainment of consciously chosen ends.

17. What is 'right action readiness'?
Right action readiness is a state of psychological and physical poise, organised from within, that releases us from the 'emergency circuitry' of our fight or flight response, and permits us to govern our feelings, thoughts and actions in a purposeful way.

18. What is a separator state?
A separator state is the state in between 'wrong reaction readiness' and 'right action readiness', in which we use the relaxation response to release ourselves from the emergency circuitry of our fight or flight reactions. In this state we still experience the symptoms of the fight or flight response, but we are not going along with them. Instead, we are 'doing nothing' and that is exactly what we need to do. By doing nothing, we let go of as much tension in our body as we can, thereby allowing the fight or flight response simply to burn itself out. If we release ourselves from tension and stop our fearful imaginings (by calmly and confidently waiting for our anxiety to calm down) our anxious feelings will first reach a peak and then they will gradually subside. In short, a separator state is a state in which our body is separating its reactions from its emergency circuitry and returning us to a state of relaxed self-possession.

19. What keeps our panic going?

Our panic is kept going by our failure to release tension from our muscles and by our continuing to fuel our fight or flight response with fearful imaginings and frightening thoughts about the terrible things that 'might happen to us'.

20.   What is the basis of tension?

Tension arises in us whenever we feel under stress. It is part of the body's automatic reaction which prepares us to run or to fight our way out of trouble or difficulty. Unconsciously held tension actually works against us. It prevents us from properly getting in touch with our reason and it therefore perpetuates indecision, which leads to a growing lack of self-confidence and an increasing susceptibility to our 'fears for the worst'. In short, tension is self-perpetuating. So long as it is not consciously released from our body it increases our sense of danger.

21. How can we use the relaxation response to master panic?

We can use it to master panic by:
> (a) regularly practising tension release, even at times when we are not anxious, so that the relaxation response can become routine.
> (b) using it whenever we feel tense and anxious, and
> (c) associating relaxation with an inner vision of ourselves as calm, relaxed and at ease in all situations.

22. What is the first rule for mastering agoraphobia?

The first rule for mastering agoraphobia is: 'Never leave a situation of panic until your anxiety is already coming down.' If we run away from situations in which we feel anxious, this simply reinforces our fear-reactions and our learned avoidance response. If we release ourselves from tension and let go of fearful imaginings in favour of a positive and relaxed inner vision of ourselves, our panic will leave us, we will calm down, and we will be learning to master agoraphobia.

23. How do expectations affect our psychological state?

Expectations affect our psychological state by acting as possible situations which our mind and body prepare us to meet. By envisaging such possibilities and expecting them to happen we engage in a sort of inner rehearsal to meet whatever we visualise as likely to happen. Our body does not distinguish between actual situations and those imagined 'in our head'. In either case our body responds by preparing us to meet the reality that we expect to meet.

24. What is 'second fear'?

Second fear is the fear that we add to our fight or flight response when we focus our mind upon frightening possibilities. Our suggestible senses react to all such frightening thoughts and expectations. In this way, our panic mounts and we become governed by the emergency circuitry which is fed by second fear.

25. What is creative visualisation?

Creative visualisation is the practice of using our imagination to envisage ourselves responding to all our life situations in a creative and confident way. Such visualisation can alter our whole psychological predisposition to life, opening up possibilities for mastering anxiety in a way that would otherwise never become accessible to us. Creative visualisation can be practised at home, relaxing in a chair, or it can be engaged in any situation where we feel at ease and are prepared to re-vision how we are going to meet and cope with situations that are not immediately present.

26. **What is worry?**

Worry is uncreative visualisation. It is the practice of dwelling upon, mulling over and thinking about what we would not like to happen. Negative inner rehearsal is involved. Worrying is always useless and destructive. The same thoughts and feelings keep on going round and round in our minds. Worry is not constructive thinking. Instead, thinking is obscured and dominated by anxiety-based feelings, tension and vicious cycles of projection and reaction. To release ourselves from worry we should focus on what we would prefer, rather than what we would not like, thereby adopting a constructive attitude. If we never worried again, we would suffer no ill-effects in consequence.

27. **How can we use creative visualisation to master agoraphobia?**

We can relax in a chair and visualise ourselves confident, relaxed and at ease in situations that put us ill at ease and tend to send us into a panic. At all times we should stay as relaxed as possible, letting go of tension. If we feel anxious, we should let the anxiety feelings rise to a peak and then slowly subside, all the while imagining what we would do in the real life situation. We can put this into words in a number of confident self-instructions, such as "Face, accept, float and let time pass", "One hundred per cent acceptance not ninety per cent", "Let go and let God". No matter how strong our feelings of panic, we should simply accept them and let them pass, possibly saying to ourselves, "This too shall pass", as surely it will. Feeling anxiety and panic is not a necessary part of imaginal practice. In fact, the more confident we feel in our imaginary situations, the better, always given that our visualisation is full and detailed and not just superficial 'thinking about'. Creative visualisation puts us in the frame of mind for going out and repeating what we have visualised. All kinds of practice make perfect!

28. What does it mean to 'practise' and 'not to test'?
This refers to a relaxed attitude to practice, where having a panic attack is considered less a measure of our failure to master anxiety as it is a further opportunity for practice. Testing ourselves means trying to do as well or better than we did the last time. This attitude brings on that wee edge of tensions which may just tip our practice session into a panic session. We should take the attitude that it really does not matter whether we panic or not, so long as we practise coping with it the right way, if and when it does come.

29. How do beliefs affect our psychological state?
False, harmful and limiting beliefs stand in the way of our growing beyond the limitations that they impose upon us. Positive, expansive and constructive beliefs set free our potential, while negative, constricting and destructive beliefs hold us captive within the limitations that our thinking predefines and projects onto our life situations. As W.I. Thomas stated, "If men define situations as real, they are real in their consequences."[3]

30. What false and harmful beliefs do agoraphobic persons need to overcome?
False and harmful beliefs that need to be overcome include those which treat the symptoms of agoraphobia to be symptoms of serious physical and psychological malfunctioning. They are no such thing. The physical symptoms experienced are usually no more and no less than the ordinary symptoms of the fight or flight response. The psychological symptoms experienced are only the result of uninformed and unregulated reaction to the fight or flight response, no more and no less. It may help you to realise that the fight or flight response is

set and limited, with the same nerves and organs responding in a set pattern to fear of fear. The symptoms you are experiencing now are probably as 'bad' or 'unpleasant' as you will ever experience them. False and harmful beliefs can best be explored through a series of questions (*see* questions 31 to 37).

31.Why do we have difficulty in breathing?

You may complain of difficulty in taking a deep breath. If you observe yourself closely you will probably find that you have unconsciously breathed all the way *in* and are holding your breath. Try breathing all the way *out*. Even try holding your breath out. After a short while you will find yourself breathing freely and normally. Sometimes people fear that if they stop breathing consciously their breathing itself will stop and they will pass out or die as a result. If this is your problem you will probably find that you are actually breathing too much. Fast shallow breathing often washes out too much carbon dioxide, so that the automatic breathing control centre in your brain, which functions in accordance with the oxygen/carbon-dioxide ratio in your blood stream, is waiting for your carbon-dioxide to increase. If you are forcing your breathing rate, your breathing centre will slow your breathing down while the levels of oxygen and carbon dioxide in your blood are adjusting. There is no need to force your breathing. There is nothing wrong with your breathing, otherwise how could you breathe while asleep? Simply relax and let your breathing take care of itself.

32. What is that lump in the throat?

A lump in the throat is a common feature of anxiety states. No, it is probably not cancer. A lump in the throat is a common feature of anxiety, representing a kind of conflict between 'wanting to scream' and 'suppressing a scream'. We often hear of the expression of people trying to 'gulp down their fear'. If you have difficulty in eating solid food as a result of this lump in the throat, try simply chewing your food without attempting to swallow it. Sooner or later, some of the food will touch the back of the throat, your swallowing reflex will take over, and at least some of your food will be on its way down.

33. Will our heart burst?

Some agoraphobics fear that their heart will burst because it is beating so very forcefully. This will never happen. The size and strength of the heart muscle makes it impossible for it to burst.

34. Will we have heart failure?

There is probably nothing wrong with your heart. A rapidly beating heart is merely responding naturally and automatically to your fearful imaginings. Some people are concerned about their heart 'missing a beat'. Heart beats are never actually missed. All that happens is that a sudden spasm of fear gives rise to a sudden rapid heart beat, which is followed by a resting pause while your heart adjusts it rate. After this pause your heart may thump. The thumping, racing heart is still under control and will always return to its natural rhythm once panic is over.

35. Why do we have 'jelly legs'?

Jelly legs are a common feature of agoraphobia. A feeling of muscular weakness often follows excessive tension. You are in all probability not suffering from a muscular disease. Claire Weekes reminds us that "Jelly legs will get you there if you let them". As long as you let go of tension and worry, and do not try to hurry, your jelly legs are quite capable of carrying you wherever you wish to go at a slow and easy pace.

36. Why do we have dizzy spells?

Some people find it hard to believe that dizzy spells can be the result of anxiety and tension, but such is, in fact, the case. Anxiety and tension may well lower our blood sugar level so that such things as a sudden shock or a rapid run across a busy street can bring on a dizzy spell. There is probably nothing at all 'wrong' with your brain or your body.

37. Why do we have feelings of unreality?

Many agoraphobic persons become quite alarmed because they experience feelings of unreality or feelings of de-personalisation. These feelings are usually the result of too much anxious introspective brooding in which we become preoccupied with our state (or our plight) to the exclusion of all other thoughts, aims and experiences. Small wonder, then, that when we return our attention to ordinary living the outside world seems 'strange' or we ourselves feel 'strange'. If we simply disregard this feeling, giving it no undue attention, it will disappear of its own accord as we accommodate ourselves to the normal give and take of everyday life.

38. How do attitudes affect our psychological state?

Attitudes are predispositions to respond in certain ways to given situations. As we think about such situations, so we inwardly rehearse how we are going to respond. Attitudes are therefore very important. If we change our thinking and acting from fearful preoccupation and avoidance to creative visualisation and regular practice, so our attitudes will change accordingly.

39. What attitudes do we need to change?

We need to change all attitudes that keep us locked into vicious cycles of anxiety and tension, including such attitudes as self-pity, procrastination, waiting for our mood to change, avoidance of feared situations, impatience, and so on, in favour of cultivating the attitude of calm, relaxed confidence.

40. What aims do we need to change?

We need to change all aims which concern our avoiding situations of anxiety, in favour of purposefully practising coping with panic and practising anxiety mastery strategies until the sudden flashing of panic is no longer feared, but is instead simply accepted as part of the programme of mastery itself. Conditional fear reactions to certain places or certain thoughts, worrying and therefore inwardly rehearsing feeling anxious and simply thinking about losing control, all predispose us to reacting with anxiety. Such, however, is *not* our aim. We should instead plan to go out and face places that we have been seeking to avoid for fear of what reactions this might bring. Facing such places, in specific ways, letting go of tension and anxious imaginings and accepting our feelings as natural, temporary and 'part of the job' form an integral part of anxiety mastery. Such is our aim.

41. What is sensitisation?

Sensitisation is the process whereby we become 'sensitised' to our own nervous reaction, our fight or flight response, so that as soon as we feel an increase in our heart-rate or tension, we react with alarm and our feelings of anxiety and panic quickly increase and intensify.

42. What does a sensitised person do?

A sensitised person takes an anxious interest in their own physiological reactions, listening in with fearful anticipation for any indication of increased heartbeat or other signs of anxiety. As a result, such people become primed, like a booby trap, to trip themselves into a panic state at the slightest provocation. Even a mild shock or a sudden loud noise can do it.

43. How can we de-sensitise our nervous system?
We can de-sensitise ourselves by becoming more informed about what we are doing to ourselves, ceasing to morbidly preoccupy ourselves with our physiological processes and practising a full-scale programme of anxiety mastery.[4]

44. How does panic mount?
Panic rapidly mounts when we hold false and harmful beliefs about what is happening to us, when we expect the worst, when we listen in with alarm to our nervous reactions, when we tense up and do not release tension and when we add 'second fear' by imagining and anticipating all the fearful things that might happen to us next.

45. How can mounting panic be controlled?
Mounting panic can be controlled by letting go of tension and fearful imaginings, taking a deep breath and letting it all go out slowly, sighing, sinking and sagging to release tension, and giving oneself confident instructions which are in line with our understanding and our aims. A simple phrase such as "Let go and let God" or simply "Accept and let go", or "This too shall pass" will do.

46. What is the difference between mastering agoraphobia and putting up with anxiety?
Putting up with anxiety means restricting our movements outside of our own home, avoiding more and more places. In this way the problem only gets worse. The more we put up with anxiety the more anxiety we will have to put up with. Mastering agoraphobia means accepting the symptoms of the fight or flight response and practising the programme in places that we have been avoiding.

47. **What common props do agoraphobics use?**

In order to bolster their confidence and give them a false sense of mastery, agoraphobics often habitually rely on the following props: understanding friends; tranquillisers; alcohol; going out only in the dark or in the rain.

48. **What is the problem with props?**

The problem with props is that, if we routinely rely on them we become dependent upon them in an unhealthy way. Props do not enable us to face and overcome our fears. Instead, they foster in us a growing loss of confidence in our own inner powers, an undermining of self-reliance and a continued dependence on props.

49. **What are the four concepts for mastering agoraphobia?**

The four concepts put forward by Dr Claire Weekes[5] as a sure way of mastering agoraphobia are as follows:

> (i) Face
> (ii) Accept
> (iii) Float
> (iv) Let time pass

50. **What does 'facing' mean?**

It means understanding and looking at the situation as it is, not trying to occupy your mind with something else, by, for example, counting or saying mindless prayers. Trying to distract yourself always misses the mark in the end. Instead, you need to apply your understanding of the fight or flight response to your situation and use tension release to switch this response off. Instead of adding second fear, it is a good idea to describe to yourself exactly what you are doing (I am doing this and this and this), and to describe your surrounding to yourself, noting what is actually there and what is actually happening rather than filling your mind with fearful imaginings.

51. What does 'accepting' mean?

It means not tensing oneself against 'unwelcome' feelings, holding the attention of others for security's sake, watching the clock, grimly gritting one's teeth. This is not accepting but fighting. It means accepting the feelings of heightened sensitised anxiety reactions as natural learned responses, while one is un-learning these extreme reactions through the acceptance method of 'desensitisation'.

52. What does 'floating' mean?

Floating means letting go of all excess tension, offering no tense resistance. By tensing up in a moment of panic, you cog yourself into a cycle of spiralling tension. By releasing yourself from the grip of tension, taking a deep breath and letting it all out, slowly, you let your panic spend itself and you go free. So long as you do not reinforce your panic with second fear, and you let go of tension instead of letting tension control you, your panic will subside. It is all in the word 'float'. Let yourself feel like a row of corks on a fisherman's net, gently undulating on the deep rolling waves.

53. What does 'letting time pass' mean?

It means not trying to hurry the panic away. The subsidence of panic will occur naturally, in its own time, if you let it. Hurry itself signifies fear and therefore means unconsciously tensing up. You must be prepared to accept your anxiety feelings one hundred per cent for as long as they last. You may also worry that your agoraphobia is taking a long time to take its leave of you; however, such release will only come with repeated practice. You have probably collected a lot of discouraging memories in your time as a 'victim' of agoraphobia. Let yourself recover now, at your own pace, with repeated practice, until the right response to anxiety becomes *routine*.. What we call 'agoraphobia' will only cease to bother you when it no longer matters to you whether you feel anxious or not. When you know how to master panic and are confident in coping with anxiety, its coming will simply cease to concern you. That is what recovery means. Letting time pass means accepting yourself under all conditions as time passes. This is the key.

54. What is imaginal practice?
Imaginal practice means using the process of creative visualisation to imagine yourself feeling at ease and confident in situations that you have previously been afraid to face. It also means inwardly rehearsing going into the 'separator state', doing nothing while you let panic spend itself. By imaginally entering into feared situations in a confident and calm way, and by practising coping with panic the right way, you gear yourself to meet situations as you imagine them. This is also called 'acquiring right action readiness'.

55. What is the Law of Inner Rehearsal?
The Law of Inner Rehearsal states that 'Whatever we think about or dwell upon we inwardly rehearse'. This means that our body responds to whatever we rehearse in our thoughts, thus creating our psychological state or 'set' for meeting situations that we visualise inwardly. In this way, whatever we visualise or dwell upon becomes our unconscious goal.

56. How does practising anxiety management fail?
It fails when we vividly recall past fears and failures in the same way as before and so, unwittingly, we rehearse our future anxiety and downfall. This is how we

inwardly rehearse and acquire 'wrong reaction readiness'.

57. What is the Law of Reversed Effort?

The Law of Reversed Effort, first stated by Emile Coue,[6] can be paraphrased as follows: "The more effort, the less effective". The law applies both to imaginal practice and to practice in real life situations. The converse of this is also true - the more calm and relaxed we are in our visualisations and our practice sessions, the more control we have over our emotional reactions. This law is echoed in research work on people who use bio-feedback to lower their blood pressure.[7] The more they 'try' to lower their blood pressure, the less they are able to do so. On the other hand, by simply letting go of all effort and passively imagining that it is going down, brings the most effective results. This process has also been called 'passive volition'.[8]

58. What is the 'Alexander Principle'?

The Alexander principle states that 'Use affects function'. This means that the use that we make of our body affects the functioning of our body. Excessive tension held in the body means not only disturbed intra-organismic functioning - joint problems, muscular pains, stress disorders in general - but also disturbed psychological states in the form of increased irritability, tiredness, anxiety and depression.[9]

59. Why is it important to walk tall and breathe freely?

This is in line with Alexander's method of better use of the body. By walking tall we lengthen the spine and achieve a more integrated postural balance. Our spine achieves an anti-gravity alignment, which leaves us feeling less under pressure. As we free the breath instead of squeezing our belly in, we feel more at ease. Walking tall, breathing freely and thinking positively all put us in better touch with our self-governing potential, which keeps us out of the clutches of panic.

60. Why should we regularly practise relaxing?

We should regularly practise relaxing (once a day at least, whether we are anxious or not) so that we can use the 'relaxation programme' as a routine to switch off the distressing effects of the fight or flight response. It we were to relax only at times of panic this would associate relaxing too closely with the panic state itself. Instead, being at ease, open and relaxed is something that we need to cultivate as a way of life, rather than just a coping routine. Relaxing may, after years of tense living, cease to be a natural way of life for us. However, by practising relaxing as a routine, we can consciously relax whenever we wish to do so. Through practice we can relax routinely so that, like the routine of dressing or driving a car, we do not have to think it all out from the beginning each time.

61. What is the first thing to do when panic strikes?

Take a deep breath and let it all out. Sagging to release tension and saying inwardly the words "Sigh, sink and sag", helps to establish the right mental attitude.

62. What are the 'terrible twins' of agoraphobia?

The terrible twins are Hurry and Worry. Hurry signifies fear and keeps our tension high. Worry is negative inner rehearsal and it constitutes negative practice. The less we entertain the terrible twins, the better we feel.

63. What will happen if we stop worrying?

Nothing bad will happen. Worry gives us some sort of immediate short-term relief from anxiety because it feels as if we are doing something, but the long-term effects are disastrous. There is no justification for worry. It is useless and harmful. Dropping the worry habit gives us a new lease of life. At the same time we need to replace worry with constructive thinking.

64. How can we reframe a worrying thought?
We should look for what we want rather than what we do not want, and see how we can attain our positive goal rather than fighting against what we do not want.

65. How can we be bluffed by our feeling?
The more frightening a thought is, the more anxious we feel when we think about it, especially when we start imagining that the frightening thought could happen to us. The stronger our anxiety, the more we become convinced that the fearful thought behind it must be true, simply because we feel it so strongly. This is how we are bluffed. Strength of feeling is no indication of the truth of a thought.

66. How can we avoid being bluffed by our feelings?
We can avoid being bluffed into thinking that strongly felt anxious thoughts must be true by understanding *how* we are being bluffed, by ceasing to hold onto or follow through our thoughts with further anxious reflection, and by not reacting in any special way as we let go of our fearful thoughts and focus on positive aims and goals instead. Whenever we are feeling sufficiently positive, we can look again at our negative fears to see if they can give us any information regarding our positive aims.

67. Is self-talk important?
Self-talk and thinking are really one and the same thing. The way we think reflects the way we are and the way we are going to be. We constantly carry on an inner dialogue with ourselves. If we pay attention to our self-talk we can easily see whether it is constructive or destructive. People who fret and worry a great deal can benefit dramatically by changing their self-talk. Instead of

engaging in destructive self-talk it may be useful to start changing the nature of our inner dialogue by simply describing to ourselves the things that we are doing. We may thus say: "I am making some tea. I am pouring water into the kettle. I switch the tap off. I plug the kettle in", and so on. Doing all these things with care and appreciation has a calming and strengthening effect on our awareness, concentration and our general purposive consciousness. Our awareness becomes focused and one-pointed. In nearly all cases, such action-appreciating and aim-appreciating self-talk can help to replace anxious inner chattering with a sense of conflict-free inner purpose and constructive attention.

68. What is a mental diet?

We choose the condition of our life by the thoughts with which we feed our mind. Mental dieting involves selectively choosing our thoughts in order to transform both our psychological outlook and the very 'substance' of our life and circumstances as we experience them.

69. How can we go on a mental diet?

For seven days, do not allow yourself to dwell for a single moment on any kind of negative thought. Under no pretext allow yourself to dwell upon or imagine anything that is not positive, constructive and optimistic. A week's diet is sufficient to transform the whole framework of our thinking. If we make a false start, or at any time find ourselves dwelling on negative and destructive thoughts, we should immediately drop the diet and start afresh in a few days time. There must be no half on, half off.[10]

70. What can we expect from going on a mental diet?

Find out for yourself. When you have reaped the benefits, encourage others to do likewise. Discuss the effects with someone who has gone through the diet themselves.

71. What are negative emotions?
Negative emotions are feelings and attitudes that negate our self-governing potential and keep us trapped in cycles of reactive bondage.

72. What are common examples of negative emotions?
Common examples of negative emotions include sulking (brooding over misfortunes); self-pity (feeling sorry for ourselves); shame (finding fault with ourselves); guilt (condemning ourselves); blame (finding fault with others); envy and jealousy (fearing that others have what we lack or will take from us what we have); and resentment (condemning others). Negative emotions give us a temporary feeling of relief, because they are fear-based reactions. Yet we indulge in them at our peril since they are self-fuelling and predispose us to wrong reaction readiness. Indulging in negative ruminations and feelings involve us in focusing on our deficiencies and reacting against (or with) our fears. This only feeds our fears, negative beliefs and harmful attitudes, expectations and aims, rendering us even more fearful and useless than we started out.

73. How can depression grow out of agoraphobia?
Depression is a psychological state which is characterised by refraining from all purposive action. The avoidance habit of agoraphobia - being afraid to go out - may well be replaced by depression - not wanting to go out and losing all hope. This is how depression can grow out of agoraphobia.

74. How can affirmations of positive belief help us?
Affirmations of positive belief can help us by establishing the framework in which we are prepared to act and

outside of which we are not prepared to act. Positive beliefs open up constructive aims and purposes for us to act upon. Every time we act upon positive and constructive beliefs and aims we strengthen them in us and we also strengthen, thereby, our positive and constructive resolve.

75. What are common examples of negative and harmful beliefs?

Here we open up a vast can of worms for agoraphobic persons. Study the following a-to-z of negative beliefs and add your own to the list if they are not already included in it:

  (a) I'm not confident enough yet
  (b) My problem is inherited
  (c) I can't
  (d) I'm afraid I will faint or my legs will give way
  (e) It's just the way I am. I can't do anything about it.
  (f) I'm afraid of what other people will think of me
  (g) I'm as bad as ever. I'm not making any progress
  (h) I've got to get out of here quickly
  (i) My nerves have the better of me
  (j) I hope I can do as well as I did last time
  (k) I'll go as far as I can
  (l) I'm not in the right mood
  (m) Life is terrifying and death is worse
  (n) I'm too uptight
  (o) Nobody wants to know me
  (p) Nothing I try ever works out
  (q) I don't think the same as everyone else
  (r) It may work for others, but it won't work for me
  (s) I haven't got the guts
  (t) It's will power I need

(u) Other people have got their lives together and
      I haven't

(v) I can't accept the way I am

(w) I'll take a rest today, I need one

(x) I'm going mad

(y) I'm a born worrier

(z) I'm too impatient

76. **What constructive and positive beliefs can be
    affirmed to replace harmful and destructive ones?**
The following list provides belief antidotes for the
destructive beliefs given above. Some of these may
overlap. Choose the antidote that feels right for you and
that you feel you can best act upon:

> (a) (I'm not confident enough yet)
> - Confidence goes places
> - Wait on no mood
> - I can compel my limbs and muscles in spite of
>   my feelings
> - Act the way you want to feel. Think the way
>   you want to be.
> - Daily practice builds confidence
> - Confidence is not a feeling, but an attitude of
>   mind
>
> (b) (My problem is inherited)
> - I'm a person not an emotional reaction
> - I have a choice
> - Don't be bluffed by your feelings
> - God doesn't make junk
>
> (c) (I can't)
> - Never say "I can't" when the thing in question
>   is an ordinary and good thing to do

- If a thing is worth doing, it's worth doing badly - at least to begin with, and while you're improving
- Easy does it

(d) (I'm afraid my legs will give way)
- Jelly legs will get you there if you let them

(e) (It's just the way I am. I can't do anything about it)
- Act the way you want to feel. Think the way you want to be
- My first reaction is a fear reaction: I will let go, let it pass and carry on, nice and easy
- I am open to receive the Power within
- Give yourself a chance
- Daily practice builds confidence

(f) (I'm afraid of what other people will think of me)
- Those who mind don't matter. Those who matter don't mind
- The best in me is for others and the best in others is for me
- Everyone has the same needs as I do. We're all in this together

(g) (I'm as bad as ever. I'm not making any progress)
- Keep right on to the end of the road
- 100 percent acceptance, not 99 percent
- In a set-back, settle back
- One step at a time
- Only if you accept yourself the way you are can you improve upon the way you are

(h) (I've got to get out of here quickly)
- Let go and let God
- Never leave a panic situation until your anxiety is already going down
- In the middle ground we come around
- My panic will spend itself, if I let it
- Relax into a vision

(i) (My nerves have the better of me)
- The best way to get a grip of yourself is to let go
- Face, accept, float and let time pass
- I am open to receive the Power within
- Panic doesn't matter - it's what you do in panic that matters

(j) (I hope I'll do as well as I did last time)
- Practice, don't test

(k) (I'll go as far as I can)
- Keep right on to the end of the road
- Be specific (about your goals)
- I've started so I'll finish
- It's not the place that matters, but the moment
- Keep on keeping on

(l) (I'm not in the right mood)
- Wait on no mood
- Avoidance adds up to panic
- Don't put off until tomorrow what you can do today
- My feelings will get better as my habits of thinking and acting get better
- Action is the magic word

(m) (Life is terrifying and death is worse)
- The best in me is for others and the best in others is for me
- The only thing to fear is fear itself
- Don't be bluffed by your feelings
- The best is yet to come
- Visualise what you want, not what you don't want

(n) (I'm too uptight)
- Never *try* to relax
- Let go and let God
- Don't react; relax and act
- Relax into a vision
- Easy does it

(o) (Nobody wants to know me)
- The best in me is for others and the best in others is for me

(p) (Nothing I try ever works out)
- Relax into a positive vision of yourself
- Try right-action readiness
- Imaginal practice makes perfect
- The less effort, the more effective
- One step at a time
- Be specific about your means and goals

(q) (I don't think the same as everyone else)
- Don't make a personal issue out of problems of adjustment
- Anxiety conditioning is unconscious, mastery of anxiety is conscious

(r) (It may work for others, but it won't work for me)

- The programme works
- Panic doesn't matter. It's what you do in panic that matters
- Face, accept, float and let time pass

(s) (I haven't got the guts)
- Easy does it
- The less effort, the more effective
- Whatever we dwell upon becomes our unconscious goal
- Daily practice builds confidence
- Hope doesn't abandon you; you abandon it

(t) (It's will power I need)
- Imaginal practice makes perfect
- The less effort, the more effective
- Relax into a vision

(u) (Other people have got their lives together and I haven't)
- The way we are depends upon our daily decisions
- Act the way you want to feel. Think the way you want to be.
- The best in me is for others, and the best in others is for me
- Everyone has the same needs as I have. We're all in this together
- One step at a time

(v) (I can't accept myself, the way I am)
- Only if I accept myself the way I am will I be able to improve upon the way I am
- 100 per cent acceptance, not 99 per cent

(w) (I'll take a well-earned rest)
- There's no such thing as a well-earned rest
- Avoidance adds up to panic
- Confidence goes places
- Don't put off until tomorrow what you can do today
- The way we are depends on our daily decisions
- Daily practice builds confidence
- 'Action' is the magic word

(x) (I'm going mad)
- Practice makes perfect!
- Don't be bluffed by your feelings
- Visualise what you want, not what you don't want
- First things first
- Agoraphobia is not a serious mental illness

(y) (I'm a born worrier)
- Whatever we dwell upon becomes our unconscious goal
- Practice right action readiness not wrong reaction readiness
- Visualise what you want, not what you don't want
- Give your hang-up a rest
- Get off the misery-go-round
- Take your finger off your pulse and start living

(z) (I'm too impatient)
- Make haste slowly
- Easy does it
- One step at a time
- When God made time, he made plenty of it
- First things first

- I can do all things through Christ who strengthens me
- A journey of a thousand miles starts with the first step

77. Why is it useful to draw up a list of avoidance situations in order of intensity?

Such a list is useful because it enables us to see where to start working on our problem, where we are heading for, and what progress we are making.

78. What is an anxiety ladder?

An anxiety ladder is the above list, starting at the top with situations most feared and ending up with situations which make us just slightly anxious, *plus* an anxiety rating for each item.

79. How can we construct an anxiety ladder?

Anxiety ratings are made on a subjective scale (from one to one hundred) with items spaced as evenly as possible in each decade. If all our items are bunched together at the top and bottom, we need to be more imaginative in filling in in-between items that approach those at the top. For example: shopping at the supermarket - 99; going to the door of the supermarket with a friend - 64. In between items can be found, allowing you to have a full range of items to be tackled.

80. How can we convert an anxiety ladder into a progress ladder?

By starting to practise facing anxiety-evoking situations at the bottom of the list, and working our way up to the top.

81. How specific should our progress ladder be?

As specific as possible. There may be a very discernable difference between going to the supermarket on a crowded shopping day, and going some time when it is likely to be less crowded. There may be a big difference between going to buy twenty items and going to buy two or three, or going with a shopping list and going without one. Hence, our item might read: "Going to the supermarket at half-past nine on a Tuesday or Thursday morning, with a shopping list to buy four items and meeting a friend afterwards." If we were to write merely "Going to the supermarket", does this mean going in? buying something? alone or with a friend? What should we do before we feel that we have succeeded in this item? To be specific enables us to know when we have successfully completed an item. Precise descriptions give us criteria to aim for and which will let us know how we have done, and how far we can reasonably hope to go next time.

82. Why are target criteria important?

Target criteria are important because, if we are going to change our ways of thinking and acting, we need criteria built into what we intend. Such criteria enable us to avoid misunderstanding about what we intend to do. We need to be certain, in our own minds, so as to avoid misunderstanding, to avoid deceiving ourselves and to avoid confusion in doing what we intend to do.

83. If we succeed in completing a practical task, what should we do next?

We should repeat the task a few more times to establish our confidence and to consolidate our progress, before moving on to a more difficult item.

84. If we succeed in a practical task, what should we not do?

We should not congratulate ourselves and 'take a well earned rest'. This simply means continued avoidance on the flimsy pretext that we've finally made it. We have *not* made it. We need to keep practising. We need to consolidate and move on. The only people who should be resting on their laurels are those who are about to die.

85. What does 'bridging the gap' mean?

Bridging the gap means solving the problem of getting stuck on one item in our progress ladder and not being able to move on to the next. What is missing is some intermediate item that will allow us to build confidence for going on to the next step. If, for example, the next item reads "Going alone to the post office to post a parcel", and we feel unable to carry this through, perhaps we could insert an item such as "Going to the post office with my friend to post a parcel [or buy stamps, or whatever]." This intermediary item bridges the gap between what we feel able to do and what we do not as yet feel able to do. Taking such an intermediary step enables us to build sufficient confidence to move onto the next rung of the ladder.

86. How often should we practise facing feared situations?

We should practise every day. If we do not, we are in danger of making a special 'thing' about anxiety management. This is avoidance. It is not a special thing. Facing ordinary things that frighten us needs to become an ordinary part of our everyday life.

87. Should we use tranquillisers?

Tranquillisers are like 'governors' that are placed on the engine of a truck, keeping the speed of the truck within certain limits whether the driver intends it or not. In this sense they can be said to stand in the way of our consciously realising our own self-governing potential. On the other hand, we might decide to use tranquillisers to 'bridge the gap' on a difficult item, so long as we practise without tranquillisers again, soon afterwards on the same site. Tranquillisers used in this way should be taken just before engaging on the practical task. It would be self-defeating simply to take them, say, three times a day, every day. This just means becoming dependent upon them. Such a crutch we do not need. Who wants to learn how to cripple themselves? On the other hand, if you are already hooked on tranquillisers you should not come off them all at once, but consult your doctor about how to gradually wean yourself off them.

88. What happens if we panic and forget what to do?

Carry a short list of rules with you. Before you practice, read through the list. When you panic, take the list out and read it. Whatever ideas help you, put them on the list. Here are some suggestions:

    (i) Panic is not harmful, just unpleasant. I will accept it and let it pass.

    (ii) I will take note of the situation and describe what I am doing.

    (iii) This too shall pass.

    (iv) Face, accept, float and let time pass.

    (v) Easy does it.

89. What happens when we have a set-back?

When we have a set-back all our old fears and anxieties return, seemingly as bad as ever, almost like a chain reaction. We feel as anxious and unconfident as we ever did. It is as if we were back to square one. So long as we do not over-react to these feelings we will come through our set-back strengthened by the experience.

90. What are the symptoms of a set-back?

The symptoms of a set-back are the symptoms of the fight or flight response.

91. What should we do when we have a set-back?

Whenever we have a set-back we should accept it as a natural part of the process of mastering anxiety. We are almost certain to have a set-back at some stage. Memory alone will bring it. But all is not lost as we might imagine. We know how to master agoraphobia and, by starting all over again, we strengthen our resolve and consolidate our previous progress. This is why a set-back may well be a very useful and rewarding learning experience.

92. Is keeping a Personal Life Book important?

In the long term, keeping a Personal Life Book is one of the most important things we can do.[11] It enables us to be continuously aware of all that we are thinking and doing, to let go of negative and destructive beliefs and imaginings about ourselves and others, and to overhaul our aims and intentions. By writing about our present and our past 'without praise and without blame', we are enabled to centre our awareness on the stream of our being and becoming in such a way that we are freed from negative traps of anxiety-based emotions. By the same token, we are released from self-conflict by the positive forces within us working in a conscious, constructive and total way. Another reason why the P.L.B. 'works' is that, by keeping it, we slow our thinking down, becoming more mindful, reflective and undistractedly attentive.

93. Why does trying to forget not work?

Trying to forget the difficulties that we have had does not work because our memories are constantly stimulated and recalled. There is nothing the matter with recalling or thinking about our difficulties, so long as we do so with the appropriate beliefs and aims in mind. Trying to take our minds off the fact that we have agoraphobia or events that surround it or give rise to it, is like trying to drink a bottle of medicine without thinking about a green monkey once we have been told "This medicine will only work if you do not think of a green monkey while drinking it." Trying to forget is a form of repression. This involves tension. It also involves a failure to accept ourselves and our situation in life. We can only master our difficulties by accepting them and understanding them, thereafter taking appropriate action to consolidate 'who we are' and 'how we are'. Trying to forget may work for a time, but our fears and memories are sure to rebound back on us at unwelcome moments. Using tension to overcome tension can never work. Instead, we need to accept and understand our past in order to plan to meet the future in a new and different way.

94. When does practising anxiety management fail?
It fails when we vividly recall past fears with the same beliefs, expectations, attitudes and aims that we had in the past. In this way our future becomes like our past through the process of inner rehearsal.

95. How important is the food we eat?
It may be very important. Diets containing large amounts of refined sugar, a large proportion of meat and lots of processed and denatured food such as white bread, are acid-producing and tend to make us feel under stress. Nervous feelings may arise because our body is using up its alkaline reserves to balance out the acid formed from the foods we eat. Eating more alkaline-forming food such as fresh fruit and fresh raw or lightly steamed vegetables, may be a major factor in enabling us better to master anxiety.[12]

96. Is exercise important?

Exercise is very beneficial. Fairly vigorous exercise every day, or at least twice or three times a week, can only be good for us. This may take the form of walking, jogging, skipping, swimming, cycling, aerobic dancing, or any other activity which raises our pulse and keeps it raised for about twenty minutes to half an hour. Among other things, exercise helps to regulate the workings of the sympathetic and parasympathetic nervous systems. It regulates hormone levels, helps lower our general level of tension, and keeps our lungs clear so that we can breathe deeply and freely.

97. What is the Law of Requisite Variety?

The Law of Requisite Variety states: "Only variety can destroy variety".[13] We cannot replace something varied and complex with nothing. We can only replace it with something varied and interesting. To replace habits of anxiety and avoidance we need to engage in activities and pursuits that are purposeful, engaging and constructive. To replace forceful anxiety-based beliefs, expectations, attitudes and reactions we need hopeful and positive beliefs, expectations, attitudes and aims.

98. Should we take up new and varied interests now or wait until we have recovered first?

Hobbies, interests, activities, vocational and recreational pursuits provide us with something definite and positive to get well for. If we have something to go out for, *now*, we are all the better equipped to master agoraphobia. The alternative is staying at home, avoidance, continued agoraphobia and possibly also depression. Therefore we need to start now to take up new or old interests, visit friends, join a club or get a job. These are important ways of helping yourself *now*. They provide regular opportunities for practice in meeting and mastering anxiety, and they help to fulfil the requirements of the Law of Requisite Variety.

99. Why is it important for us to tell others about our anxieties and our progress in mastering them?

It is important for us to tell other members of the group about our presenting difficulties and our progress in mastering them, for a number of reasons:

(i) It helps others to identify with our problems rather than leaving them feeling alone, isolated and without anyone to understand what they are going through.

(ii) It enables others to envisage possibilities for their own progress.

(iii) It enables us to be positive and constructive about ourselves, to credit ourselves with progress, and to practise reframing our thoughts and feelings in a positive and purposeful way.

100. Why is it important to let others talk out their anxieties?

It is important for a number of reasons:

(i) It allows them to face, accept and articulate their experiences, their memories, their expectations, their beliefs, their attitudes and their fears.

(ii) It allows them to talk about their problems rather than feeling that they simply *are* their problems.

(iii) It gives them emotional release.

(iv) It allows us to enter into dialogue with them so that we can work to shift their beliefs, expectations, attitudes and aims, reframing these in anxiety management terms.

(v) It gives them a chance to consider alternative ways of thinking, acting and feeling.

(vi) It gives everyone else an opportunity to establish identification, a sense of solidarity and a desire to help.

(vii) It provides material for reframing and for the setting of practical tasks to consolidate understanding and acquire confidence.

101. Why should we learn to understand, ask and answer these questions?

Because this will replace our ignorance, confusion and bewilderment with understanding, direction and a framework within which we can help ourselves and others. We, of the Northern Ireland Agoraphobic Society, have found that the self-help approach brings to full fruition any and all advances made in individual therapy and counselling. Agoraphobics learn a great deal from listening and talking to one another. When they see what others like themselves are able to achieve, they learn to strike out on their own account, so adding to the collective accomplishments of the group and establishing a place for themselves in the group's developing oral history, achievements and positive self-understanding.

PROGRESS REVIEW ONE

Anxiety mastery: reflection for action.

CENTRAL IDEA: If we think we can solve our problems and difficulties without understanding them, we are on the wrong track. If we abandon our mental and physical health to outside agencies that prescribe no more than chemical solutions to our problems, we foolishly send the human side of our human being into chemical enslavement. We need instead to replace fear and confusion with clear-sighted understanding and practice. Constructive thought and positive action need to be the hallmarks of our progress.

Advancement in self-discovery means studying our problems objectively. Properly understood, a problem becomes an opportunity to make progress.

'Understanding' is the consciousness 'under' which we 'stand', the knowledge that we use to live by.[1] Our understanding needs to be deep, full and dynamic, like the flow of life itself.

The quality of our life depends upon the quality of our awareness and the choices that our awareness makes available to us. When we explore what these choices are, recognise what we need to do and what we need to avoid doing, we start to make clear headway. We begin to think and act in ways that are good for us, *because* we recognise their goodness and what they can achieve.

Read Chapters 3, 4 and 5, and put their precepts into practice.

Criteria of Attainment
1. You checked out your experience of anxiety in terms of the various components of the 'fight or flight'

response; you recognised this response to be normal, given your thinking, and you were able to consider the response itself as physically set and limited. You saw it as understandable and controllable, certainly not harmful.

2. You reviewed your beliefs concerning what you thought was happening to you and were able to recognise those beliefs that were not only false but also frightening and self-limiting. You were able to replace such beliefs with a more constructive and realistic understanding of what was going on.

3. You became aware of 'listening in with alarm' to check out your emotional state. You realised that this practice, in itself, brought on the very components of the stress response (the fight or flight response) that you feared. In the long run it 'sensitised' you to your own nervous reactions. You realised that you had been intensifying a vicious cycle of worry - checking up - anxiety. You committed yourself to a programme of 'desensitising' yourself, by accepting the symptoms of the fight or flight response, 100%, for as long as they lasted, without reacting to them, without trying to get rid of them or hurry them away. Instead, you practised letting go of tension, letting your breath out and breathing slowly and deeply. You let go of frightening thoughts. You replaced them with calm, confident commands and affirmations.

4. You recognised your tendency to avoid people and places that you associated with anxiety. You made a list of situations you felt anxious in and avoided. You rated these situations, as described, in an 'anxiety hierarchy' and you started to work your way through this list from the *least* to the *most* anxiety-provoking situations. By using imaginal rehearsal and graded practice, you converted your 'anxiety hierarchy' into a 'progress ladder'.

5. You understood the difference between 'first fear' and 'second fear'. You ceased to try to avoid or be afraid of first fear, namely the stress response. Instead, you practised dealing with it by ceasing to stoke your anxiety with worry, fearful imagining and frightening anticipations. Rather than do this, you practised giving yourself calm, confident instructions such as "Sigh, sink and sag", "Let go and let God", "Face, accept, float and let time pass", "Jelly legs will get you there if you let them". You followed these commands and affirmations without inner contention, 'as if' you believed them to be completely true. You discovered that your feelings were able to turn around and assume the pattern of your thinking and acting.

6. You practised relaxing each day - letting go of all tension in your body - so that you were able to develop a routine for 'letting go' whenever you wanted to or needed to. You made use of the relaxation response to accept all your feelings, let go of tension, and let anxiety pass.

7. You understood what was involved in the process of inner rehearsal. You practised avoiding *negative* inner rehearsal (worry). You replaced it with *positive* inner rehearsal (positive visualising). You used positive inner rehearsal to practise entering feared situations with 'ease' and 'confidence'. You dealt with panic 'the right way', whenever it arose.

8. You built on imaginal rehearsal with graded practice, using the four concepts - 'Face', 'Accept', 'Float', and 'Let time pass' - to master anxiety, whenever you felt a panic attack threatening to break on you. You *let* it break on you harmlessly and spend itself.

9. You accepted your set-backs as a natural part of the recovery process. You refused to 'awfulise' about them and 'catastrophise' them. Instead, you accepted them, learned from them what you needed to do to make

progress, and got back to work again with the minimum of fuss.

Notes, References and Suggested Reading

1. See Nicoll, M. *Living time and the integration of the life*. Watkins, London 1981. "If the doctrine of potentiality is true and man is incomplete but capable of reaching further states of himself, any psychological system that does not take these possibilities into consideration must be inadequate." p.47.

PROGRESS REVIEW TWO

Positive inner rehearsal.

CENTRAL IDEA: We are thinking, feeling and doing beings. This is what we are aware of when we think. The thoughts that we dwell upon create physiological changes in us. Through these changes, that we experience as feelings, our body prepares us to meet the reality that we visualise and think about. In this way, our body creates in us a particular 'response readiness'. It is the interaction of our thoughts and feelings that ultimately determines our behaviour. Recognising this, we realise our power to prepare ourselves to meet situations 'the right way'.

Listen to the tape "Mastering Anxiety". This will enable you to practice coping with panic and visualise yourself being relaxed and confident. It will help you to inwardly rehearse letting go of tension, accepting the stress response (i.e. anxious feelings), facing and entering feared situations and putting the whole programme of mastering anxiety into effect.

Criteria of Attainment
1. You were able to let go of unhelpful attitudes like "This tape only makes me feel anxious", "This tape reminds me too much of my problems and difficulties", and so on. Instead, you practised *facing* your problems, as they were presented to you on the tape: *accepting* the feelings that the tape gave rise to; remaining as *relaxed* as possible as you listened to the tape; and *letting time pass* while you let anxious feelings break on you, until they spent themselves, like a big wave.

2. You selected affirmations and autocommands that felt right for you. You found it helpful to use them.

3. You discovered for yourself that your feelings were able to turn around to assume patterns of thinking and acting - or relaxing - that you adopted.

4. You replaced bewilderment with calm understanding and you ceased asking yourself the questions "what is happening to me?" and "why is this happening to me?". Instead, you practised replacing 'wrong reaction readiness' with 'right action readiness'.

5. You took stock of what you expected to happen and changed your fearful expectations into coping strategies with positive aims.

6. You understood the Law of Reversed Effort and, in both imaginal rehearsal and graded practice, you realised how success follows the dictum 'Easy does it'. You recognised how tension, effort, hurry or fighting your fears meant forcing yourself against inner resistance. You recognised how 'nice and easy does it every time'.

7. You understood what it meant to be bluffed by your feelings - the strength of fear generated by a frightening idea convinces you that the idea itself *must* be true, simply because you feel it so strongly. You chose to change the nature of your inner dialogue. This made your thoughts, actions and feelings more workable and more in line with a higher level of understanding and truth.[1] Basic confidence developed.

8. You ceased to use tranquillisers in a general non-specific way. Instead, you used them only to face new and difficult tasks and situations. Later on, you practised facing these same tasks and situations without the assistance of artificial chemical agents. If you were *not* using tranquillisers before, you decided to keep off them altogether. If you *were* using them,

you decided to wean yourself off them gradually, under your doctor's guidance.

9. You understood the relevance of the Law of Requisite Variety ('only variety can replace variety'), and you practised replacing worry, fretting and avoidance with meaningful plans of action, socialising, entering feared situations and joining a self-help group. You gave yourself all the reasons you could to want to change and get better.

Notes, References and Suggested Reading

1. Maurice Nicoll. *Living time and the integration of life.* Watkins, London 1981. "Only the recognition that there are higher degrees of reality, and the emotions that such a recognition can arouse, can begin to give the right starting point."

PROGRESS REVIEW THREE

Dialogue for change.

CENTRAL IDEA: Each person's history of problems and difficulties brings out many unique personal questions. Yet common threads run through them all. Each person's development of problems and false solutions stems from the same capacity to experience, remember and acquire 'self-sabotaging habits'. Yet we also all share the ability to unlearn such habits and become confident persons. Problems shared are problems halved in the caring, problem-solving dialogue of a self-help group.

The dialogue process, central to the sharing and caring of problem-solving groups, helps anxiety sufferers to appreciate that they are not alone, not 'freaks', not 'going mad'. There are issues to be faced and other people to meet - people who are all facing the same problems and issues. Self-help groups enable people to explain themselves to one another, see what they need to understand, encourage one another, and feed back what has been found to be helpful. Not only is attending and participating in the group helpful and confidence building, but so is staying for tea afterwards - just for 'the craic'.

We either master anxiety through understanding and practice, or we remain as we are, dominated by tension, worry and misgivings. Guidelines for mastering anxiety are put forward in this book, yet there is nothing quite like meeting others who are also learning how to master anxiety and who 'know the score' from their own experience. As Etta Jennings says, "It takes one to know one".

To master anxiety we need to be able to let go of tense resistance and place wholehearted trust in our body's self-regulating functions. An extension of this trust, that helps us to believe in ourselves, is putting faith and trust in others. This kind of trust is essential to more complete self-discovery. Without it we will have difficulty realising that great 'something' that is 'beyond us, yet ourselves'. Without such trust, we cannot go beyond our insecurity, defences and defensiveness.

See if you can find an anxiety self-help group in your area, one like the Northern Ireland Agoraphobic Society group (a society founded by Etta Jennings, herself an ex-agoraphobic). Attending meetings regularly and participating in them, in the right spirit, will enable you to realise the following:

Criteria of Attainment
1. You talked about your problems and difficulties to other members of the group. You listened to their experiences, what they had felt like, what they had done and what they had found to be useful and helpful. All this helped you to feel less isolated. You experienced sharing a common problem and a shared way to make progress.
2. You gave up 'awfulising' ("isn't it awful!") and focused instead upon what you and others were finding helpful. You learned what was useful to think about and do. You set yourself tasks and goals for the week ahead.
3. You credited yourself with progress when you made it, and shared this progress with the group. You were specific about what exactly you had set out to do, what you did, how you felt at the time, and how you felt afterwards.
4. You helped others to talk about their beliefs, expectations, attitudes and aims. You helped them to think constructively about what to do and what to avoid doing.

5. You discovered that talking about your problems helped you to see them more clearly and 'in perspective'. You also discovered a sense of fellowship with others who experienced similar dilemmas to yourself.
6. You understood the benefit of dialogue. You reflected on your actions and acted in new ways because of your reflections. You understood and appreciated the benefit of looking at and seeing things from different points of view. You saw that different points of view meant different aims and different ways of thinking, feeling and acting.
7. You found yourself able to identify with others in what they were doing, feeling and thinking. You discovered this to be a great source of encouragement. It led you to want to help others. A spirit of enthusiasm and group togetherness developed.
8. You were able to look at many experiences and understand them in terms of the principles of anxiety mastery. Useful practical tasks helped you to consolidate understanding, develop confidence and broaden your horizons.
9. You brought other anxiety sufferers into the group and were able to regard yourself as 'one like others', no more thinking of yourself as 'unique' or 'freaky'.

Section Three

Mind-Body Training & Transformation

6   *Love's Body*

"The human physical senses must be emancipated from the sense of possession, and then the humanity of the senses and the human enjoyment of the senses will be achieved for the first time."

Norman O. Brown[1]

To understand the body, we need to understand the field of which the body is a part. This field is perhaps best identified with the Tao or Logos, which can be thought of as the 'totality of oneself', a concept that includes our potential to grow and to discover ourselves beyond the way that we currently are.

MIND-BODY ATTUNEMENT AND ANCIENT MYSTICAL KNOWLEDGE

The conscious attainment of union with the totality of oneself through the practice of Hatha Yoga has two components:

   (i) the attainment of desirelessness
   (ii) the experience of inner contentment arising from awareness of the self-regulating processes of our own being.

In hatha yoga, we use certain postures to redirect the energies in our body and we use the awareness that we attain to realise stress-free states of mind-body attunement. The non-conflicting unity of thinking, feeling and doing attained in the practice of hatha yoga can be

143

thought of as translating into everyday life in similar states on inner unity. But this ideal is also accompanied by moral precepts and attitudes, which parallel similar attitudes practised in hatha yoga itself; namely, injunctions that prescribe the exercise of patience in unfavourable circumstances and the practice of restraint in favourable circumstances.

When something that is in our favour happens to us, we may feel tempted to seek more of the same. By not giving in to this temptation, we learn to accept and enjoy things as they are, without letting our desires and our imagination run away with us. Similarly, when results are unfavourable, we are encouraged not to yield to feelings of fear or anger or self-pity that this may stimulate. Instead, we are counselled to use the energy changes that these experiences bring about to act with a high degree of awareness. As Krishna is portrayed saying in the Bhagavad Gita:

> "Arjuna, when one thoroughly abandons all cravings of the mind and is satisfied in the self through joy of the self, then he is called a man of steadfast wisdom." (2:55)

This indicates the effects of attaining union with the Ground of our being, namely an experience of profound inner joy, an experience that we should not be tempted to block in favour of following the dictates of some petty feeling-of-the-moment that might deprive us of our intimate relatedness to the joyful depths of our own being. The message is repeated in a slightly different form as we read on in the Gita:

> "He who is unattached to everything and meeting with good and evil, neither rejoices nor recoils, his wisdom is steadfast." (2:57)

In the practice of yoga, in everyday life, the Gita advises that we can best enjoy the processes of our own being, in action and reflection, by not becoming so emotionally entangled with the results of what we do that we lose awareness of the depth of our being, our essential Ground (the Fire, Tao, Logos, Brahman of our being), and the essential non-duality of our psyche and its Logos - our atman (soul) and Brahman. A conscious experience of this unity is achieved in the practice of hatha yoga, and, as I will attempt to show, in other (related) body-minding practices.

THE WAY FORWARD

Through attaining and retaining contact with the essential depths of our being, the forces that would otherwise be exerted by our senses become less troublesome. They do not distract us from the task of Self-discovery in all that we think and do, in the creative freedom that we experience. In-depth deliverance from the reactive bondage of ungoverned feelings puts us in control of our responses to external events. We are then able to go inwards and deal with the subtleties of the pressures and problems that we encounter in our life in the world - a life that we understand to be non-different to our way of embracing and being embraced by the depth of our being.

7   *Hatha Yoga -The Practice of Mind-Body*
          Attunement

"We don't come into this world.
We come out of it, like a wave from the ocean."
                                        Alan Watts

Our body is evolved from the Universe and is attuned to its essential rhythms, balance and harmony. Our body is not merely ours - yours and mine - it is Love's body; it belongs to the all-in-all, whose name is 'Love'.

We have within us a self-regulating source of balance, evolved from the universe and sharing in the cosmic order of its rhythms, its integral harmony and its wholeness. This, our 'Universal Essence', is most clearly evident in the stress-free functioning of our body, that is to say, when we are able to return to a state of rest that is free of inner stress and worry. When we let go of any claims that the world may make upon us, letting go also any claims that we would like to make upon the world, we enter into a state of self-regulating inner balance. This state may be called 'pre-personal'.

The Biological and Psychological Functioning of Our Being

Although our body functions in accordance with inherent biological principles, it also functions in accordance with psychological laws and principles. These latter do not over-ride principles governing our biological base, but rather build upon them, using them as a foundation for

147

discerning and evaluating what is, what is possible and what is desirable.

Our body responds to the way we think. It responds to symbols and images that we present to it. Whatever we think about, our body prepares us to meet. It develops a response readiness that enables us to relate to what we anticipate or imagine to be possible, relative to what we have experienced and reflected on in the past.[1]

Whenever we consider what is, what is possible and what is desirable, we scan and review what we can do and be in relation to what we have already experienced, thought about and understood. Such processes of scanning and evaluating constitute the psychological foundation of our being. We are able to relate self to circumstances - and possible self to possible circumstances - in terms of symbols and images. Because of this, we are able to grow and develop beyond anything that is possible for less psychologically evolved creatures.[2]

Our Strength and Our Vulnerability

Our ability to scan and evaluate is a double edged sword. When the possibilities that we focus upon fill us with tense inner resistance, anxiety and worry, our biological base reacts in ways that actually prevent us from scanning and evaluating possibilities. At worst, our reason may be swallowed up in feelings of terror, despair or dread. These feelings now become, instead, a source of reactive bondage to the ungoverned reactions that they generate.

Our ability to scan and evaluate possibilities is finely balanced. What it is balanced upon is our ability to release ourselves from the stress-generating effects of certain remembered, anticipated or otherwise imagined possibilities.[3]

The Spirit in Which We Live

Two dynamics function in us - one putting us creatively in charge of our choices and our destiny, the other taking control of us.

The spiritual foundation of our being lies in our capacity to consciously limit the stress-generating effects that our thoughts and images might otherwise have on us. Our capacity to maintain this balance is the foundation of our creative freedom.

Spiritual practices, enabling us to maintain states of mind-body attunement, are explored in this book.

THE PRACTICE OF HATHA YOGA

The term 'Yoga' means 'union', and this refers to union with God. God is considered, in yoga practice, to refer to the source and ground of our being. God is, in fact, considered to be non-different from ourselves. The idea is that, if we could only free ourselves sufficiently from self-limiting blocks that prevent us from realising this fact, we would be able to attain to a direct, undistorted awareness of our 'advaita', our non-duality from God, our unity with Him, in the depths of our being.

Hatha Yoga involves a set of mind-body practices, which, when properly undertaken, enable us to realise our Universal Essence. The practice of hatha yoga requires that we disengage from external pressures and demands, in order to free ourselves also from worries and stresses. Then, by achieving a direct, simple relationship with our body, we become able to focus our awareness upon its self-regulating processes. This, in turn, enables us to enter into an inherent balance that awaits us there.[4]

Conscious realisation of our Universal Essence arises out of a control of emotional distortions of consciousness. The aim of hatha yoga can be said to be "The control of mental modifications".[5] The state of yoga (union), thus attained, is called 'sat-chit-ananda' (being-consciousness-bliss). It is the union of our existence and our experience, achieved through a realisation of our Universal Essence.   When the control of distortions in consciousness is attained, the practice of yoga can be said to have realised its aim. Such realisation is existential. At this moment, the desire to realise sat-chit-ananda is replaced by its direct experience.

Hatha yoga - 'ha' meaning sun, and 'tha' meaning moon - uses 'asanas' or postures to attain a steady awareness of the state of our mind-body relationship. We hold the postures that we adopt until body and mind (sun and moon) directly reflect and mirror one another in a state of self-regulating balance.

The high level of physical health that is cultivated plays an important role in maintaining body-mind co-ordination and balance. Regular practice of these postures eventually enables us to secure and maintain mind-body balance even in situations that might otherwise unsettle us.

"Be still and know that I am God," says the Psalmist.[6] At deeper levels of physical and mental ease, deeper levels of meaning and value are able to become apparent to us. To quote Lonergan, "Judgement proceeds rationally from the grasp of a virtually unconditioned state."[7]

The asanas of hatha yoga are performed without any undue strain and without any undue regard for the time involved. All instructions for engaging in yoga postures either explicitly or implicitly include the following: "Stretch (bend or twist) as far as you comfortably can. Now, just a little further."

The postures include not only the extreme position attained during the 'holding phase', but also the 'moving phase' leading to it. Ease in assuming the postures is achieved through practice, regularly undertaken. Where necessary, the practice of yoga will involve accepting whatever experiences of discomfort are necessary to enable us to achieve eventual ease of execution. Such discomfort, patiently endured, leads ultimately to an experience of the postures that is steadying and conducive to meditation.

Patience in assuming the postures results in physical strength and endurance, together with an improved ability to focus and govern our thinking. Practising yoga asanas in only a partially competent manner, enables us to achieve deeply satisfying experiences of body-mind co-ordination and balance. We are able to release ourselves from many of the emotional, mental and physiological underpinnings of those 'cycles of reactive bondage' that prevent us from acquiring inner contentment, peace of mind, and an ability to think through problems and issues. Anxiety-based thinking and feeling, that previously may have characterised our state of mind, is replaced by a grounding of our everyday experience in the self-regulating processes of our Universal Essence.

In addition to the quieting and balancing properties of the postures, we also find certain pressures being applied to redirect the flow of physiologically organised energies.

Combining mental focus with breath regulation, while holding the postures, helps us to release ourselves from habitually held tensions. We are, thereby, also released from those processes of repression that kept certain mental and emotional conflicts out of our awareness. Because of the presence of mind that we acquire, we are now able to consider and work with such conflicts at a conscious level, instead of being controlled and dominated by them at an unconscious level.[8,9]

'Pranayama' means 'breath control'. It is an integral part of the practice of hatha yoga. The movements of breathing and the movement of our mind are closely related to one another. Hence, partially suppressed and irregular breathing is reflected in unbalanced, restricted and distorted thinking. Conversely, breathing that is rhythmic, quiet and easeful is reflected in balanced, sensitive and aware consciousness.[10]

Calm, serene, balanced states of consciousness, having been realised in yoga practice, can be maintained also in everyday life, and used as a basis for scanning and evaluating possibilities.

Asanas and pranayamas also break down and expel acid waste products that collect in tensely held and immobile areas of the body. In addition, they serve to promote good circulation, improve elimination, cleanse the body and lungs, and co-ordinate the activity of voluntary and involuntary nervous systems.

While holding the asanas, it is good practice to focus awareness on the area of maximum tension, stretch or pressure in the body. Such a focus, combined with awareness of one's breathing, stabilises and calms our thoughts and feelings. Other thoughts and feelings are effectively excluded. As a result, we arrive at a state of mind-body attunement. Subsequent ability to remain aware of tensions and tones in our body helps us to maintain a good standard of 'Use' and 'Use-perception'. (The meaning of these terms will be explained when we consider the Alexander Method.)

Instructions for engaging in various asanas and other mind-body practices are set out in the following order:

1. Hip rotation
2. Shaking loose
3. Ardachandrasana (Half-Moon postures)
4. Natrajasana
5. Brahma Mudra (head rotation)
6. Vajrasana and shoulder stretch

7. Uttitha Kummerasana (raised waist breathing posture)
8. Astangasana
9. Bhujangasana and Svanasana (Snake and Dog postures)
10. Salabhasana (Locust pose)
11. Dhanurasana (Bow posture)
12. Supta Vajrasana or Matsyasana (Back-bending Radiant posture or Fish pose)
13. Vatnyasana
14. Paschimotanasana (lower back stretch)
15. Bhadrasana
16. Yoga Mudra (reintegration posture)
17. Navasana (Boat posture)
18. Savasana (Corpse position)
19. Jatara Parivartanasana (legs left and right)
20. Toning (long outbreath, "aaah")
21. Laughing meditation
22. Side-to-side rocking (laughing meditation continued)
23. Folded leaf position
24. Sarvangasana (Candle position/Shoulder stand)
25. Ardachandrasana (lying down variant)
26. Halasana (Plough position)
27. Chakrasana or Shoulder position (Crab posture)
28. Ardha Matsyendrasana (spinal twist)
29. Ushtrasana (Camel posture)
30. Spinal Massage
31. Savasana (Relaxation and Meditation)

1. Hip Rotation

Stand with your feet about 18 inches apart, hands on your hips or left hanging loosely by your sides. Let your whole head ease upwards and let your whole spine follow that upward movement. Shoulders relaxed.

Keeping your head and feet fairly still, move your hips around in a wide arc. Imagine that you are on the inside of a very big barrel and touch all sides of the barrel, with your hips, as you go around. First rotate your body clockwise, and then . . . after a while . . . counter clockwise. Keep all your movements relaxed, smooth and flowing.

As you rotate your hips, you will, at best, feel the weight of your body shift over the full spread of your feet. Breathe deep down into your belly. Keep your knees slightly bent, staying low down.

Benefits
Daily practice of hip rotation (25 x clockwise, and 25 x anti-clockwise) morning and evening, each day, should yield the following benefits:

(i) reduction in overall body tension in everyday life
(ii) greater flexibility and range of body movement
(iii) shoulder and neck tensions reduced
(iv) whole body feelings experienced
(v) whole body movements delighted in
(vi) greater overall freedom and zest for life experienced

2. Shaking Loose
Stand with your feet about 8 inches apart, knees slightly bent, pelvis loose, back straight. Bend and straighten your knees in a 'bouncing' movement. Let your whole body shake free. Let your head and neck also be loose and free. For a while, let your breathing go with the shaking of your body and pant like a dog.

Benefits
Tension release, freedom of the breath.

3. Ardachandrasana (Half-Moon Postures) and Squat

Stand with the feet about 8 inches apart. Raise the arms as high as possible above your head, linking your thumbs. Bend back as far as possible, knees slightly bent. Bend forward as far as possible, buttocks moving backwards. Bend down as far as you can. Stand upright, raising the arms above the head once more. Bend to the right side, exhaling. Inhale while returning to the upright. Exhale, while bending over to the left side. Inhale, as you return to the upright position. Twist your whole body as far as possible to the right. Twist your whole body as far as you can to the left. Return to face the front; now, with toes facing outwards, lower your arms, bend your knees and go into a squatting position. Repeat this whole sequence twice.

Benefits
The twisting, stretching and bending postures improve flexibility and prevent fatty deposits from forming on the spine. They also bring good circulation to the chest, face and brain, thereby helping to counteract fatigue. The squat increases spinal elasticity.

4. Natrajasana

This posture come from the words 'Nata' meaning dance, and 'Raja' meaning Lord. It refers to the cosmic dance of Siva. To achieve it, stand upright, transfer your weight to your right foot. Bend your left knee and draw your left foot up behind your back with your left hand. Raise your right arm up into the air. Focus on an imaginary point in space or on the wall in front of you. Now, lower your raised arm as you bend the top half of your body forwards, keeping your left foot raised behind you. Repeat this with the other arm and leg.

Benefits
This posture helps to develop poise, toning the leg

muscles and keeping all the vertebral joints of the spine in good order.

5. Brahma-Mudra (Head Rotation)

Kneel on the floor, sitting on your heels, your feet flat. This position is known as 'Vajrasana', the radiant posture. Place your hands behind your back, shoulders straight, without being tense. Place your fingers between your insteps. Keeping still, bend your head as far as you comfortably can to the right, then just a little further. Do the same on the other side. When you have done that, face the front. Now roll your head back, so that the muscles of your neck are stretched. After a while, bring your head forwards, pressing your chin into your chest. After some time, head upright, turn your head to the left. Turn it as far as you comfortably can, then just a little further. Face the front. Turn your head to the right, as far as you comfortably can - now, just a little further. Using all these movements, freely roll the head about through many positions, very slowly. Focus attention on the area of maximum stretch.

Benefits
Easing of body-mind tensions.

6. Vajrasana and Shoulder Stretch

Sitting on your heels, with feet stretched out behind you, cross the fingers of your hands behind your back. Turn them in such a way that the palms face downwards. Now, lowering your head to the ground in front of you, raise your arms as high as you can. If possible, raise them above your head. Hold.

Benefits
Easing tensions in the shoulders and neck.

7. Uttitha Kummerasana

'Uttitha' means 'raised, 'Kummer' means 'waist'. This is a posture that raises the waist.

Kneel on the ground and place your hands on the floor. In this all-fours position, breathe all the way in, while hollowing the back and looking up. Hold. Then breathe all the way out, arching the spine upwards, while emptying the lungs completely. As you do this, contract the muscles of your stomach to expel the last traces of air from your lungs. Hold this position, with your breath out. Continue to move and breathe in this way for some time.

Benefits
This posture relaxes the back and relieves tiredness.

8. Astangasana

'Astanga' means 'eight'. In this posture, eight parts of the body touch the ground, simultaneously. Kneeling, arch your back and place your chest and chin on the floor. Keep breathing freely, deeply and easily. Elbows bent and arms kept by your sides. If you find it difficult to place both chest and chin on the ground, move your knees back or bring your head and chest forwards a bit. Be sure to keep your backside up in the air, your back and neck arched.

Benefits
This position exaggerates the natural curves of the spine, removing tensions and toning up the entire spinal musculature.

9. Bhujangasana (Snake Posture)

'Bhuj' means 'bend', 'ga' means 'going in'. This position raises the body like a cobra raising its head.

In the first phase, lie flat on the ground, place your hands under your shoulders. Raise the front half of your body into the air, without using your arms. When the back muscles are contracted, the muscles of the thighs (but not the calves) are also tensed and the whole weight of the body rests on the stomach. Relax.

In the second phase, use the arms to raise the front half of your body up into the air, your hips resting on the ground. The arms take the strain this time, with the muscles of the back relaxed. Keep breathing free, deep and relaxed. Keep the head proudly raised above the shoulders.

Benefits

This posture combats constipation and genito-urinary disturbances. It is good for the kidneys and it gives suppleness to the spine. It also helps to strengthen back muscles.

9(a) Svanasana ("Adho Mukho" Svanasana - Face-down stretching Dog Posture)

'Svana' means 'dog'. This posture resembles that of a dog stretching himself.

From Bhujangasana, keeping your hands and feet in the same position, turn the toes inwards and raise yourself up on your feet, pushing your heels down towards the ground. Focus attention upon the stretch in the calf muscles and the tension in your abdominal muscles, as you do this. Hold.

Benefits

This pose stretches the calf muscles. It relieves any pain and stiffness that may be present in the heels, and it also strengthens the ankles. This pose helps to get rid of stiffness in the shoulder blades. Abdominal muscles are strengthened and, because the diaphragm is lifted to the chest cavity, the heart-beat is slowed down. This is a vitalising and refreshing pose.

9(b)

Return to Bhujangasana, going down first onto the knees, then bring the hips down to the ground. Chest and head raised once more, in the snake pose.

10. Salabhasana (Locust Pose)

'Sa' means 'sharpen', 'Labh' means to perceive'. This posture is meant to sharpen one's perception.

To realise it, lie flat on your front. Making your hands into fists, place your arms along your sides. Keeping both legs straight, raise your right leg into the air. Hold. This is known as the 'Arda Salabhasana', the Half Locust Position. Relax. Repeat on the other side.

Now, placing both arms underneath you, raise both your legs and your hips into the air. This constitutes the full locust pose.

Benefits

While Bhujangasana works on the middle part of the back, Salabhasana works on the rest of the back, particularly the lower part. It draws blood into the base of the spine, recharging, as it were, the nervous system that is so highly concentrated there. There is a high concentration of parasympathetic nerves in this body zone. It also gives a deep internal massage to the kidneys and digestive system, increasing peristaltic action in the latter. Furthermore, it helps to improve the functions of the liver and pancreas.

11. Dhanurasana (The Bow Posture)

'Dhanura' means 'bow'. In this posture, the arms resemble the string of a bow, while the legs and trunk represent the wooden portion. The 'dhanura' can also be thought of as being made up of two terms, 'dha' meaning 'bestowing', and 'nura' meaning 'stillness'.

(a) To attain this posture, lie face down and fold the

lower legs back over the thighs. Grasp your ankles with your hands and pull your body up by keeping your arms straight, using the muscles of your thighs to raise your torso and thighs off the ground. The whole body is then balanced on your lower belly. The back muscles themselves are totally relaxed. Breathe slowly and regularly, focusing attention on the small of the back or on the stomach. Touch the big toes of both feet together, as this ensures that the back is not irregularly twisted.

Benefits
Stimulation of the nerve centres of the spine, leading to a feeling of exhilaration. The suprarenal glands are stimulated. This leads to the raising of a depressed person's overall level of vitality. This posture helps to combat various forms of rheumatism. In addition, psychosomatic tensions in the lumbar region and in the front of the legs are relieved, all of these being innervated by lumbar nerves.

(b) A dynamic version of this posture can be engaged in by rocking the body backwards and forwards, like a rocking chair or a rocking horse. At first, this rocking will be small and limited to the abdomen. With practice, it can be gradually increased until both the chest and the thighs are alternately touching the ground. At this stage, of course, it will be impossible to keep the back totally relaxed.

Benefits
The liver is compressed, helping to decongest it. Blood circulation in the gut is increased. It also helps to dispel constipation by assisting peristaltic movement in the intestines. It is a good exercise for men who wish to lose abdominal fat, and for women who suffer from menstrual disturbances.

(c) Two completing stages to this posture:
  (i) Take hold of the feet, pull the heels down to the buttocks. The chin remains on the floor.
  (ii) Finally, use the arms to pull the feet up the back, raising knees and thighs off the ground. Arms and back are now tensed, whereas the legs are relaxed.

12. Supta Vajrasana (Radiant Sleep Posture)

Kneel on the floor, sitting on your heels, your feet flat on the floor. Lean back, placing first your hands and then your elbows on the floor behind you. Now, take your elbows away, resting the top of your head on the floor. Place the palms of your hands together, with fingers pointing upwards. Gently squeeze your sides with your elbows. Breathe normally. Focus attention on the base of your neck.

Stage Two: Using your arms as levers, lower your shoulders and the back of your head to the ground. With your shoulders flat on the ground, relax, breathe gently and focus attention on the sacral region of your spine.

Benefits
This posture benefits the spine, especially the lumbar and neck regions. It relieves aching and tired legs and recharges the pelvic area.

12(a)   Matsyasana (The Fish Pose)

This is a variation that some may prefer to the Supta Vajrasana.

Sit in padmasana, the lotus position, or, if this is too difficult for you, sit on the ground with legs stretched out in front of you. lower yourself back onto your elbows. Arch your back and, lowering yourself down, rest the top of your head on the ground. Breathe up into your chest.

If in the lotus position, take hold of your feet or toes.

Stage Two: This involves using your elbows to lower the back of your head and your shoulders onto the ground.

Benefits
Spine and lumbar region relaxed and loosened. It can also help thyroid and parathyroid glands to function well and is said to 'tone up' pituitary and pineal glands.

13. Vatnyasana
Lying on your back, bring your right knee up to your chest. Taking hold of your shin with both hands, lift your head, placing your forehead on your knee. Hold. Relax. Repeat with the other leg.

Now, raise both knees up to the chest, and, holding them there, raise your head, placing your knees in your eye sockets. You will find your breath constricted in this position. Concentrate on breathing mainly out, holding the breath mainly out before the next in-and-out breath.

Benefits
Neck region of the spine is benefited, as well as the abdomen. Feelings of depression are lifted. Because blood is pressed out when the legs are clasped to the chest, breathing in and out vigorously, massages and carries blood to the gut.

14. Paschimotanasana
'Paschima' is Sanskrit for 'the West'. In yoga the back is always considered to be facing the west, the front the east, the head north, and the feet south. 'Utana' means 'to stretch'. Hence paschimotanasana means 'the posture that stretches the back'.

Begin by stretching the arms out, behind the head. Relax briefly. Slowly raise the arms up to the vertical, linking the thumbs together. Following the arc of the arms' circle, lower them in front of you, until your hands rest on your thighs. As the arms go down, raise your head and eyes to watch them.

When the hands touch your thighs, push them forwards towards the feet. The trunk is now being raised to a sitting position, in readiness for leaning forwards. Following these instructions leads to a progressive curling of the whole spine, from top to bottom. Now, move the hands forwards. Take hold of the toes or ankles. Pull the head forwards and down, towards the knees. Hold.

After this, gradually uncurl the back, lowering it to the ground. Make sure that you do not remove your hands from your thighs until your back is on the ground. When the back is down, raise the arms up in a slow arc, lowering first shoulders, then head, then the arms, replacing them in their starting position, behind the head.

Benefits
The slow curling and uncurling of the spine keeps it supple along its whole length. The abdominal muscles are strengthened as well.

In the holding phase, the base of the spine is stretched. Stretching the muscles of the back strengthens them.

Paschimotanasana also acts on every organ in the abdomen. Constipation is brought to an end. Spinal curves are corrected and posture is improved.

14(a) 'Hook' variant of Paschimotanasana
Raise arms, head and shoulders as before. Then slowly come up into a sitting position. Place the thumbs just behind the kneecaps with fingers below and behind the knees. Pull the arms back so that the nose is brought

towards the navel. Bring the head as close as possible to the knees and stomach, curving the top of the back as much as possible. Hold. Let go, slowly uncurling the back.

15. Bhadrasana

'Bhadra' means 'prosperous' or 'happy'. This posture is supposed to release hormones that enhance the practitioner's appearance. Sit on the ground, back straight, place the soles of your feet together and pull them towards your body. Bend forward, touching your forehead on your toes. Hold. Slowly come up.

Benefits

This asana removes calcification from the hip joints and relieves tension in the sacral region as well as the thighs, knees and ankles.

16. Yoga Mudra

Sit in a lotus or half-lotus position. Take hold of alternate knees with arms crossed. Bring your forehead down towards the floor. Hold. Place other foot on other thigh, if in half-lotus. Repeat.

Benefits

This posture relieves constipation and improves digestion.

17. Navasana

'Nava' means 'boat'. The posture resembles a boat with oars.

Balancing on your buttocks, raise your legs and your trunk into the air, with your arms stretched out in front of you.

Benefits
This posture has beneficial effects on the liver, gall bladder, and spleen. It also brings life and vigour to the back.

18. Savasana
'Sava' means 'corpse'. The aim is to allow the body to lie still, with no movement.

Lie flat on the back, with arms a little away from your side. Palms face upwards. Ankles are allowed to fall outwards. Breathe deeply down into your lower belly. If you wish, place your hands on your lower belly, feeling it rise as you breathe in, and fall as you breathe out.

Benefits
This posture brings calmness of mind and relieves fatigue.

19. Jatara Parivartanasana
'Jatara' means 'stomach' or 'belly'. 'Parivartana' means 'turning'.

Lying on your back, stretch your arms sideways in line with your shoulders so that the body resembles a cross. Raise both legs until they are straight up in the air. Bring both legs down to the side, keeping as much of the shoulders and back on the floor as possible. Keep breathing freely and deeply, the legs turned mainly from the hips. Hold. Repeat on the other side.

Benefits
Intestines are strengthened, and liver, spleen and pancreas are toned up, removing sluggishness.

20. Long Outbreath: Toning - "Aaah . . ."
Lying on your back on savasana, continue to breathe freely and deeply right down into your lower belly. This is called 'abdominal breathing'.[11]

Now, breathe deeply in and slowly let the breath out, vocalising as you exhale, with the sound "aaah".(12)

This is called 'toning'. The "aaah" sound resonates with the whole body when the toning is done correctly, yet it resonates particularly in the abdominal region. Likewise the sound "Oh" resonates in the chest, "u" in the throat, "mmh" in the head, and "nnh" at the top of the head.

Benefits

Toning leads to a deep sense of mind-body-spirit unity. It harmonises whatever is inharmonious within us. We become aware of the deepest sources of our being - our Universal Essence. This essence is pre-personal - impersonal - a 'just being'.

21. Laughing Meditation

Lying in savasana, let a smile come upon your face, and let a chuckle begin to develop in your belly. Let it work its way up into your chest, your throat and jaws and . . . if and when it wants to . . . let it come out of your mouth.

At first, *you* will be doing it, but the sound of your laughter and the heaving and shaking of your body will soon cause genuine *spontaneous* laughter. When this happens, let yourself go. Abandon yourself to the spirit of laughter. Lose yourself in it.

Benefits

Laughter has a deeply cleansing effect on the whole person. All blocks dissolve. Laughter and tears open up a deep source of being within us. We become able to speak and sing from this source also. Laughter releases special hormones in our body. It lightens us during the day. We let ourselves go into laughter whenever we feel moved to laugh. This gives a light and free (yet deep) quality to our life. (13)

22. Side-to-Side Rocking (Laughing Meditation continued)

Bringing the knees up to the chest in a lightly held vatnyasana (without placing the knees in the eye sockets), roll from side to side, still engaging in the laughing meditation.

Benefits

This rolling about increases the extent and the intensity of one's laughter. It also gives the back a pleasant massage.

23. Folded Leaf Position

The Folded Leaf Position is a relaxing position. Sitting on your heels in vajrasana, bend forwards. Place your head on the ground in front of you, your arms by your sides. Sigh, sink and sag. Let all your tensions melt away.

Benefits

This posture is for relaxation. Your body is folded in three, thighs against calves below, and against chest above. Full, deep relaxation is possible. This posture is also called 'the position of the child'.

24. Sarvangasana

'Sarva' means 'whole', and 'anga' means 'body'. This posture inverts the whole body. It is also known as the 'shoulder stand' or 'candle posture'.

Lying on your back, bend your knees up to your chest. Keeping your arms on the floor, raise your trunk up into the air. Bending your arms at the elbows, support your back, raising your legs up into the air. Your whole body now rises up from the shoulders, with chin resting against chest.

The feet are raised as high as possible through contraction of the stomach muscles. Breathing is slow and even. Attention is focused on the throat, where the thyroid gland lies. Hold.

After some time, lower one leg down from the vertical, keeping the other upright. When you have touched the floor behind you with the toes of the lowered leg, raise it to join the other in a vertical position. Now repeat this process with the other leg. Once both legs are together again, in the vertical position, lower both legs down behind you. Touching the floor behind you with both feet, do not pause but bring both legs up again. You will have been in 'halasana', the plough posture, for a brief moment.

After returning to the upright position again, lower the trunk to the ground, bending the knees against the chest as you do so. Then straighten the legs, lowering them to the ground very slowly. When they are about 6 inches off the ground, keep them there. Hold. After some time, relax.

Benefits
Blood circulation in the legs and stomach is reversed, with relief for sufferers from haemorrhoids and varicose veins. Blood flows to the brain and the thyroid gland is irrigated through a suffusion of blood, thus improving or helping to stabilise its effect on the body's overall metabolism. Headaches can be cleared. Because thoracic movement becomes limited, breathing automatically becomes diaphragmatic. This can prove helpful to people who suffer from asthma. Finally, this posture brings blood to the face. It nourishes the roots of the hair and it gives the face a good colour.

25. Lying Down Ardachandrasana
This is the half-moon posture achieved through lying on the side with your head cupped in the hand of the arm you are lying on. The other hand is placed in front of the

belly. Now raise both legs into the air and hold. Repeat on the other side.

Benefits
This pose improves elasticity and prevents fatty deposits forming around the waist and hips.

26. Halasana (Plough Position)
'Hala' means 'plough'. Halasana can be thought of as ploughing bodily energy back, making it available at higher levels of conscious control.

Raise yourself up into the candle position, sarvangasana. Then, lower both legs behind the head, keeping them straight, until your toes touch the ground. Now, hold your breath in as you push your feet back as far as they will go behind your head, your chin pressing hard into your chest. Breathe normally, but shallowly, as the throat is now constricted. Hold. Then bring your feet back a little towards your head, easing the breathing. Hold. Finally bend the knees, bringing them next to your ears. In this posture, breathe deeply, giving yourself an abdominal massage.

Benefits
This posture works on the spinal column, strengthening the surrounding muscles, while keeping the spine itself flexible. Stretching the muscles of the back expels blood from them. Then, when they return to normal length, a fresh in-flow of blood benefits nerve centres surrounding the spinal chord.

The liver is cleansed and decongested in this posture and the pancreas is also massaged and purified.

27. Chakrasana (Crab Position)
The word 'chakra' means a 'centre' or 'nodal point'. This posture is thought to benefit all the chakras of the body.

Lie on your back, bend your knees and bring your

feet up to your buttocks. Take hold of your feet and raise
your stomach up into the air, as high as you can. This
position is called 'the shoulder position'. If you are able,
you may proceed from here into the full chakrasana, also
known as the 'crab posture'. Placing the palms of your
hands on the ground beside your head, your fingers
pointing towards your body, use your arms to raise your
head and shoulders up into the air. Breathe gently. Focus
your attention on the small of the back. Hold.

Benefits
This posture stretches the whole spine, giving full spinal
stimulation and spinal correction. All in all, it keeps the
whole body alert and supple. It strengthens the back and
makes one feel full of life. It also strengthens the arms
and wrists and has a soothing effect on one's head. It
gives the whole person a great sense of stability, energy
and lightness.

28. Ardha Matsyendrasana (Spinal Twist)
This posture is named after a great teacher of yoga called
Matsyendra. The complete posture is difficult to
accomplish. We shall therefore go into the half posture.

   While most other asanas bend the spinal column,
Ardha Matsyendrasana twists it throughout its whole
length.
   Sitting up, with both legs stretched out in front of
you, bend the right leg and place the foot against the
outside of the left knee. The right foot is parallel to the
left leg. Now, looking to the right, place your left arm
down the outside of your right leg, taking hold of your
right foot with your left hand. Using your knee as a lever,
twist your whole body to the right, sitting tall and
straight with your right hand on the floor behind you.
   Throughout this asana, the back remains passive.

The stomach is compressed on the right side against the raised leg. Hold. Repeat on the other side.

Benefits

This asana keeps all the vertebral segments of the spinal column free and flexible. It stretches and lengthens every ligament and muscle in the spinal column, and it suffuses the sympathetic ganglia on either side of the spinal chord with blood, helping to rejuvenate the whole system.

When the twisting movement is carried out first to the right and then to the left, this works in the correct direction of peristalsis, so preventing constipation. Apart from the large intestine, liver and right kidney being massaged and stimulated during the first half of the exercise, the spleen, pancreas and left kidney are benefited in the second half.

Fusion of spinal segments is prevented. This posture also helps to combat obesity.

29. Ushtrasana (Camel Posture)

'Ush' means 'the warming light of dawn', 'ushtra' implies the throwing of light on previously hidden areas of understanding. This posture is also known as the 'camel' posture because it reflects the camel's ability to use its hump as a source of nourishment in a barren environment.

Sitting on your heels in vajrasana, place your hands on the floor behind you. Raise your stomach and entire torso up into the air. And place your hands on your feet, your heels on your ankles. Bend your head backwards, looking over your head. Press your pelvis forwards, hollowing your back. Breathe up into your chest.

Benefits

This posture benefits the lumbar area of the spine and it strengthens the thigh muscles.

30. Spinal Massage

Sitting up, cross your ankles. Take hold of alternative feet. Rock backwards and forwards on your back, with great gusto and enjoyment, giving yourself a spinal massage.

31. Savasana (Relaxation and Meditation)

Lie down, once again, in savasana. This posture balances the tensions in the body. Now go through all areas of the body, relaxing the muscles in each area, starting with the eyes, going to the mouth, jaws and throat, down the front of the body, around the feet, up the back of the body, neck, head, scalp, face and body as a whole.

Practice acceptance of Self in this posture - self experienced as Universal Essence, balanced and co-ordinated with all things and in all things.

Benefits

Savasana is an excellent stress antidote. High blood pressure declines rapidly as circulation in the veins become easier, blood vessels in the skin expand and circulation of the blood becomes equal throughout the body. The heart is relieved as its pumping is much easier and complete rest and rejuvenation is achieved.

BODY-WORK AND SPIRITUAL AWARENESS

A freely creative and fulfilling life is really only possible when we are able to control the state of our consciousness, even in adverse circumstances. Such control needs to be cultivated and this, in turn, is only possible once we look at our 'Sadhana' - our practice - not as a 'trick' or 'technique' that will enable us to feel good if only we 'do it often enough', but rather as part of a *total way of life* that enables us to determine the quality of our being and becoming.

Whatever practice we use to govern the state of our being, this needs to become an integral part of our spirituality. Only when it is able to penetrate, suffuse and govern our everyday thoughts, feelings and actions will its purpose have been realised.

Lacking such a spiritual practice, the kind of dynamic control that we seek to exercise over our mind-body-circumstance relationships comes to be largely determined by the circumstances in which we find ourselves, or by our tendency to 'worry'. In this worry process, it is as if we were forced to remember, focus upon and anticipate what we would not like to happen to us. Another name for this is 'negative inner rehearsal'. It may well lead to anxiety-generating avoidance of certain circumstances, or to withdrawal into inaction, leading to depression, or, through the use of artificial chemical agents - that interfere with the way our body responds to our thinking - to a state of chemical dependence.

8   Use-Perception and Creative Freedom

"We lie open on one side to the deeps of spiritual nature,
to all the attributes of God."

Ralph Waldo Emerson

F.M. Alexander referred to the way we use our body as 'Use', spelled with a capital U. "Use affects function", that is to say, the way we use our body affects the way it functions.[1]

We can learn to maintain states of inner control even in stressful situations. The less tension of inner resistance there is within us, the less we are likely to discover ourselves 'under stress'. The Alexander Method enables us to maintain a balanced resting state, achieved within our own body, to secure proportion, harmony and balance in our thinking (and acting) regardless of the kind of circumstances in which we find ourselves.

Inability to return to a balanced resting state means that we end up holding onto tension that serves no useful purpose and is of no benefit to us. On the contrary, it may even prove harmful, by generating uncontrolled stress and worry in us, thereby dissipating energy and robbing us of both inner peace and zest for life. A balanced resting state is, conversely, self-energising, enabling us to regain a positive, self-integrating outlook.

To restore our capacity for self-integration and spirit-centred living, we need to be able to break whatever cycle of inner tension and resistance may be operating in us.

One way of doing this is to begin to apply the Alexander Method of Use in a continuous way, utilising what he calls 'The Basic Movement', not merely 'now and again' or 'when we remember', but in all movements of the body. To make this possible, Alexander supplied students of his Method with the following instruction:

> "As you begin any movement, move your whole head upwards and away from your whole body, and let your whole body lengthen by following that upward movement."

The Basic Movement is a 'principle' of movement. It serves as a basis for governing the quality of our whole mind-body-spirit being. Using it as a principle of movement in all that we do was something that Alexander considered to be tantamount to "the next step in human evolution". Indeed, this claim may not be as exaggerated as it first appears.

When we become aware of the way that our human biological functioning supports our capacity for self-reflective awareness, the next logical step we can take is to use this awareness to govern the state that we are in. If we could use our awareness to combat mind-body stress, we could prevent ourselves from entering into those states of being that deprive us of self-reflective control of our own thoughts and actions. Alexander's 'Basic Movement' promises to make this possible.

Before we are able to use the Basic Movement routinely - almost as 'second nature' - we need to practise engaging in it through paying attention to its component processes. These, in turn, can be learnt through following the instructions given below:

(a) Neck free, head facing forwards and lengthening upwards
(b) Shoulders relaxed
(c) Back lengthen and widen
(d) Breathe easily and naturally through the nose
(e) Breathe right down 'into your pelvis'
(f) Pelvic basin feels balanced, not tilting up or down
(g) Knees free of tension

In the words of Wilfred Barlow, an Alexander teacher, "The Alexander Balance throughout the whole of the body . . . seeks to establish a resting position in which all the joint surfaces are lengthening away from each other, and since it is now realised more and more by neurologists that awareness of muscle balance derives from an awareness of the lengthening of muscle, a newly ordered 'wisdom of the body' is likely to be facilitated by such lengthening."[2]

USE PERCEPTION

Alexander's method of Use also emphasises performing all actions at our own pace. To be able to achieve this, we need to discover the pace that best suits us, at the same time remaining free and flexible in all our movements.

Through employing the Basic Movement, we arrive at what Alexander called 'Use-perception'. This is a state of mental-physical co-ordination that we experience clearly and directly. It is free of excessive, functionally harmful tension. It enables us to be aware of the way we feel, while at the same time allowing us freely and creatively to decide what to do about our feelings.

Because harmful and destructive emotions are able to take root in us through bodily tensions,

177

employing the Basic Movement, routinely and continually, enables us to perceive these emotions before they develop to a point where they are likely to undermine our self-control. By releasing ourselves from the tensional underpinnings of such emotions, we are able to release ourselves from self-feeding cycles that might otherwise spiral out of control, leading to an overall lack of balance, harmony and skill in our life. Using the Basic Movement thus helps us to reclaim our creative freedom. It also keeps us free from the following states and processes.

- compulsive behaviour
- a 'racing brain'
- anxiety states
- rigidity in our thinking and acting
- worry
- resentment
- self-pity
- guilt
- shame
- depression

In learning to use the Basic Movement we realise the benefits of Use-perception, discovering how a practised routine release of tension actually results in more spontaneous awareness of our feelings and greater freedom to choose what to do with the way we feel. In short, Use-perception enables us to adopt a certain basic attitude *to* our feelings. This attitude has both mental and physical components. It helps us to achieve distance, flexibility and leeway with regard to what we feel like doing. Among other things, it frees us from any impulsive behaviour to which we might otherwise be drawn. It is also able to liberate us from any compulsions to which we may previously have been inclined.

Two alternatives thus present themselves to us:

(i) the unhealthy alternative of releasing muscle tension only a little, without resolving underlying tensions, so that a state of excessive tension can arise in us, once again, at the slightest provocation; or

(ii) the healthy alternative of totally resolving tension by returning to a balanced resting state, leaving no unconscious predisposition for tension-based states of mind to develop in us.

Ultimately, we have the choice of learning to live in accordance with principles that we can understand and put to good use, or of remaining 'helpless' and 'victimised' by the way we feel. The choice is ours.

IN-PUT, THROUGH-PUT AND OUT-PUT

If we consider the selection of what we attend to as constituting 'input' and our response to that input as 'output', then we can think of the selecting-organising process itself as 'throughput'.

High levels of tension held in the body predispose us to react to certain people, places, thoughts and situations in an emotionally charged and consciously ungoverned way. Conversely, freeing ourselves from such excessive tensions enables us consciously to choose and refine whatever response we wish to make.

Stressful input usually creates a need in us to produce stress-relieving output. Such output may well suffer from a woeful neglect of throughput. As a result, the response that we make may well be impulsive, compulsive or otherwise unskilled. Furthermore, a tense inner state is also likely to arise in us, once again, leading to a repetition of the same or similar in-put/output mayhem.

END-GAINING

All attempts to gain relief from tension-based emotions that neglect 'throughput' Alexander called 'end-gaining'. When relief from such emotions is gained without resolving underlying tensions, our predisposition to experience these emotions once again remains. The alternative to end-gaining is Use-perception. By routinely employing the Basic Movement, we find ourselves able to overcome unconscious habits of shortening our necks, hunching our shoulders, pulling our chest down, and shortening/arching our back. Consciously and routinely letting our whole head ease upwards and letting our whole body follow suit by following that upward movement, we find ourselves enjoying the healthy anti-gravity posture thus adopted. Excessive tension disappears and moving without strain becomes a pleasure.

When our body is able to stand easily erect, without strain, the segments of our spine balance naturally on top of one another, maintaining a naturally balanced S-shaped curve. As a result, our mind becomes free of racing chatter and our naturally deepened breathing gives a tonic massage to all our internal organs. This keeps these organs all in a healthy state. It also enables us to achieve clear 'presence of mind' and an aware value-realising openness to our own experiences, actions, words and relationships.

PROGRESS REVIEW FOUR

Yoga Practice

CENTRAL IDEA: Hatha Yoga is a discipline that employs our bodymind in the service of the life that is in us and around us. It restores our bodymind balance, strengthens our muscles and helps us to achieve a balanced resting state. It cleanses our organs and increases our vitality and aliveness.

Hatha yoga is said to be a preparation of the body for conscious union with God. As we employ our bodymind to serve the life that is in us and around us, we realise a desire to express this life in every muscle, organ and cell of the body. We are - body, mind, spirit - becoming servants of Life itself. As we serve Life, so Life serves us. We are, in fact, manifestations of Life and, as such, our body, mind and spirit are created to serve the Life that is in us. This realisation, in the fullness of yoga, fills us with a feeling of gratitude that is a celebration of the glory of it all.

Practice the yoga postures as illustrated and presented in the "All-in Yoga" tape. Read about the principles behind yoga and other body-oriented practices. Even if yoga postures are performed with only partial competence, they yield remarkable results.

Criteria of Attainment
1. You engage wholeheartedly in the 'All-in yoga session', attending as much as possible only to the postures you are engaging in and nothing else.
2. In all yoga postures, you stretch as far as you comfortably can, and then you stretch a little further.
3. All your movements during the session are slow, relaxed and expansive, rather than fast and forceful.

4. In each posture assumed, you focus attention on the area of maximum pressure, stretch or tension, to the exclusion of all other thoughts.
5. You find that these postures calm and stabilise your feelings.
6. You understand in greater detail what the tensions and tones of your body are all about.
7. You are more mindful of your body in everyday use.
8. You understand the rationale behind yoga and other body-oriented practices.
9. You develop a more complete sense of your own awareness and meaning as a person.

Section Four

Meditation Training and Transformation

9   *The Living Flame of Love*

"A fly that touches honey cannot use its wings, so the soul that clings to spiritual sweetness ruins its freedom and hinders contemplation."

St John of the Cross

Only when we go beyond that which is 'merely practical' can we realise our full potential. This realisation involves our entering into a level of consciousness that we cannot 'master'. We can only learn to submit ourselves to its processes, so as to discover ourselves in it.

FIRE CENTREDNESS

Fire-centred work focuses primarily on awareness, rather than on persons. People in the process of training and transformation seek to transcend prejudgments, in favour of getting in touch with a 'something else' that may be called the 'Tao' or 'Logos' or 'Fire' of being, which is mysteriously active in all life. As well as balancing and integrating all things within itself, the Tao/Logos/Fire also functions in such a way as to balance all things within themselves. Hence, it is to the essence of being that all training and transformation directly or indirectly points. And it is within its 'way of going' that all such training and transformation needs to be integrated.

We can represent our initial hazy awareness of a

'something' that has an important bearing on our life as an elliptical section of light within the darker circle of our self, as we currently know it.

In itself, our work is transpersonal. It transcends the individual person. And yet, by so doing, it does not in any way diminish the significance of our individual selfhood. On the contrary, it places that selfhood within a wider integrating context, in which we are somehow destined to find ourselves profoundly 'at home'.

We can represent this as a circle in which the largest light section is our growing awareness of the Tao or Fire or Logos of our being, within which our psyche or soul participates and from which it derives its existence. We see ourselves, now, as servants of the Tao/Fire/Logos of our being, which is the master and overlord that we love and serve.

It may be said that the larger whole, of which our self or psyche is a part, is the real subject of our being. However, we cannot say this with conviction unless we have somehow experienced it to be so. By identifying ourselves with the self-governing processes of the Tao, we experience the Tao/Logos/Fire of our being, now, *as* our 'true self'.

We can represent this as a circle in which our psyche is but a small dot in the centre of the Logos that it now considers as its true being, relating to its awareness of this fact as a speck of personal awareness within the stream of the Tao's flow.

As our participation in the Fire/Tao/Logos develops, we develop an appreciation of its Process as the all-in-all of our being. At this stage, we recognise our being as one with its Ground. And so complete is this identification that we do not even recognise ourselves as having any independent existence from the Fire/Tao/Logos itself. The Zen saying "True mind is no mind" makes absolute sense to us now. We experience no hindrance to the flow of the Tao in us. Everything that we do is wu-wei, effortless effort. Nothing interferes with the flow of being-awareness in us. We have no personal edges that conflict with or challenge our complete identification with the action of the Fire/Tao/Logos in us.

We can represent this state of being in the form of a circle, in which all that is included within the circle is the Fire/Tao/Logos itself. There is no separate individual self. Atman and Brahman are one. There is no duality.

Is there a further state of realisation that we can attain? There is. This state represents our 'return to the market place', in which we re-integrate ourselves into the everyday world, with its dualistic thinking, its erroneous understanding and its clinging to individual form, its reactive and defensive emotional bondage and unaware conditioning. Now, however, we recognise all of this as a manifestation of the Fire/Tao/Logos - and we are an integral part of it also. And yet we do not belong to the reactive bondage and unaware conditioning of the world, in the sense of being subject to it, as a puppet is subject to the pulling of its strings. We belong to the World process, but in an aware, awake, enlightened, liberated way. Because of this, we can perfectly tune in to what is happening, still without the interference of any personal edges but with a deeply penetrating awareness of the processes that operate both within and beyond the operation of these edges.

We can represent this as a circle whose centre is perfectly filled in with the darkness of ignorance and reactive bondage, but which, nonetheless, no longer functions in us as darkness, ignorance and reactive bondage. This is a state that we experience as the ultimate liberation, in which we experience nirvana (the changelessness of deep awareness and understanding) and samsara (the constantly changing process in which all things participate) as one and the same.

In understanding the process of progressing

through a living awareness of these different states and stages, we realise the nature, the purpose and the value of meditation.

Although we may be able to understand something before we experience it, yet it is only through experiencing it that we are fully able to understand its meaning and value. Only then are we able to live our awareness to the full. And this is so because we experience its goodness and know that there is no higher goal for us to seek - except to enable others to know what we know and be where we are.

So it is, then, that bringing others to where we are becomes the crowning glory of the being that we have become, not by our own efforts but rather as a result of our transformation in that totality of being that realises itself in us.

THE 'HOW TO' OF MEDITATION

The practice of meditation requires that we set time aside for silence and solitude. Having done this, we use our awareness to detach ourselves from involvement with the outside world. Then, after noticing the nature of the thoughts and feelings that stir in us, we let go of these thoughts by refocusing our attention upon a simple repetitive process - one that occurs in us of its own accord, a process such as our breathing. At the same time, we accept the way that we feel and we do not allow our feelings to distract us - at least at this stage - from the focus of our 'second attention'.

With practice, we are able to empty our consciousness - our primary awareness - of all distracting thoughts and to accept our feelings, without reacting to them in terms of our primary awareness. At last, we find ourselves able to rest in fully undistracted, 'blissful' awareness of the stress-free processes of our breathing. In this way, we become aware of the totality of our being in one exemplary form of mind-body attunement. And the state of awareness that we attain, in this form, is without conceptual content. It constitutes a state of 'sat-chit-ananda' - a state that St John of the Cross characterised as "night more lovely than the dawn".[1]

In this practice, which Buddhists call 'samatha' meditation, we do not let our mind wander to other things but keep returning its focus to a natural self-repeating process, chosen in advance. When we are able to focus our attention solely upon this process - a process that takes place in us without our intending it - we experience ourselves in an unconditioned state of being. In this way, we pass from an awareness that there is a higher state of being, one that governs our existence in some unknown and mysterious way, to a direct experience of that higher state functioning in us. Although we do not need to intend this process, nonetheless when we attend to it, we become enchantingly aware of the way in which our whole being, conscious and unconscious, is grounded in the larger process of which it is a part. Through entering into the way our breathing happens, we enter into the Tao/Logos/Fire of our being, in this particular state of mind-body attunement.

Through our continuing practice of breathing meditation, our experience, in this state, becomes increasingly more expansive, seemingly unlimited, giving us a limitless sense of our own existence, unbounded by such conceptual processes as comparing, contrasting, choosing or intending. Still less is it limited by edges of awareness that lead us into confusion, embarrassment, fearing, attacking or defending.

When we become aware of - and selectively receptive to - the flow of our body's own self-governing process - *and nothing else* - we become consciously able to identify with the flow of these processes - *and nothing else*. This results in an experience of 'advaita' - an experience of the non-duality of the self-governing essence of our being in the self-governing essence of all being. While we are aware of this non-duality, we still remain conscious of the psyche that is one with its Logos, yet is not totally absorbed by it.

There is something highly paradoxical about this awareness. We are like a dot in a circle, but what is that dot and what is that circle? We stay with our meditation. Perhaps we will find out. Perhaps not.

EMPTY AND MARVELLOUS

The 'I' that we seek to secure against attack or hurt, or the 'I' that we seek to enhance in other people's eyes is not the 'I AM' of "Christ who lives in me"[2], nor is it the "Me" of Krishna "who neither slays nor is slain".[3] All diharmony or inner contending within the self is dissolved in the kind of Self-knowledge that results from a realisation of the supreme Self, within.

Such realisation cannot be intellectually superimposed upon our everyday awareness and experience. It can, however, be used to develop a deeper consciousness of the meaning of our everyday life as we are living it, even as a hunter stalks his prey, through the use of second attention. We can also use it to creatively transform our everyday life. On the other hand, we can use our realisation to stay with our second attention in that other realm of being, the Kingdom of Heaven, leading to a new kind of subjectivity - the "not I but Christ" of St Paul, the "neti neti" (not this, not that) of the Upanishads.

Religiously speaking, we see the aim of meditation to lie in "an escape from the corruption that is in the world because of passion " and in our becoming, instead, "partakers of the divine nature."[4] When the Divine Ground realises itself in us, we become a "new being", recognising ourselves as "living and moving and having our being" beyond our previous consciousness.[5]

And yet, before we can come to such an experience, we must necessarily first pass through experiences that come about because we have let go of our defensiveness. As a result, we may well come to experience ourselves as impoverished, defenceless and vulnerable. What Ken Keyes calls our "security, sensation and power addictions"[6] block our progress, so long as we are not able to let go of them. Embracing what we feel to be our inner poverty and vulnerability means accepting the "via negativa" of our path to wholeness. St John of the Cross addressed this path and his experience of it as a "Living Flame of love", which he said "tenderly wounds my soul at its innermost core."[7]

The via negativa would hold that we will not enter into a process of inner transformation and we will not be transformed unless we first embrace our poverty and hold onto what seems like 'nothing', while our habitual ways of thinking, feeling and reacting are dissolved in a new spirit of being, one that is discovered through the 'letting go' of meditation - a spirit that seems to wound us even as it transforms us.

THE SPIRIT OF MEDITATION

In the spirit of our inner poverty, we can now use another form of meditation. Now that we know that we can enter into and experience a new kind of consciousness in the 'neti neti' of 'just breathing', we can begin to use our meditation to enter into a 'neti neti' through use of the contents of our primary awareness.

To do this we need to accept our powerlessness to control the way that we feel. As we accept whatever feelings arise in us, we use the information contained within and behind our feelings, in various sensory channels, to uncover the meaning of what we feel. We also discern the value of our feelings and their underlying meaning by comparing the experiences to which they give rise with the being-consciousness-bliss of mind-body attunement.

All this we do by allowing ourselves to enter what the mystics call 'the dark side of God', the 'shadow' in our Logos. As we wander through the labyrinth of our unconscious conditioning, we eventually reach "the Light that enlightens every person born into the world". This is a light that, as St John describes it, cannot be overwhelmed by the darkness, that is to say, it cannot be overwhelmed by the darkness of our unaware, unenlightened fears and ignorance. This whole process is something that St John of the Cross saw fit to sum up in one word, "humility".

By entering into the dark night of our soul's journey, we discover, through staying there, that there is a power greater than our conscious ego, able to govern our thoughts and feelings, if we submit ourselves to it.

Arnold Mindell[8] suggests, likewise, that we follow the thoughts and feelings that arise in us during meditation. When what he calls an "existential fantasy" assails us - an experience that occurs simultaneously with variations in our breathing rhythm - he suggests that we check out what channel it is using. Any stirring that interrupts the second attention that we are using to focus on our breathing, we can treat as a secondary process that conflicts with our capacity to experience sat-chit-ananda. We can use this conflict to amplify and follow perceptual signals that are reaching us, by attending to them and observing where they lead us. What are we seeing, hearing, feeling or wanting to do? As we pay attention to whatever is occurring in us, we amplify the process and follow it. When the conflict that entered our awareness has revealed its meaning to us, it will have served its purpose. In all of this, the basic attitude that we adopt is one of humility. In essence, we are saying to ourselves, "Who am I to interfere with what comes into my awareness? I will accept it and go where it wishes to lead me." Having followed the course of our existential fantasy, with choiceless awareness, we find ourselves once more able to return to our original meditation practice.

This way of meditating resembles what Buddhists call 'vipassana' meditation - insight meditation. In this form of meditation we do not so much seek to retain a single focus of awareness, as we seek to enter into, flow with and observe everything that enters our conscious awareness. In this way, we become able to free ourselves from our intense reactions to the appearance of things. Changing conditions arise and pass away within the continuing functioning of our body's self-regulating Tao. We realise, as a result of this kind of meditation, that all changing conditions which arise within us - and outside of us - do not change the essential nature of our being. In our awareness itself, we discover a changeless self-governing process that reveals to us the ultimate Ground of our being.

Vipassana meditation - insight/conflict-following/awareness-following meditation - is an integral part of the practice of journalling and the practice of speaking-and-listening, described in the following two sections.

THE BENEFITS OF MEDITATION

Those of us who meditate, discover within ourselves something universal about the inner divisions and inner contending that come to all of us in our personal growth and development. We discover, in fact, that the practice of meditation, leading as it does to a direct experience of the Tao or Logos of our being, also passes through the same kind of problems and predicaments that face every person in the course of their life. In this way, we discover the truth that sets us free - the truth about an unconditional acceptance - an unconditional love - that embraces all people, because it participates in the same essence of being that we all share.

Meditation transforms us into mystics. It leads us to love all human beings, everywhere. It does this because it teaches us compassion - compassion for the psyche that needs to escape from its reactive bondage in order to enter into the Logos of its creative freedom.

Since the Logos, Tao, Fire, Brahman of our being includes all that I am, I cannot any longer conceive of it as an object. Rather, I realise it to be the larger Subject of my being. This, in turn, gives me a deeply respectful attitude towards the deep essence of every person that I meet.

St Francis of Assissi counsels that we should "ask nothing and refuse nothing; but leave ourselves in the arms of Divine Providence, without wasting time in any desire except to will whatever God wills in us."[9] But how can God will anything at all in us, except that we have been able to re-integrate ourselves at a deep level of psychological awareness, such as the level that we experience in meditation? How else can we experience God's being in our own being? How else can we experience God's being *as* our own being? Of course, it is impossible. We will not be capable of following a counsel such as this, until we experience a new centre of orientation in ourselves as ourselves.

THE ULTIMATE LIBERATION

The duality between what we know as 'the individual' and what we know as 'the universal', in the world of everyday experience, is precisely what we overcome in the attainment of moksha (liberation) - the satori (enlightenment) to which our practice of meditation brings us.

A further edge now enters our consciousness, a conflict existing between our awareness of the truth of our existence, realised through meditation, and our awareness of ourselves as people among people, in everyday 'non-spiritual' living. How are we to retain the conscious awareness of our advaita (non-duality), realised in meditation, and still be able to function as a person among people, in the ordinary give-and-take of everyday living - especially when that give-and-take is based on quite different premises to those upon which we wish to base our lives?

The basic attitude of 'humility', adopted in meditation, comes to our aid, here. If we are going to exercise our creative freedom to live among others, especially among others who are less liberated than ourselves, we need to adopt towards them the same attitude that we originally adopted towards ourselves. This, we recognise, will be increasingly necessary to the extent that we identify with others whose lives are dominated, to a lesser or greater extent, by emotionally bound ego-centric and ego-defensive reactions.

In order for us to remain free from such reactively bound emotions, we may seek refuge in the state of exemplary mind-body attunement that we experienced in samatha (single focus) meditation. In this state we realised our essential unity with the self-governing essence of all being. And yet, we used our awareness of this essence to pass from single focus meditation into insight meditation. It is the same now. How else will it be possible for us to influence events in a creative, growth-promoting and transformative way? How else enable others also to realise their creative freedom?

We are at an edge. We recognise our need to go beyond this edge.

This is where the wisdom of insight meditation becomes most clearly apparent to us. Instead of seeking merely to take refuge in an exemplary state of tension-free mind-body attunement, we recognise the need to let ourselves flow beyond the edge of our still fragile identity, by entering into and exploring those differences and distinctions that are challenging our sense of how we are and how we can be. In this way, we explore the full meaning of the conflict that exists between, say, what we feel like doing or saying and what we are holding back. We become able, thus, to reconcile, at a more profound level of awareness, those contradictions that previously prevented us from thinking, feeling and acting of one accord.

Castaneda's don Juan spoke of the dangers of the power and clarity that come to all men and women of knowledge. If we have had an enlightening experience, we try to hold onto it. As a result, instead of humbly exploring new edges that become apparent to us - so as to be able to discover their meaning and value - we try to recapture the clarity or power or peace that we felt, before. This is obviously a false solution. Not only does it prevent us from '"being here now", as Ram Dass would say,[10] but it also represents a vain attempt on our part to sustain our identity within the subtle dimensions that belonged to the experience that we are tempted to glorify as the high point of our awakening, enlightenment, liberation or whatever. The fact is that there is still a higher point that we have not yet attained.

The only way that we can overcome this false sense of our identity is a radical letting go of all attempts to hold onto an image of enlightenment that actually contradicts the true reality of the ultimate enlightenment that awaits us.

No matter how remarkable or admirable the state of mind-body attunement that we attain, and no matter how deep and pure is our realisation of the true essence of our advaita, we need to learn how to remain unattached to it. Only by so doing can we allow all information coming to us, through different channels of perception, freely to enter into the wider and deeper realms of our awareness. By so doing, we come to recognise that every state of exemplary self-integrating awareness - no matter how enlightening, beautiful and good it may be - cannot be regarded as the ultimate goal of meditation.

When we come to this conclusion, an even more profound realisation of the truth of our being dawns upon us. We realise that our ultimate liberation lies in our becoming able to let go of everything, even what we take to be the most precious fruits of our meditation, thereby opening ourselves to what lies beyond all identity.

This ultimate goal corresponds to Mindell's characterisation of the value of enlightenment, namely that it enables us to remain open and flexible in all situations and under all conditions. He says, " 'Liberation', in process language, means being aware of your edges and being able to move with them or around them. Liberation means being free of your edges to your secondary processes."[11]

An archetypal model of this process is given by St Paul in his Letter to the Philippians. He says, "There must be no competition among you, no conceit. . . . In your minds, you must be the same as Christ Jesus:

> "His state was divine,
> yet he did not cling
> to his equality with God
> but emptied himself
> to assume the condition of a slave,
> and become as men are;
> and being as all men are
> he was humbler yet,
> even to accepting death,
> death on a cross."[12]

St John of the Cross characterised the experience of

spiritual death and rebirth as a "dark night of the soul". In this process, he says, we should not be attached to anything, however much good there may be in it. "Todo nada" was his motto - "absolutely nothing". This precept is held also as an ideal in Buddhism in the form of 'anatta', self-lessness, non-attachment, not clinging to any idea of self because we realise that there is no self other than the 'just so', the 'thus come', the 'suchness' of the way things are and of the way that we are in our particular circumstances. Similarly, we can recognise how the 'unknowing' of St John of the Cross corresponds to the dynamic readiness of all 'souls on Fire' to let go of the primary focus of their awareness - with which they identify themselves - in favour of tuning into what is happening in alternative channels of awareness.

Arnold Mindell, the father of process-oriented psychology, seems to exemplify the ideal of 'letting go' and refusing to be tempted to hold onto any image of himself. He writes, "I wish I believed more in my work. I am recommending something simple, too: that my reader trust and follow the inner process. You need not trust any human being, not even me. I have as yet to meet a guru or wise, enlightened, educated, shamanic, mediumistic person who is as intelligent as the process which unfolds in the channels of your own perception."[13]

What more can I say? Are we in the Process that the Fire is?

10 Meditation, Choiceless Awareness & Creative Freedom

*"He is the transparence of the place in which He is
and in His presence we find peace."*

Wallace Stevens

All action that is the outcome of tension and inner struggle is not centred in meditation. Only when we are free of anxiety, defensiveness and inner contending can our mind become still. Such stillness is characteristic of the meditative state. From a therapeutic standpoint, the meditative state can be seen to establish a kind of baseline, a foundation, from which to make a fresh start. In meditation, we discover an integrated state of being that sets a standard for all further states of integration, personal growth and development.

A NEW BEGINNING

The practice of meditation is an art that delivers us to what may be called 'a state of higher consciousness'. In this state, we are free from the effects of past conditioning. While we are in the meditative state, our reactions remain uninfluenced by all previous experience. At the height of meditation, we enter into a totally unconditioned state of being.[1,2] Such an unconditioned state cannot be put together by thought. It can only be achieved by systematically letting go of the thinking process itself.[3] As the Spanish mystic, St John of The

Cross, puts it:

> "I entered into unknowing
> And there remained unknowing
> Transcending all knowledge."[4]

Thought always takes place in relation to memory. Without the relationship of thought to memory the 'me' that compares, judges, decides, intends, and acts simply disappears. Beyond memory, judgement and choice is innocence. Choiceless awareness is free of self-evaluation, guilt and defensiveness. It is like a river whose course is not blocked or tampered with, flowing entirely peacefully and undisturbed.

> "Such a tide as, moving, seems to sleep,
> Too full for sound or foam."[5]

The choiceless awareness of meditation seems to lead, quite naturally, to a certain austerity, in which everything that would otherwise interfere with being-consciousness-bliss is simply allowed to fall away.

> "I will never lose myself
> For that which the senses
> Can take in here,
> Nor for all the mind can hold,
> No matter how lofty,
> Nor for grace or beauty,
> But only for I-know-not-what
> Which is so gladly found."[6]

This austerity serves to lay a foundation for our seeking and securing a whole new way of life. Meditation does not, of itself, secure this way of life for us, yet it establishes access to a new field of experience, against which other states of being and consciousness can be compared, and in which they can be transformed. St

John of The Cross expresses this transformation in terms of it being a 'mystical union' or 'mythical marriage', in which our everyday consciousness is penetrated by the meditative state (the 'Lover'), so transforming our everyday thinking-feeling-doing self (the 'beloved'). This is how he puts it:

> "O guiding night
> O night more lovely than the dawn!.
> O night that has united
> The Lover with His beloved,
> Transforming the beloved in her Lover."[7]

The practice of meditation enables us to look at, understand and transform vicious cycle processes in us, processes that create and sustain states of worry, guilt, resentment, self-pity, greed, envy and so on. The emotional traps involved in these states can be dispensed with, simply by virtue of our becoming aware of how they function and letting go of those parts and processes that keep them going. We can then set about replacing these parts and processes by the kind of thinking and acting that contradicts and excludes the misery-go-round of our emotional traps.[8]

In the process of releasing ourselves from such traps we rise above their influence simply by seeing them as 'false solutions', instead of reacting to them. This, in turn, clears a path in our consciousness for discerning the real issues of life that we face. We can now look at the possibilities that seeing these issues enables us to discover and invent.[9]

One mystical poet has referred to the nourishing influence of the mystical state in terms of it being a 'pasture' or 'meadow'. It feeds us by giving us the space to see new possibilities for creative thought and action. When we act on what we see this action transforms us. He describes the meditative state as a 'made place', that we can return to. Although we do not live our everyday lives in this 'made place', yet we are able to return to it for personal renewal and inner growth. Thus, he writes:

> "Often I am permitted to return to a meadow as if it were a scene made up by the mind, that is not mine, but is a made place, that is mine, it is so near to the heart, an eternal pasture . . ."(10)

Freedom from cycles of reactive bondage is intimately related to our capacity to be alone. This capacity, in turn, is rooted in the kind of self-acceptance that enables us to transcend those inner processes in which our feelings uncontrollably dominate our thinking. Anxiety, for instance, since it is one of our strongest emotions, may well convince us that the thoughts that give rise to it must be true, simply because we feel them so strongly. This is called 'being bluffed by our feelings'. We need to see through the error of this bluff in order not to feel obliged to pay undue attention to such thoughts. If we fail to do this, it will be difficult for us to be alone. Instead we may find it necessary to seek for the sense of security and identity that only other people seem able to give us. To be alone means always to be an outsider to the pettiness, power-plays and divisions that dominate so many relationships in everyday life. Such domination ceases to affect us only when we are free of its influence in our own consciousness.

> "Alone, mind empty of form and figure,
> Finding no support or foothold,
> He tastes there I-don't-know-what
> Which is so gladly found."(11)

A mystic is a person whose life springs mainly from his or her practice of meditation.(12) As a result, his consciousness, by and large, is free of emotional confusion, inner division and contention.

> "Until you call yourself my own,
> I shall not be what I am."(13)

Meditation is movement in stillness. In the deep flow of the meditation experience, brain processes are not caught up in projecting, reacting, defending and asserting. In the silence of meditation, simple awareness replaces reactive bondage. True creativity develops out of such awareness.

> "In safety, in disguise,
> In darkness, up the secret stair I crept
> - O happy enterprise! -
> Concealed from other eyes
> When all my house at length in silence
> slept."(14)

The 'house' mentioned in this poem refers to the poet's consciousness, which, after a long period attempting to realise the unconditioned state of meditation 'at length' becomes silent.

WORRY AND INNER DISTRESS

The futile struggle of worry involves continually visualising what we would not like to happen and how awful it would be if we were unable to cope. Worrying is not constructive thinking. Instead, the same emotions chase the same thoughts round and round in our consciousness, with seemingly no way out. Worry is never helpful. It is the opposite of constructive thinking. It merely ties us up in knots and exhausts us. (If we never worried again for the rest of our lives, no harm would come to us as a result.) Worry and similar states of inner contending distort awareness. They hi-jack our capacity for clear thinking, visualising options, evaluating possibilities, choosing what to do and acting resolutely. Worry is negative inner rehearsal. It prepares us to repeat our mistakes without learning anything useful from them.

Helpful learning experiences have an entirely different effect. Like meditation, they provide us with a refuge or 'safe harbour' in which emotional turmoil is laid to rest. Distressing experiences, by contrast, prevent us from learning anything useful. We find instead that our body becomes primed to fight or run because it is governed by the 'fight or flight' response.[15] This response is a primitive inborn set of bodily changes that prepares us to take immediate vigorous physical action. Whenever we are faced with danger, regardless of whether this danger is real or imagined, remembered or anticipated - and we have no coping response with which to meet it - the 'fight or flight' response is automatically brought into play. Our capacity for clear thinking is thus simply replaced by the stress response and, in this way, it becomes 'unavailable'. Faced with such a situation, we find that our creative freedom 'disappears'. Whatever we do in this state, therefore, tends to add more distress to our already existing distress. This, in turn, gives rise to distress-laden memories, together with intensified expectations that we will not be able to cope with a similar situation, in the future. Indeed, if we do not review our distress experience in a calmer and more stable frame of mind, our expectations will almost certainly prove to be correct. Next time we meet a situation that 'reminds us too much' of this distressing event, our distress pattern will be called into play, repeated and added to with more distressing memories.[16]

THE UNDOING OF DISTRESS PATTERNS

Meditation takes place beyond the realms of everyday personal and social expectations. This allows our mind to be opened up to its inherent self-regulating processes. Rich in its own quietness, such a mind is able to let go of all goal-seeking, goal-striving, distressing memories and anxious anticipations. In this way, it is able to rest in an anxiety-free, undivided state.

> "Oh, who my grief can mend!
> Come, make the last surrender that I yearn
> for,
> And let there be an end
> Of messengers you send
> Who bring me other tidings than I burn
> for."[17]

Worry is self-feeding. It generates the stress response in us, preparing us to fight or run. But what from? Against whom? Where to? If fighting and running are so inappropriate that we engage in neither, we are bound to be lumbered with a state of tension. Tension and worry are the 'messengers' that bring us the same messages over and over again, depriving us of the 'surrender' that we 'yearn' and 'burn' for.

Only when the movement of our mind ceases to pass from one judgement to another, or from one conclusion to another, does meditation begin.[18] Meditative consciousness is untouched by conceptual thought. It ceases to accumulate information. In itself, it is free of all purposefulness. Past and future have no meaning for it and in it. It simply involves an ongoing being that has no other aim but to be, and that aim is unconscious, the life in us simply taking care of itself.

> "I entered into unknowing

> Yet when I saw myself there
> Without knowing where I was
> I understood great things;
> I shall not say what I felt
> For I remained unknowing
> Transcending all knowledge."[19]

SHARING THE WORK OF PERSONAL GROWTH AND DEVELOPMENT

Psychologists often think of their work in terms of temporarily detaching people from their involvement in the outside world, helping them to inwardly reorganise their response to that same world, so enabling them better to fit back into it. Our work here will be similar yet different. We will seek to help one another to realise a high standard of wellbeing so that peace, joy, love and creative power can permeate our lives, enabling us not only to change our own consciousness and aims, but also to enable others to do the same. This will have a knock-on effect, leading to changes in the very structure of those relationships in our society that keep patterns of reactive bondage in place, thereby blocking personal growth and development on a large scale. The foundation of this whole process we see to lie in making available those practices whereby individuals may discover the underlying reality that meditation discloses to us, a reality in which we experience the interconnectedness of all that is - an all-in-allness that calls forth in us a feeling of unrestricted love, love that knows no boundary, separation or division.[20]

> "After I have known it
> Love works so in me
> That whether things go well or badly
> Love turns all to one sweetness
> Transforming the soul in itself."[21]

UNCONDITIONAL SELF-ACCEPTANCE AND UNRESTRICTED LOVE

The practice of meditation frees our mind from self-deception, delivering us to a state that is untouched by anxiety, despair, struggle, ambition and even an awareness of the passage of time itself. The meditative state is filled with great intensity - the intensity of unrestricted, unconditioned love, bliss and innocence. Free from all anxiety-based reactions and projections, a wonderful quality of awareness comes into being. In this awareness we give ourselves over to a profound acceptance of what is. This acceptance in turn, enables us to come into contact with a new centre of being in us. Traditionally, this contact has been called, variously, 'God-realisation', 'Self-realisation', or 'spiritual rebirth'.

> "I know there is no other thing so fair
> And earth and heaven drink refreshment there
> Although by night."[22]

Anxiety-based patterns of living - patterns of reaction and projection - cannot be overcome without the development of states of choiceless awareness that enable their 'host' to observe these patterns, understand what is leading to what in them, and finally let them fall away, replacing them with more worthwhile ways of meeting and resolving the issues that, in themselves, they obscure and prevent us from addressing. In short, only if we first accept ourselves the way we are, can we improve upon 'the way we are'. Without acceptance, understanding is not possible. We cannot understand what we reject. Acceptance of 'what is' enables us to do away with a profitless inner contending with the way we are so that we can see the essential error involved in 'the way we are', dispose of this error and work away from there. One Japanese mystic has expressed the 'suchness' of this kind of profound acceptance as follows:

> "Mount Fu in misty rain, the River Che at
> high tide
> When I had not been there, no rest from the
> pain of longing
> I went there and returned . . . it was nothing
> special
> Mount Fu in misty rain, the River Che at
> high tide."[23]

Meditation puts us in touch with our universal nature, putting an end to our 'pain of longing' by allowing us to be who we essentially are, and to see things as they essentially are.

MYSTICAL TRANSCENDENCE AND CHEMICAL DEPENDENCE

Among the alternatives to understanding that people have attempted to use to improve the quality of their lives, is the use of artificial chemical agents to change the quality of their consciousness. Pursuing this alternative can well become a problem in its own right. It can give rise to a debilitating reliance on chemicals, whose rate of consumption needs to be increased, over time, so as to be able to induce the same desired effect as before. This is because our body is so designed that it is perfectly attuned to the way we think, and consequently it always attempts to overcome any interference to this attunement. When our body successfully manages to overcome the interference of artificial chemical agents on the functioning of our bodymind, we call this achievement 'increased tolerance'. There is a price to pay for continuing to try to overcome this increased tolerance. A vicious cycle of increasing addiction is the inevitable result. In the end, increasing levels of consumption serve only to relieve the harrowing 'side effects' that they bring in their train. When this cycle becomes viciously self-feeding, it needs to be overcome, in its own right, before any other problems and difficulties can be faced and resolved.

Our body not only responds to the way we think, it also responds to artificial chemical agents that interfere with the way our body prepares us to meet whatever we are thinking about. The practice of meditation involves a development of the skills of letting go of tension, judgement and finally thinking. Some people use alcohol or some other drug to achieve much the same results. Letting go of words, concepts and images, we let go of those elements that relate present awareness both to past experience and to future expectations. Our consciousness therefore is able to withdraw from all involvement in fearful forebodings and debilitating self-recriminations. This is how meditation puts us in touch with our unconditioned nature, a state of being that the Zen Buddhists call 'empty and marvellous'. We could speculate that it is just this state that chemically dependent persons are seeking to realise in the first place. As St John of The Cross puts it:

> "The current that is nourished by this source
> I know to be omnipotent in force,
> Although by night."[24]

The mystical state that we achieve in meditation is a state of inner accord, in which there is no division or conflict. This experience is tantamount to our discovering a new source of identity within ourselves.

> "The man who truly there has come
> Of his own self must shed the guise

> For all he knew before the sum
> Seems far beneath that wondrous prize."(25)

The mystical state that we achieve in meditation is a state of inner accord, in which we are not in any way divided against ourselves. Instead, we find that our inner processes are so attuned to their own natural functions that our energy is able to regenerate itself, leaving us rested and refreshed. Even outside our practice of meditation, now, we find ourselves in a similar divided state, our everyday thinking, feeling and acting itself becoming increasingly integrated. This is what we mean when we say that the meditative state 'sets a standard' for everyday living.

> "He who masters himself
> Will, with knowledge in unknowing,
> Always be transcending."(26)

Every time we deviate from this state of inner harmony, we become aware of the disharmony, tension, discord or inner contention within us. Such a standard is thus closely related to what has traditionally been called our 'conscience' or 'the Holy Spirit within us'.

> "This life I live in vital strength
> Is loss of life unless I win You:
> And thus to die I shall continue
> Until in You I live at length."(27)

We are now in a position to relate the state that we attain in meditation to such therapeutic practices as intensive journal keeping and Fire-centred speaking and listening. Both of these practices provide us with a way of reliving distress-dominated experiences in a 'safe' situation - a situation of relative detachment from the demands, expectations and obligations of everyday society. When our experiences are explored in such a setting and put into words, we are able both to see 'what led to what' in them and to release ourselves from the emotional trap of being 'parasited upon' by their distress-dominated patterns. We learn thus to *understand* our experiences instead of merely being forced to *relive* them. This transformation is brought about through our expressing and exploring the realities behind our experiences. Moreover, our experiences are expressed, explored and re-experienced in states of non-judgmental, choiceless awareness. Therefore, instead of our being re-traumatised, the components of our experiences are, instead, articulated and separated out into manageable bits of useful information. In this process, we become able to compare and contrast aspects of our past experiences with aspects of reality currently being experienced. Having reviewed our past experiences, in this way, we understand them. This is how we are able to 'make sense' of both our past and our present experiences, as far as all available information allows.[28]

We understand our present experiences not only in terms of our past experiences, but also in terms of our present aims and intentions. Because we are able to compare and contrast past aims and intentions with present ones, we are able to see the difference that this difference makes to what we choose to do and what we choose to refrain from doing. At best these choices will reflect the core values that govern the spirit in which we wish to live and outside of which we do not wish to live. Such core values undoubtedly bear an intimate relationship to the essential ground of our being. At best, they enable us to stay attuned to it, thereby giving us an overall capacity to live the kind of free, creative and self-sustaining life, that is going to be good for all of us.

PROGRESS REVIEW FIVE

Relaxation and Meditation

CENTRAL IDEA: The anxiety sufferer needs to become skilled at releasing tension from his or her body so that they are able to use the relaxation response routinely to defuse panic and regain self-control. This is a discipline that is acquired with regular practice. It yields enormous benefits.

Each anxiety sufferer experiences his or her unique fears and problems, tensions, projections, reactions and misgivings. At the same time, each sufferer's anxiety state is founded upon a common inborn response to danger known as the 'sympathetic response', the 'stress response', or the 'fight or flight response'. The danger that we experience can come to us in the form of an external threat, or in the form of imagined and anticipated fears of what might happen to us. Whatever the source of our 'danger' experience, be it external or internal, our nervous system is bound to react to it in the same predictable way. Our heart beats faster to get a good supply of blood coursing through our body and lungs; we breathe fast and shallow to wash out carbon dioxide and take in oxygen; our blood pressure rises as blood vessels in our skin and gut constrict (supplying blood to our muscles of action); we sweat in order to cool down; our muscles tense up in preparation for immediate vigorous action. This can happen simply in response to the way we think! We do not need to mystify ourselves by looking for 'other' or 'deeper' reasons for what is happening or to terrify ourselves with extravagant ideas about what might happen next. The anxiety response is set and limited. The safest and surest antidote to this response is the 'relaxation response', also known as the 'parasympathetic response'. This, too, is a physiological process. It occurs when we do not feel under pressure or under threat or when we cease to experience ourselves as 'in danger'. Our heart-beat slows down, we breathe slowly and deeply, blood flows back into our skin and our digestive system, we stop sweating, our muscles relax, we feel calm, at ease and at peace.

This relaxation response is the perfect antidote to the stress response, the perfect antidote to anxiety. We can induce the relaxation response as a way of defusing anxiety and fear. This is where relaxation practice comes in. Use my "Relaxation-Meditation" tape, on a daily basis, once or even twice a day. By so doing, you work to develop a routine way of inducing the complete 'parasympathetic' response. By engaging at least some of the elements of total relaxation, you signal to your nervous system to 'switch off' its stress response. By inducing some of the elements of total relaxation, you release tension from your muscles, you breathe slowly and deeply, and you change the pattern of your thinking. These three changes transform your whole bodymind state from 'tense anxiety' to 'relaxed ease and peace of mind'. Having a practised relaxation routine at your disposal means that, like the routines of dressing or driving a car, you do not have to work it all out, from the start, every time. You just go ahead and put the routine into practice.

For this to be possible and for such a routine to be available, you need to practise relaxation and meditation on a regular basis, regardless of how you feel, regardless of how tense or relaxed you are before you start. In fact, if you practise relaxing and meditating only when you are tense, this will tie tension and relaxation too closely together in your mind, and you will have difficulty relaxing when you need to.

Regular use of the "Relaxation-Meditation" tape will not only help you relax, it will also enable you to think, feel and live with a profound sense of personal wellbeing.

Criteria of Attainment

1. You are able to release all tension from your body, while listening to the tape and following its instructions.
2. You are able to stay relaxed and tension-free while affirming that you accept, without any reservation, your body and all its processes, your mind and all its powers, your 'self' as a whole person.
3. You are able to extend this total acceptance, during meditation, to people in your family and community, people you work for and with, people you resent, and so on.
4. You are able to extend this process of acceptance, forgiveness and love to all people regardless of race, religion, colour, class, nationality, sex or age.
5. In this total acceptance of yourself and all humankind, you experience yourself at one with the whole human family. In that unity, you accept that you are also one with God and open to receive His love for you.
6. You are able to take this bodymind state with you into your daily life.
7. You use the relaxation response, routinely, to 'let go' of tension in the face of anxiety and panic. In this way, you learn to govern the state of your being in different situations.
8. You use the relaxation response and the affirmations that feel right for you to inwardly rehearse meeting and handling all situations with peace, joy and love.
9. You use your relaxed and accepting bodymind state to engage in the graded practice of entering and dealing with situations as set out, in a step-wise fashion, on your 'progress ladder'.

Further Reading

Carlos Casteneda, *The Fire Within,* **Penguin.**

> *"Self-importance is our greatest enemy . . . our*
> *self-importance requires that we spend most of*
> *our lives offended by someone."*

Section Five

Journal Training and Transformation

11   *The Inner Eye of Love*

"You have also proclaimed me to be a new Darwin, or Marx, or Pasteur, or Freud. I told you long ago that you would be able to talk and write like me, if you only would not always yell Hail, Hail, Messiah! For this victorious yelling deadens your mind and paralyses your creative nature."

Wilhelm Reich[1]

If we are emotionally unbalanced and our thoughts and actions are driven by inner contending, then, whatever we do in this state is likely to create more problems than it is able to solve. Nor does withdrawal into inaction help us to resolve our problems. Instead, such withdrawal may well give rise to a sense of hopelessness. The less we do, the less we feel able to do. Nor can our problems be resolved through trying to right the imbalance within us through the use of artificial chemical agents. All such agents merely interfere, at some level, with the manner in which our body responds to the way we think.

MEDITATION AND JOURNALLING

In the practice of meditation, we see how detachment from the outside world, together with a detaching of our thoughts from all conceptual involvement with outside events eventually enables us to pay attention to the natural stress-free functioning of our body. This practice enables us to deepen our conscious awareness of the universal essence of our being - free of all aims and purposes, free of inner contending and judgement - functioning of its own accord, in an entirely balanced and intrinsically harmonised way.

By remaining centred in this state, we create, within ourselves, a pool of uncommitted energy which constitutes an uncommitted potential for personal growth and development. Such energy is experienced as a 'blessing' or as 'grace' that flows into us, enabling us to be more aware than we were before and enabling us to become more (or other) than who and how we are now. Thus we experience how it is that the 'samatha' form of meditation - e.g. one-pointed awareness of our breathing - constitutes a practice that is able to restore us to creative freedom.

"At first", Chogyam Trungpa tells us, "Meditation is pure frustration."[2] The reason why meditation is so frustrating, in the first instance, is because of the functionally ungoverned feelings that rise up in us when we practise remaining tension-free and inwardly focused. The fluctuations that we experience in our bodymind are what Patanjali[3] called the 'vritti' in the 'chitta'; that is to say, the fluctuations that arise in us and disturb our consciousness. Through continuously letting go of all thoughts that enter our conscious awareness and through accepting all emotions, neither tensing up against them nor reacting to them, we learn to let the state that we are in govern itself. Remaining conscious of our self-governing, self-balancing bodymind state, both the depth of its balance and the depth of our awareness increase. Ultimately, the deep state of being-consciousness-bliss that comes to us creates a frame of reference and a standard of being that is able to transform both our inner life and our life in the world.

In the "Living Flame" section we looked at the ultimate goal of meditation, namely a form of openness and flexibility that enables us to be free and creative in our responsiveness to all situations. In relation to this flexibility and openness, we looked at the possible superiority of 'vipassana' meditation - insight meditation - over and against one-pointed 'samatha' meditation. However, both forms of meditation have their merits and are not in competition with one another.

As in insight meditation, so also in life-journalling and speaking-and-listening. We notice what thoughts and feelings are stirring in us and we express and explore whatever images, memories, anticipations or impulses give rise to these thoughts and feelings. We both express what we see, feel or hear, and we allow what we express to stimulate further thoughts, feelings and memories in us. This is how what we alternately 'express' and 'contain' enables us to enter into new fields of personal growth and development, leaving us more open and flexible in our responsiveness to all life situations.

BASIC ATTITUDE

As we continue to respond to all that we experience, express and explore, further thoughts and feelings stir in us. All such thoughts and feelings need to be framed within a basic attitude of unconditional self-acceptance, as we write. This is the sole condition that we need to keep, if our writing is to be of any real growth-promoting benefit to us - a condition of no conditions! Only by holding to a basic attitude of unconditional self-acceptance are we able to prevent the awareness-blunting effects of shame, guilt, self-blame, remorse and so on that might otherwise arise in us, from short-circuiting our awareness and our explorations.

The boundary that frames and limits our primary awareness is not only established by a defensiveness concerning who we are and how we think we should be, it is also established by our primary *beliefs* about what is, what is possible, and what is desirable. These beliefs lead us to expect certain things to happen - and not others.

They therefore tune our perceptions in to picking up and responding to what we expect. This, in turn, creates a certain attitude in us. At the same time, however, this attitude can be influenced and modified by our aims. And this is why the aim of being open to processes taking place in all our perceptual channels makes information accessible to us that would not otherwise be accessible. In all of this, the basic attitude of unconditional self-acceptance takes us beyond a limited framework of intent, giving us greater access to all that lies 'above and beyond the merely practical'.

In Chuang Tzu's words:

> "If you persist in trying
> To attain what is never attained
> (It is the Tao's gift!)
> If you persist in making effort
> To obtain what effort cannot get;
> If you persist in reasoning
> About what cannot be understood,
> You will be destroyed
> By the very thing you seek."[4]

EXPLORING BEYOND OUR EDGES

The boundary of our primary awareness separates information that is available to us from information that is not available to us, that is to say, it keeps information from us that is irrelevant to our aims and purposes.

It is only when signals that do not usually constitute information conflict with or contradict the intentional framework established by our beliefs, expectations, attitudes and aims that we do become aware of them. Otherwise our primary awareness generally tends to exclude such signals and events, ignoring them, treating them, by and large, as irrelevant, as 'noise', not constituting what we would call 'information' at all.

222

We can represent this as a circle, created by our attending to signals that let us know were we are in relation to where we are going. Only such signals are treated as information. All other signals are, by and large, excluded.

The boundary of our primary awareness faces both ways, inside and out. It relates inner signals, such as 'relevant' feelings, memories and anticipations to external events. What makes such signals 'relevant' is our 'practical' aims and intentions plus our identification of who we are in and through these signals. However, when we cease to preoccupy ourselves with 'the merely practical', much information that we would probably otherwise ignore becomes available to us, unless, that is, such information is felt to threaten our primary identity.

In the circle of our awareness, internal and external events 'line up', as it were, to create a perspective that makes sense, giving us a possible avenue of development for our reflections, evaluations and possible actions.

Thus we can say that our primary awareness is specialised for selective processing of a wide variety of perceptual signals that we are potentially open to receive. Such selectivity is in line with what is relevant and what is not relevant within the framework established by our intent.

The selective processing of perceptual signals creates, sustains or transforms 'who I am' and 'how I am', in my circumstances. By governing and directing our actions to certain definite ends, our primary awareness creates a particular perspective in us. This perspective enables us to engage in selective learning experiences, within the perspective adopted. It also enables us to explore the meaning, the value and the limits of our perspective, as well as enabling us to relate to alternative perspectives.

When we explore our own perspective, by comparing it with alternative perspectives - with which we can identify, in some way - this makes it possible for us to transform our beliefs, expectations, attitudes and aims, so long as we are basically accepting of ourselves and our circumstances, rather than being defensive about ourselves and our situation in life. We can selectively expand our awareness along certain lines and thereby allow our way of processing certain kinds of information to be transformed. This, in turn, transforms our perspective and our identity itself, insofar as that identity is tied to a given perspective and way of responding to events and situations.

Our primary awareness allows for expansiveness and inclusion of certain types of information when we do not feel threatened or under pressure. By the same token, however, our primary awareness becomes constricted and exclusive of alternative points of view, whenever we feel threatened or under pressure. Thus the boundary of our awareness - our edge - comes clearly into focus when something seems to threaten our identity - and may even seem to threaten our survival. Our aim must be thriving, not simply surviving.

In soul-on-Fire work, we seek to enable people to let go of their defensiveness, in order to go beyond their edges. To do this, we teach ways of 'taking' experiences that enable ourselves and others to dismantle our defences and trust ourselves to a deep process of acceptance. If we have been resisting looking at ourselves and our experiences in perspectives that are not infolding, this may lead us to experience great vulnerability. But, then, we remember - "It's OK to feel vulnerable" - and we continue to go with the flow. This is where an overall attitude of unconditional self-acceptance proves its worth. It enables us to let go, unconditionally, letting secondary processes that have been excluded from our primary awareness to transform the very nature and purpose of our awareness itself.

We can say, as a general rule of thumb, that all organisms open up for incorporation and growth when they feel 'safe', just as they close down for exclusion and defence when they feel 'threatened'. At the same time, however, we can organise ourselves to take our experiences in such a way that what we would normally regard as threatening, we come to accept as safe.

This basic attitude may well contradict an anxiety-based tendency in us to 'get it wrong', as it were. When we do get it wrong, instead of being able to organise our overall response to life in a creative and flexible way, we unwittingly use our conscious awareness to dwell almost exclusively on possibilities that generate fear and tension in us, so serving to negate our creative potential. This we may do, for example, by visualising ourselves being unable to cope with certain situations, or, alternatively, by looking for faults and limitations in ourselves and others. All in all, what we are doing is to generate forces in our body that 'shut down' our awareness, rather than 'opening us up' to the whole picture. Even in safe situations, therefore, people who are governed by tension and anxiety-based worry fail to control the state that they are in. This makes it well nigh impossible for them to come to a full awareness of what is, what is possible, and what they want to go for.

The type of actions and reflections that a person who is dominated by tension and anxiety engages in, become their 'symptoms'. If, suffering from such symptoms, we fall into the wrong hands, we may not only find ourselves identifying with our symptoms but we may also find ourselves beholden to people who label us and our problems, in a way that shuts down our ability to work with the processes involved. As a result, we become even less able than before to liberate ourselves from the cycles of reactive bondage in which we have become trapped.

Various kinds of soul-on-Fire work have been evolved to enable us to release ourselves from tense, constricted, defensive states and to help others to do the same. This same work also enables us to release ourselves from the symptomatic (uncontrollable) false solutions that keep us in these states.

Only by exploring what lies beyond our edges can we become free and creative on our own account. This, and this alone, enables us to make meaningful, value-realising choices about who we are and who we can be, when all is said and done.

PERSONAL GROWTH AND DEVELOPMENT

To grow and develop as a free whole and creative person, life journalling is an invaluable aid. Once we have adopted the exclusion clause "no praise, no blame" to create a basic attitude and framework for our writing, we become able to write everything down without either defending or justifying ourselves. Our habitual way of dealing with situations and issues is thus able to reveal itself to us.

Once we see this, alternative ways of thinking and dealing with issues also begin to reveal themselves to us. We explore these also. This, in turn, enables us to evaluate the pattern that has been governing our choices. Yet this kind of evaluation is only able to take place when we have said *all* that comes to us to be said.

Life journalling is not analysis. If we attempt to analyse our experience before we have freely explored it, this would imply that we already understood what our experience was all about. And of course we do not. We do not understand what we have not as yet allowed ourselves to express and explore.

Perhaps the feelings that stir in us, as we explore various themes in our life, would overwhelm us, were we not able to contain them and express them in a manageable way; for example, through the journalling process. By thus rendering our feelings manageable, the journal process gives us a way to integrate our life. It both records and promotes our journey to wholeness.

Our Lord tells us a parable of what the Kingdom of heaven is like.(6) The servants of a landowner come to him to tell him that an enemy had come "in the night" to sow tares among his wheat. They ask him if he would have him gather the tares up. "No," he tells them, "Don't do that in case you pull out the wheat also." He advises them instead to let both the tares and the wheat grow up together, side by side, until the harvest. Then, when all has been gathered in, the wheat and the weeds can be separated. So it is also with the journalling process. We let everything be recorded on the pages that we write, good and bad together, making no distinction between them. We let all be recorded together, passing no judgement. We let it all grow 'side-by-side'. And only when all has been expressed and explored, will it be the right time to evaluate all that has been written down. The moral, here, is that prejudgement only interferes with the process. Prejudgement, evaluation or analysis only blocks the effectiveness of the practice of keeping a journal. The time to evaluate is not before everything has been said. Only when all has been put into writing - without praise and without blame - can what is, what is possible, and what is desirable be seen and felt in its full extent. Only when the full harvest has been gathered in can what is desirable and what is undesirable be weighed and balanced within itself.

Another metaphor for the journalling process is the Greek myth of Theseus. Through the use of Ariadne's thread he is able to find his way through the labyrinth, without losing his way and perhaps being devoured by the minotaur. This thread enables him to explore all the passages of the labyrinth, without his becoming confused about where he has come from or where he is going. He finds out as he goes along. Thus the thread helps him to trace his way out of the labyrinth. It enables us to express and explore the totality of our experiences in the life that we are living. By so doing, it enables us to understand our journey. Such understanding develops because we do not panic. We are not daunted by the apparent complexity - or the apparent hopelessness - of our life. The writing process helps us to see where we have gone and where we still need to go, what we have done and what we still need to do. As we hold to the integrity of staying aware and continuing to respond to all that enters our consciousness, we become able both to secure our own liberty and to enable others to do the same.

As we unravel our thoughts and feelings by putting them into words, we ask, "Is there anywhere else to go?", "Is there anything else stirring in me?", "What do I see?", "What do I feel?", "What do I hear?". Eventually we come to the end of our explorations, and, when this happens, all that we have thought, felt, seen, heard and expressed is able to become inwardly related to itself. In this way, particular 'themes' within our existence reveal themselves to us. We see, perhaps for the first time, what they involve and what they mean.

Only through accepting ourselves, the way we are, can we improve upon the way we are. Keeping a journal helps us to realise such acceptance. By re-experiencing, expressing and exploring the way we think and feel and act, we become able to see what is leading to what in us. We see patterns and processes. We gain insights into why we think and act the way we do. This in turn enables us to break the mould of our habitual reactions. It enables us to re-evaluate the patterns and processes in which we have been unconsciously locked. The journalling process enables us to express and explore not only the way things are, but also the way that we would prefer things to be. To plan and write about what we visualise, and what 'feels right', prepares us for decisive action. When we act on what we prefer, this confirms us in the meaning and value of our intentions. And when we write about what we have done and what the outcome was, this deepens our total appreciation of the process.

All of this makes the practice of journalling one of the most liberating and life-transforming enterprises that we could ever embark upon. The basic method, as set out, enables us to generate a total acceptance of ourselves and it enables us to use this acceptance to live the kind of life that we always knew, deep down, was possible.

HOW IT HAPPENS

When the flow of our writing, that springs from a certain constellation of experiences, comes to an end, we are able to reflect back on the entire sequence which, articulated in its many parts and processes - yet forming a coherent theme as a totality - is at last both understood in an objective way and appreciated in a purposeful and feelingful, subjective way. It is this dual perspective that generates insights in us, letting us know who we are and what we really want, when all has been 'gathered in'.

Life journalling helps us to know what our feelings are about and it helps us to feel what we know. We come thus to understand our inner processes, our moods and our states of mind. States of mind, we find, are constituted by the nature of our beliefs, expectations, attitudes and aims that selectively draw information from the pool of our potential awareness. As we continue with the journalling process, we see how our perspective revolves around the values or principles in relation to which our thoughts and actions 'make sense' and 'have meaning'.

All this becomes apparent to us. As a result, a subtle and deeply moving reorganisation starts to take place in us. We grow because of what we feel and think and see and hear and do and know. We also grow in ways that we do not fully understand, except that we experience ourselves living more fully and more consciously, in a world that is meaningful and precious to us.

Criteria by Which to Evaluate Progress

If ever you are in doubt as to whether or not your journalling is as it should be (i.e. could be), you may like to check your process and your progress against the following criteria:

1. You do not spend much time thinking about what to write. Instead, you simply get on with writing down all that stirs in you, all that you feel and think about, all that you remember and anticipate, all that develops in your seeing, hearing and feeling channels, when you let it do so.
2. Inner contending drops away as you allow yourself to experience, express and explore, freely and openly, various avenues of possibility that you permit to develop in you.
3. You replace destructive self-criticism with emotional honesty and unconditional self-acceptance. You see where you are coming from, emotionally and reactively. You see how you can think and respond differently about yourself and your life. You enter into perceptual channels and ways of awareness and responsiveness that you discover yourself preferring.

You recognise this as the unfolding of your creative potential.

4. Bewilderment and confusion give way to meaningful and purposeful insights.

5. You let various channels of awareness evoke memories in you. As you express and explore these memories, further memories and associations are evoked. You allow these memories and associations to flow in you to whatever conclusion they take you. You respond and you keep on responding. In this way, you explore realms of being and becoming that lie beyond the edges of a narrow, purposeful 'merely practical' frame of reference.

6. You cease to feel trapped within narrow functional limits or within narrow emotionally bounded limits. You find that you no longer feel compelled to react as you did before.

7. Instead of trying to analyse your own motives - asking yourself 'why do I feel like this?' or 'why did I react that way?' - you write down all that is going on in you, switching channels whenever you feel stuck. This you do, for example, by asking yourself 'What am I hearing?', 'What do I see?', 'What do I feel?'. In this way, you come to understand, in a new way, the patterns and processes that are operating in you. You also tap into new possibilities that are able to evolve in you, if you let them.

8. Awareness blocks caused by guilt, self-blame, resentment, self-pity and so on are replaced by more creative, energising emotions generated within the framework of acceptance, in the dynamics of love, the dynamics of the Tao - the Logos - that you discover in your life and in your awareness.

9. Through recognising what lies behind your emotions, you gain control of your feelings. You see things coming, in your everyday living. You recognise and you appreciate what you wish to avoid doing and

getting yourself into, in the future. You also recognise
what you would like to do and how you would like
to be, instead.

10. You feel closer to other people and are better able
intuitively to fathom and appreciate what is going on
in their inner life.

11. You develop a strong attachment to the journalling
process and you look forward to journalling each
day. It keeps you feeling alive, growthful, dynamic,
creative and optimistic.

12. Your emotions are able to flow easily and they are
able to work spontaneously for your personal growth
and development.

12   *Keeping a Personal Life Book*

"The symbol has the power of expressing what logic abhors: the existence of internal tensions, incompatibilities, conflicts, struggles, destructions."[1]

In order to deepen our appreciation and understand our personal life, it is useful to keep what Terence O'Brien calls a "Personal Life Book".[2] In this Personal Life Book, or PLB, a particular structured way of writing can help us to realise how it is that our life functions at the level that we 'understand' it. Our life does not merely go the way we want it to go. Instead, our life goes the way 'I AM'.

Personal growth has as its aim conscious living, popularly called 'maturity'.[3] Growth to maturity is personal work to be done by the person who is me. Just as only I can eat my own food, so too on the level of personal growth it is only I who can grow as a person. This is a natural process of inner development. Just as we cannot make a plant grow, so too we cannot make ourselves grow to maturity. We can only create the right conditions for this growth to occur.

For me to be capable of personal growth means that I need to be able to respond to all that I am in the life that I am living. It is only in this way that I can become responsible for my own life. Only in this way will I be able to respond to my whole life and circumstances, to respond from within myself, without being dominated and controlled by outer and inner pressures and complexes. If I am being controlled, I am not 'in control'. Responsibility requires freedom and it requires that I be in control of my own responses.

Consider your own understanding in this respect. 'Understanding' is the consciousness 'under' which you 'stand'. It is conscious awareness of the knowledge you use to live by. Understanding is, therefore, your meaning as a person. It follows thus that the level of your understanding is the level at which you live.

The person who is me stands between two worlds: an external visible world which I can see, touch, taste, smell and hear - a world that I share with others in a matter-of-fact sort of way - and an internal world that none of the senses meets and is shared by no-one.

If you doubt the existence of this inner world, ask yourself the question: 'Are my thoughts, feelings, plans, hopes, disappointments, joys, desires and sorrows real to me?'. Of course, if you come to the conclusion that they are not real and only a table and chair that you can see and touch are real, then the idea of personal development will have little or no meaning for you. On the other hand, given that you accept the reality of your inner world, ask yourself which is the world in which you really 'live and move and have your being?'. Is it the 'outside world' revealed by the senses, or this 'inner world' that no-one experiences save yourself, and only you can observe? I think you will agree that it is really in this inner world that you live all the time and think and feel and suffer and come to know yourself. It is only in this inner world that we can learn for ourselves how to grasp and shape the causes of our own actions.[4]

People who are difficult to get on with are in personal difficulty and need help. People who are difficult are not living mature lives. They are not seeing and understanding things at a conscious level. They are not able to account for what is happening in their inner world. Perhaps they never realised that their inner life was something to think about, or perhaps fear of their own inner turmoil has kept them going at an unconscious, unreflective level. Such persons often try to live in their imaginations only and try to 'play to an audience' in the outside world. They attempt to 'pass themselves' as people who they are not, or rather as people they would like to be but feel that they cannot be. Within themselves they engage in fantasy purely at the level of wishful thinking, or they engage in uncontrolled worry dominated by fears of what might happen to them, quite devoid of constructive thinking.

The prescription to write down our thoughts, feelings and reactions 'without praise and without blame', firstly allows us to see that is leading to what in us, and secondly it generates a new consciousness in us, governed by an attitude of total acceptance, where awareness replaces the blunting of awareness through automatic evaluation, prejudgement and defensive reactions.[5]

As a replacement for conscious living, wishful thinking, bluff, worry and defensiveness present us with a false internal reality. When we choose to fight the negative processes that arise in us, as a result, we merely continue to strengthen and entrench them.

In the short term, then, we should refuse to be taken in by and be dictated to by negative thoughts and emotions. Instead, we should simply let go of them. Some specific strategies for doing this are outlined in this book. The general principal involved is for us constantly to make contact with love-centred beliefs and feelings and to think and act in terms of these. When negative states are in control, we are not in control. On the other hand, when love is in control we are self-governing and self-regulating. We should, in practice, have no difficulty in distinguishing which is which.

In the long term, we should let the basic unresolved problems in our lives work through our consciousness by writing about them in the manner outlined. In this way, we will be able to let go of the negative reactions associated with our unresolved problems, while at the same time allowing our problems to resolve themselves by continuously responding to their hidden meaning in our lives, recognised and explored as we write about our lives as a whole.

It is good to be able to see that our way of 'taking' life creates the states and processes that make our life the way it is. Then we can begin to work on our way of 'taking' it. Our habitual reactions to life seem to be 'ourselves' before we begin to live more consciously. Now we can begin to see that it is not our external circumstances that we need to change so much as the way that we are unwittingly reacting to all that seems merely to 'happen' to us. Once we grasp this idea, then no matter what the outer conditions of our life appear to be, we realise that we are no longer compelled to react in unconscious ways to them. Instead, we discover that we have within us a power whose value is beyond price.

The PLB can most usefully be kept by writing it under four headings:

1. The Day
2. Dreams
3. My Life, Past and Present
4. Realisations, Insights and Understanding.

These sections are discussed below.

1. The Day

In this section, you write fully and completely about your day, putting everything down on paper. In so

doing, you begin to attend to everything and an automatic and mechanical selection process is overcome.
    (a) all must be written down
    (b) all must be written down without self-condemnation or self-justification

The prescription to write 'without praise and without blame' must become your motto. Keeping this in mind means that you stop short-circuiting your awareness and your appreciation of what is leading to what in your thoughts, feelings and actions.

Writing in this way means that you are consciously open, relaxed and accepting of the whole of your personal reality. By not condemning, judging, criticising or justifying yourself, you cease to block your awareness of the nature of thoughts, images and beliefs upon which your emotions and actions turn.

To illustrate what I mean, imagine that you saw a drunk man sleeping the night away on a public bench. Your reaction would not simply be 'Oh, there is a drunk man spending the night on a bench'. Instead, this sight would more than likely reflect some ideas that you have about yourself or society or drink or being homeless and down-and-out. It acts, in other words, as an image or symbol that reflects upon yourself and your life. The situations that you meet and think about function in you as 'possible personal realities', in which you are or could be involved. You go further than just looking at and recognising situations, events and circumstances. In the same way, whatever you see or hear or think about can become a symbol for you - a personal experience that relates to you and involves you, by pointing to some hopes or fears or beliefs of your own. This is what the 'symbolic' is all about.

A second illustrative example might simply be a large bird, flying majestically across the sky. This, too, can function as a symbol in us, something which points to, and participates in, say, your sense of freedom or your desire to be free of some undesirable 'inner' state or 'outer' hardship of circumstance.

Writing down all your thoughts, feelings and actions generates an acceptance of yourself that allows your consciousness (your 'psyche' or 'soul') to work for the growth of the whole person that is you.

As you 'tell yourself' in your PLB, insights begin to emerge spontaneously. These insights do not emerge as a result of analysis. In fact, analysis is likely to interfere with the direct awareness of what is going on in you that your writing opens up. Direct awareness can be obscured by an analysis artificially superimposed on it. Instead, your honesty in what you write and your openness to yourself (no praise, no blame) allows your self-reflective awareness to come to an understanding of itself. We see our own thoughts, we understand our own understanding and we come to know how our own beliefs and convictions operate in us. This is how and why insights begin to flow.[6]

Direct awareness, which transcends the limitations of the judgements, criticisms and defensive oppositions of good-bad, strong-weak, guilty-innocent, well-sick, and so on, overcomes all sense of 'wrong' or 'lack' that we might unwittingly be generating about ourselves. The practice of writing everything down without praise and without blame takes us into the realm of direct awareness, because it derives from a self-accepting and non-defensive attitude towards ourselves. It enormously expands our awareness and creates a sense of God-given and God-like freedom in us. This sense of freedom is thorough-going and is not merely superficial or lacking in a secure foundation.

The exclusion criteria 'no praise, no blame' create in us a mental frame of self-acceptance. Letting everything flow (writing everything down), while at the same time letting go of negative judgements or defensive rationalisations about ourselves (even if we are describing ourselves as having them at some earlier stage of the day) includes all our experience of ourselves. At the same time, this practice allows us to 'take' it all in a new, self-liberating and creative way. Insights begin to flow as new, creative and fulfilling possibilities present themselves to us. An awareness and understanding of less desirable patterns might also emerge in the light of our contrasting new mental and emotional 'set'. We know what belongs to 'positive' and 'negative' mental processes in us.

We lack integrity and a capacity for self-understanding if we fail to recognise in ourselves what we are thinking and doing and yet are aware of these things in others. We may even accuse others of thoughts and acts similar to our own, without such accusations making us aware of our own thoughts and deeds. Letting go of our accusing and self-justifying frame of mind (no praise, no blame) creates in us a capacity for integrity and a clear and uncluttered perspective towards our life and its meaning.

As insights dawn upon you, write them down in the fourth section also, 'Insights and Realisations'.

When writing in the Day section of your Personal Life Book, let your thoughts flow freely out onto the paper. The PLB is a purely private affair and no-one save yourself has a right to read it, except with your permission, should you wish to share what you have written down with another person. The PLB is not written for others. It is written for oneself. It is to enable you to 'tell the untellable to yourself'.

As you write, you should feel free to put on paper any images that have been entering your mind at the time of writing. Images and symbols, as I have discussed earlier, are of great importance and should be freely experienced and expressed in writing. Images and symbols are created out of our experience, our memories

239

and also our desires, hopes and expectations. They are also, of course, created out of our fears and dreads. It is through these images, which represent certain possibilities to us, that we organise our mental and physical 'set' to meet the future or to take immediate action. They evoke a 'response readiness' or a 'reaction readiness' in us. We either use such images to persuade ourselves into a positive and constructive mental attitude, or we use them to unwittingly sabotage our potential.

There is also a sense in which our images take on a life of their own in us. In some ways, they live through us as much as we live through them. Hence, we can, as it were, 'interview' our symbols and images by seeing not only how we are living in them with them and through them, but also by seeing how our symbols and images are taking root in our lives and how we are 'embodying' them, as they infuse us with 'their' spirit.[7]

Symbolic images are embedded in us with particular emotional sets which both define and limit the scope of possibilities that they open to us. By letting go of our excessive tensions through freely expressing the opposing aims, attitudes and assumptions underlying them - 'no praise, no blame' - we are able to free ourselves from negative and destructive mental states into which some of our images habitually impel us. By the same token - 'no praise, no blame' - we are able to enter into and draw upon the growth potential and possibilities opened up by new and emerging symbols, images and perspectives.

You may find yourself writing about a river, the sea, a house, a boat, a field, a mountain or a cave. The symbolic meaning of what you are writing about does not become clear to you through analysis. Instead, if you let the symbols 'speak for themselves', as it were, you let them work through from less conscious to more conscious levels. The symbol has its own reality, meaning and relationship. It has its own framework and momentum and this can be destroyed through analysis, which in and of itself, cuts into the symbol's own framework, meaning, momentum and flow.[8]

In keeping your PLB, what is essential is that you be free and open to what you write and its effects upon you. When you write, write as a whole person without prejudgement, defensiveness or preconceived ideas. Whatever is already shaped in your mind, leave aside. Leave aside judgements already formed. Let go of negative judgements - let them evaporate - let them simply disappear. Let go all biased, partial and egocentric feelings. Be open. Write. Then the psyche - your consciousness - is able to get on with its work. The work of your consciousness is to become self-regulating, enabling you to become self-governing in relation to the life you are living by promoting its wholeness and meaning. Use your negative feelings to explore, observe and understand what lies behind them.

We do not grow because of the direction of others. We grow because of the development of our own awareness and understanding. The freedom we desire is freedom from the domination of fearful imaginings and cycles of reactive bondage to which these imaginings and associated beliefs tie us - self pity, resentment, hostility, guilt, jealousy, shame and so on. We see how these negative feelings function and are able to let go, transform and replace the processes involved.

The act of writing slows down our thinking and increases our awareness.

2. Dreams

We all dream every night. The reason that we forget or do not remember our dreams is either because we do not see the point of remembering them or because we have some block to our personal growth. This block can be overcome.

Terence O'Brien suggests that when we write about our dreams we do so with the attitude 'I go along with the work of the psyche in the dream, anything else I leave aside.' Do not worry about what the work of the psyche is or should be. If you have that attitude it will all work out by itself.

The dream state itself has some qualities in common with the meditative state which is reached by:

(a) release of mental and muscular tension
(b) letting go of all striving
(c) directing the mind's attention inwards

There is a receptive attitude towards the elements of consciousness, together with a letting go of defensiveness (no praise, no blame) allowing an exploration of depth and meaning to take place.

In our dreams, our mind scans our most recent experiences and aims, in terms of our past experiences. In the dream it is as if our psyche (consciousness, soul) were attempting to realise and represent to itself some kind of 'balance' or a 'forward momentum that is self-stabilising'.

Our dreams can advise us. They can also encourage us and warn us, in various ways, if we are open to them. The images contained in our dreams are symbols that represent our personal reality to us. They usually contain more meaning than their face value would ordinarily suggest. They often hold within them some dynamic meaning related to our life. They belong to the 'all in allness' of our life. They represent, as it were, attempts to make sense of contradictions in our experiences, aims, actions and beliefs.

Our dreams are symbols that usually have some very real place in the total 'circuitry' of our life. They reflect back to us something of where we are and what we are. They represent where we are headed for and what our values and priorities are. As such, they are a key to our personal reality. They both conceal and reveal their meaning at one and the same time. It is for us to 'read' the symbolic images of our dreams by writing freely and fully about them and being open to their effects upon us.

Write your dreams down and also write down any thoughts that occur to you about them.

There is a lot of fear deep down in all of us. In the process of trying to neutralise this fear our psyche produces dreams in which we become very frightened. If we accept such dreams and open ourselves to them we let their meaning work through our consciousness. In this way, we can come to understand ourselves and totally free ourselves from the fears that our dreams relate to. If we reject such dreams - because they are frightening - the fear gets pushed down again. It continues to act as a negative and destructive force in us. Recurring nightmares give us repeated opportunities to come to an understanding of and a freedom from our fears and destructive inner forces.

The symbolic images contained in our dreams crystallise relationships in our life in a marvellously condensed form. What they are actually representing to us is our self-regulating processes.

Start by writing down any dreams that you may have had earlier in your life, if possible, in chronological order. If not, it does not matter.

Write down any recurring dreams.

It should be remembered that not all dreams are important. There are trivial and insignificant dreams, just as there are trivial and insignificant events in life.

Do not try to analyse or interpret your dreams. Just be aware of any insight or understanding that comes to you in the dream. Just be totally open to the symbols as you write the dreams down. Put references to the fourth section (Insights and Realisations) with the

day and date, as insight and understanding dawns upon
you.

3. My Life, Past and Present

The advice 'forget about the past - leave it alone' is very
bad advice indeed. While we may consciously manage
to forget what we do not like or fear, all such buried
unexamined memories still work in us at an
unconscious, emotionally driven level. They are
triggered in particular situations in such a way that we
feel compelled to act in the same way that we did before.
In this way our past - which we want to forget - becomes
also our future.[9]

Instead, it is a good thing to be open to the truth
of your life, as far as possible, from the beginning. It
becomes possible for us to be open to the truth of our life
(as far as possible from the very beginning), by writing
about it with an attitude of self-acceptance and a sense
of gratitude for the gift of consciousness itself. Keep in
mind, once again, the motto 'no praise, no blame'.[10]

Start writing from whatever point in your life
you like.

It is necessary for us to recognise one thing from
the outset. It is this: we all have a distorted view of our
own life. Terence O'Brien suggests that our attitude
should be as follows: "I am open to the whole of my life,
painful or pleasant, totally open. If I remain shut off
from any part of my life this means that only part of me
is living in the present.'[11]

The parts of me that I refuse to face and do not
wish to look at, remember or relive, act in me as
'negative traps', ready to take me over at unsuspecting
moments.

Whenever we feel unable to give ourselves to
what we really want to do, we should sit down and
write about it in this section - letting it all flow out on

paper, without omission, without judgement, without editing, hiding nothing. This will let the whole issue unfold itself and give the psyche a chance to work at the real problem which is not simply the situation that we currently face, but what is underneath it, buried in our unconscious processes, taking this opportunity to express itself and take us over. The fact of the matter is that our whole life is contained in any real problem that 'confronts' us.

In the process of growing up, awareness and understanding are more likely than not to be overlaid at some point by rejection, fear, anger and misunderstanding. Children often push down into forgetfulness what they find unacceptable and live instead with a fantasy image.

Negative feelings such as hatred, fear, resentment and so on should be recognised. It is possible to recognise now, what these emotions are doing in us. It is possible also to realise that they are neither necessary, useful nor growthful. They keep us stuck where we are.

As the situations which give rise to these feelings in us are recalled and explored in writing, these feelings themselves can be allowed to flow in us and be transformed. Negative emotions imprison us in the past, being triggered off by events and situations in our present life. They do not allow us to move forward with that total responsiveness which is a feature of self-regulation and growthful awareness.

While negative emotions, belonging to unresolved conflicts and dilemmas in our life, can imprison us and force us to 'act out' our conflicts and tensions once again, it is good to realise that we are not willy-nilly obliged to go through the same 'soul-destroying hoops', over and over again.

We can instead voluntarily choose to consciously relive our past, instead of re-enacting it. By writing about it, letting go of the negative emotions involved and letting the dynamics of love take their course in us, we can become permanently free from our negative traps, transforming them instead into opportunities for personal growth.

Personal growth can only take place within the dynamics of love, which generates a spontaneous positive responsiveness of the whole person. When love is present, positive feelings spontaneously emerge and the whole self can then act. By contrast, when negative emotions take us over, conscious direction and positive intention is lost. Part of the self takes over the whole self.

When we feel ourselves being taken over by our feelings, we should always seek to discover what these feelings relate to. In this way, we are able to see what 'part' of ourselves is in control of us and what its relation to the whole of us is. A problem or difficulty should not turn us upside-down. In so far as it does 'I am not whole', 'I am not in control', 'Love is not operating in me'.

When we are writing about our experience with parents and other relatives, it makes no difference whether they are alive or dead. Our 'inner relations' with them will always be alive. On the other hand, our parents can take part of us with them to the grave - that part of us which has not resolved certain life issues that are tied up with them. 'We can live with one foot in the grave.' O'Brien states - that part of us that we have not explored and opened up to the dynamics of love.

Allowing memories of the past to surface and be re-experienced and explored in a positive and accepting way resolves our 'blind spots'. Love works through our 'false premises' and 'false solutions'.

In writing about the past, it should be clear that we are not trapped within those historical events which have left issues and relationships unresolved. Instead, we can re-enter these events and relationships and carry them forward in an imaginal dialogue where we enter into the consciousness of the persons involved and imaginally re-open our relationships with them, perhaps in an entirely new way. If we let this dialogue continue, the issues will work through and insights and resolutions of dilemmas will spontaneously emerge. All internal dialogue that is carried through and not broken off will culminate in clarification, a new foundation of understanding and a new continuously liberating, creative and love-centred way of being.

4. Realisations, Insights and Understanding

In this section, insights gained at any time - from dreams, from daily writing, from writing about the past or simply spontaneously can be written down. This section is all about 'personal understanding' and 'personal wisdom'.

In keeping a PLB we come to an observation and understanding of the beliefs, thoughts, feelings and actions that constitute our personal life. In keeping it, we come to recognise what is growthful - leading to a choice of continued awareness, knowledge and self-government. We also learn what prevents growth in us - negative emotions and attitudes, repression of painful experience and self-justifying. The alternative to the choice of 'awareness' and 'growth' becomes clear to us.

Personal growth requires that we create the right inner conditions. We cannot make ourselves grow, but we can become conscious of the emotion-backed beliefs that undermine us, thereafter excluding them by transforming them. We can arrive at a personal understanding of those beliefs and principles that enable us to replace stagnation, destruction and negativity with the dynamics of consciousness and love.

What we realise and understand from keeping a PLB will be integrally based on our own living

247

experience and a refined personal wisdom of our own.

Keeping a Personal Life Book is never to be considered an end in itself, but only an aid to personal growth and further development - the best one I know.

May you grow in wisdom and in love.

PROGRESS REVIEW SIX

Keeping a Personal Life Book

CENTRAL IDEA: Wholehearted acceptance of yourself and others, just the way you are, means transforming 'emotional reactions' into 'responsive awareness'. It does not mean being unconditionally involved with anyone and everyone. Rather, it means knowing yourself and others in a lovingly aware way. Keeping a Personal Life Book is an aid to living a satisfying and meaningful life. It allows the whole spirit and inner movement of your being to work for the good of all that you are.

The Relaxation-Meditation tape introduces you to a whole new way of life. You can grow into this life when you supplement its use with the practice of keeping an intensive journal, also called a 'Personal Life Book'. This practice is set out in depth and in detail in this book. Undertaken daily, keeping a Personal Life Book is one of the most liberating and life-transforming enterprises that you could ever embark upon. The basic method, as set out, enables you to generate unconditional acceptance of yourself and others. It enables you to steer clear of judgement and inner contention in favour of awareness and insight. It enables you to unfold your experiences and to explore their meaning and value. Everything you do and everything that happens to you, because of this practice, begins to make deeply meaningful sense. The total effect is satisfying, insightful and life-enhancing. Instructions for keeping a Personal Life Book, set out in this book, are elaborated on the reverse side of the 'Self-Realisation' tape.

An animal is conscious of the outside world, but is not conscious of its own mental operations. It knows but it does not know that it knows. A dog may experience pain, but it is not able to feel sorry for itself. It cannot distinguish its own consciousness from sensations of the outside world. It cannot relate such sensations to inner states of being and purpose, responsiveness and meaning. Hence it cannot discover its 'self', or learn how to develop its self. We can.

It is through our consciousness that we are able to recognise an 'inner' self. We are able to describe and comment upon our own experiences, saying "I feel", "I hear", "I think", "I act". These words reflect recognition of mental states and processes. They also reflect an 'I' that experiences these states and processes. This develops into an 'I' of self-reflective consciousness.

While we, human beings, experience the outside world through our senses, it is the 'I' that perceives and not the senses alone. What the senses perceive is the raw material upon which the mind works. There is an inner world that illuminates and informs our sensations and perceptions. By keeping a Personal Life Book, our self - and the range and intricacy of its perceptions - develops and grows. We discover 'unconscious processes' that underlie our conscious acts. We recognise how it is that every conscious act involves processes of reproduction, comparison and inference. Everyday sensations are combined into patterns of meaning that reach our consciousness. In this way, our consciousness is continually being influenced not only by conscious aims and reasoning but also by unconscious processes and assumptions Generalisations, drawn from past experience, influence our present way of selecting and processing information, coming to us through *sensations*, and transformed into *perceptions*.

Keeping a Personal Life Book helps develop our self-awareness. We express, explore and re-experience what we have come through and what is leading to what in us. We gain a more intimate knowledge of the processes and outcomes of our thinking, feeling and doing. As we write 'without praise' and 'without blame' we cease to short-circuit our understanding through excuses and defences. We also cease to cast shame and blame on ourselves.

When we have no idea what would be better, how we could improve ourselves and our life situation, our guilt, shame and self-blame are worse than useless. Instead of helping us, they only make us feel 'bad' about ourselves - and unable to cope!

Keeping a Personal Life Book helps us undo negative cycles and destructive self-fulfilling prophecies. The process is simple and does not involve analysis of any kind. Instead, an artificial analysis, superimposed on our experiences, is likely to distort experience. If, on the other hand, we simply allow things to 'work through', as we express and explore everything that comes into our consciousness, insights begin to flow and connections and understanding emerge spontaneously.

If, instead of repressing our feelings, we explore what lies behind them, what they remind us of and so on, we gain valuable insights into why we do things and what we would really prefer to do instead. This is very different from nursing our hurts, fear and anger so that we feel predisposed to react in the future just as we did in the past.

As we write about our past, our present, our dreams, and our hopes for the future, we become aware of an underlying unity in our life and we are able to live in this unity through the wholeness of our 'self' as we know it and experience it changing and growing.

Criteria of Attainment

1. In keeping your Personal Life Book, on a daily basis, you find yourself able to replace judgement with awareness. You discover yourself replacing inner contention with an ability to look at everything in an open, receptive and workable way.

251

2. You are able to write about your day-to-day living, your past and your dreams without praise and without blame. This means, in effect, retraining your mind and your attitudes. You are better able to see things, without defensiveness, self-justification, repression or inner struggle. You find yourself becoming more and more accepting and responsive to everything, in a free-flowing, flexible and insightful way. As you express and explore your feelings their function changes. They resonate your own meaning and depth. As you experience them fully they become transformed. As you become aware of the new form of your feelings, their changed form becomes, for you, an inner resource.

3. You are not afraid to experience, express and explore your feelings. You use your feelings to explore what lies behind them, not repressing any of them, positive or negative. Instead, you use your feelings to explore what has led to what - and what can lead to what. For example, exploring what is behind such 'negative' feelings as resentment, guilt, self-pity or shame enables you to gain a deeper understanding of yourself and your circumstances - instead of brooding or worrying, in the sort of unconstructive and emotionally driven way that is usually characteristic of these emotions.

4. Insights flow as you write everything down - everything you remember or are thinking about, everything that is entering your mind at the time of writing. In this way, you express and explore the whole of your experience. There is no need to analyse. You recognise how an artificial analysis superimposed on your experiences merely gets in the way. On the other hand, letting yourself write everything down allows a more lucid and penetrating understanding to evolve. Insights dawn on you, one

after the other, as everything 'works through' from a less conscious to a more conscious level.

5. You appreciate how it is that ideas and images entering your mind at the time of writing act as stepping stones to a fuller consciousness. You recognise how such ideas and images, and the feelings that go with them, have been informing your attitudes, all along, and shaping your beliefs. As you explore these ideas and images - without praise and without blame - you find the inner life of your mind renewed and transformed. You find yourself growing into the kind of person that you recognise you were always, somehow, 'meant' to be.

6. You allow yourself to respond emotionally to what you write, as you write. In this way, you become aware of the underlying unity that is shaping the nature of your consciousness. It becomes clear to you how your very consciousness is something like the sum of all the entrances and exits of various elements contained in the vast reservoir of your body-mind-being. This being is energy aware of itself and able to transform its own operations and processes.

7. As you become aware of what has led to what and what can lead to what, in certain situations, you learn correctly to anticipate possibilities and respond appropriately.

8. Mental contents that usually make their presence felt only in obscure ways become appreciated and understood for what they are and what they mean. An organic inner growth and transformation takes place. As your interest develops in what is happening, your being and becoming are carried forward through automatic inner rehearsal, intending, expectantly hoping and doing.

9. As your interest and attention to your own being develops, new choices and response options open up for you. These options are consciously explored and

worked through. Vital new possibilities are recognised and realised. You understand how it is that keeping a Personal Life Book is not an end in itself, but is rather an aid to life, enabling you to cultivate your mind, as an instrument for understanding and creative work.

Section Six

Training and Transformation in the Speaking and Listening Process

13   *Here Comes Everyone*

"If you are to penetrate your own silence and dare to advance without fear into the solitude of your own heart, and risk sharing that solitude with the lonely other who seeks God through you and with you, then you will truly recover the light and the capacity to understand what is beyond words."

Thomas Merton[1]

The spirit of speaking and listening points to and participates in a whole way of life that extends beyond the practice of speaking and listening. Our practice itself leads us to this way of life.

A SPIRITUAL PATH

Once we have entered the depth of our being, there is no turning back. Once we have entered the Fire - the Tao, Logos, Dharma, Brahman - of our being, we cannot pretend to ourselves that we know nothing of that 'something beyond us yet ourselves' that extends beyond us yet includes us. In our practice, we see and recognise our fears, grasping, insecurity and helplessness, yet we pass beyond these experiences as we deepen our awareness of their reality and our reality. By so doing, we find ourselves entering into an experience of the depth of our being, an experience that makes our need to secure ourselves against our felt vulnerability and insecurity fundamentally unnecessary.

When we let ourselves experience, express and explore the difficulties that we have always avoided, our heart softens. We experience what the Buddhists call 'the quivering of a pure heart'. Through entering fully into the realities of our life beyond our habitual defensiveness - and not being destroyed by what we experience - we wonder at our heart's courage, and in this wonder, we discover our 'Big Self', our 'Logos Self', our 'Atman-Brahman' identity.

The deep peace that we find in this openness to our life, far from being an escape from the realities of living, turns out to be, rather, a deep embracement of these realities. The peace that we experience is a peace that rejects nothing. It is, in fact, a peace that 'surpasses our understanding' because it proceeds from a level of being that exists prior to the processes of reasoning and evaluating that an experience of the depth of our being makes accessible to us. It is a peace that touches all that we are with compassion, because it contains all things in an acceptance and a love that knows no limits.

As we learn to enter all the channels of our awareness, we re-experience aspects of our being in a complete, undivided, non-contending way. The opening up of our being to this judgement-free totality of experience may allow an inner upheaval to enter our conscious experience. And this upheaval may last for days, weeks or even months. It feels like defeat, even a kind of death. And yet it is all necessary. Transforming some of our cycles of reactive bondage into cycles of creative freedom may require a continuing stripping away of our defences, so that we flow with the turbulence of the feelings involved over a period of time. And yet, if we are constant in our resolve to accept all, we can learn to flow with this turbulence until it gives way to our entering the realms of our creative freedom. It is only a matter of time.

Our practice of speaking and listening, journalling, meditation and yoga - in fact, all the practices described in this book are only what they are because there is a whole way of life that lies beyond anxiety. Taken together, all of these practices create a spiritual path leading to a way of life that accords with our 'original nature' - the universal essence of our being.

In religious terminology, these practices can be described as 'sacramental' in that they both point to and participate in a whole spirit-centred (Fire-centred) way of life. They enable us to gain entry into this way of life so that we may embody it and live it to the full, in fact, finding our personal fulfilment in it.

THE DYNAMICS OF SPEAKING AND LISTENING

Thoughts that keep repeating themselves over and over, in the same way, are kept going by edges or boundaries that prevent us from penetrating the feelings that fuel these self-repeating cycles. To move from reactive bondage to creative freedom does not mean being free of the feelings that press for our acknowledgement, acceptance and penetration. It means, rather, being free to enter these feelings so that they can take us through all our awareness channels into an experience that is rooted in the Logos itself, enabling us to be 'open', as Emerson put it, 'to all the attributes of God'.

Before we have fully expressed, explored and experienced our feelings, they tie us up in tortuous entanglements of reactive bondage. We remain prisoners of our reactions until we decide to let go and let our feelings flow through all our perceptual channels, leading us into an appreciation of new possibilities in our world and in our relationship to others. Allowing ourselves to become aware of information flowing in all our perceptual channels enables us to follow self-repeating patterns past the defensive edges that lock our feelings in and prevent us from exploring the significance of all that lies behind our feelings.

The person who is listening to us encourages us to go beyond our edges, bringing our attention to visual, auditory, proprioceptive and kinaesthetic signals that are thus made available for us to follow. We use these signals and the information that they potentially contain to enter into deeper levels of being-awareness. We let ourselves accept, with open-hearted compassion, all the signals, messages and perceptions that the edges of our fear or judgement have, until now, kept out of our awareness. In this way, we allow to unravel patterns of reactive bondage that are like jumbled-up knots of energy which have bodily contractions, emotions, memories and images all tangled up in them. As we follow these emotions, memories and images to wherever they lead, we eventually enter states of consciousness that are naturally filled with qualities which reflect our wholeness - peace, exuberance, joy, spontaneity, clarity, compassion, confidence and innate wisdom. All these qualities reflect the flow of our total self-balancing process as it passes through all our experiences, enabling us to know it and serve it as the dynamic source of our wholeness.

GOING WITH THE FLOW

Our human destiny lies in that realm of creative freedom which is excluded by cycles of reactive bondage. And yet it is in following through the feelings, kinaesthetic and proprioceptive, and the memories and images that are bound up in our reactive bondage that we are able to realise our true human destiny.

We need to honour the whole of our being in the process of our self-discovery. This includes taking to heart any feelings of vulnerability that may arise in us, so that we may seek out the kind of situation or relationship that will allow us to penetrate these feelings in an atmosphere of safety and trust.

Whenever we experience hurt and deep wounding in our lives, we create defences and boundaries around areas of presumed vulnerability to protect us from further wounding. And yet the key to the healing of our wounds and the overcoming of our fear-based limitations lies in our experiencing, expressing and exploring the way that we are.

If we are able to face and follow difficult states of being around their edges to the extreme points at which they seem to 'threaten' to take us over, then we become better able to relate to the energy and the information that these states contain. Not only does this energy lose its menacing hold upon us, but it also comes to be transformed and thus is made available for our future use. Instead of seeing only one part of the picture - one that is bounded within our edges and our defensiveness - we become able, rather, to see the whole picture by viewing it through different perspectives. It is these perspectives that enable us to use the flow of our energies in a functionally free, creative, value-realising way.

When we release ourselves from those reactions that form an edge against our emotional flow, the initial force of this flow eventually becomes more manageable. We pass beyond what Ron Kurtz calls 'shooting the rapids' to less turbulent experiences, enabling us better to ride the current and control our exploration of what we find.[2] We do not get out of the river. Instead, we stay in it, until its flow carries us along in a more consciously aware and responsive way.

As we learn to go with the flow, we discover the fulfilment that was in it, from the start. It is 'just so', a dynamic aware connectedness with the way that we are, here and now.

In all of this, we discover a way of dying to our

old self so that we might be 'born again' as a new and total Self. Thus we come to see and understand what the Buddha was referring to when he spoke of the suffering (dukkha) caused by the process of our grasping onto what we feel will give us security and seeking to avoid whatever we feel will threaten our insecurity. In this way, we cease to identify ourselves with our limited ego. We see also what Jesus Christ meant when he said, "He who would save his life will lose it", and conversely, "He who would lose his life, for my sake, will find it."

Co-counselling and focused speaking and listening enable us to free ourselves from our inner conflict, insecurity and defensiveness so that we can rediscover ourselves in an undivided realm of experience. Our spiritual search is able to bring us to fulfilment of our being only when it is able to connect us with self-reflective value-realising truth, embraced as our own.

TO FLOW WITH OTHERS

The truth of our life is always a truth that includes others. Our spiritual practice is an ever-widening circle that infuses our hearts and minds with a consciousness of ourselves that is inclusive of their consciousness also. Furthermore, this takes places in a way that makes them no longer 'other' than who and how we are. When we understand others in the same spirit that we understand ourselves, we feel naturally inclined to flow with their experience, as we come to know all things as an extension of the larger Self that we essentially are.

Only when we accept ourselves the way we are can we improve upon the way we are. This sounds paradoxical. By the same token, only when we accept others the way that they are can we enable them to grow beyond the way they are. Improving ourselves and our circumstances is not a rejection of the way we are.

Rather, we find a way to lead the process on, gently yet effectively, enabling what is there to grow and develop towards its potential, without any interference of an 'ideal' being artificially superimposed upon the way we are and possibly contradicting it. As Shunryu Suzuki puts it, "If you are ready to accept things as they are, you will receive them as old friends, even though you appreciate them with new feelings."[3]

To incorporate others into our practice means coming to know ourselves and others more openly and less defensively. It also involves developing our awareness of what Arnold Mindell calls the 'relationship channel'. It means living in the truth of our own experience, with others, while they simultaneously live with and share the truth of their experience with us.

This open responsive flowing with our own experience liberates us from preoccupation with our presumed need to defend ourselves. And why do we no longer need to defend ourselves? Because we have found the ultimate thing worth living for - our Fire.

The kind of open-ness that frees us from attachment to creating a particular impression on others enables us to forget about defensiveness and pass beyond impression-management into true Self-discovery. The spirit of it all may be summed up in a well-known saying of Elizabeth Kubler-Ross, "I'm not OK, you're not OK, and that's OK." So we discover ourselves beyond the edges of our impression management, and what we are there is 'perfectly imperfect'.

We do not speak in order to impress others, but only to express and explore our experiences. In this way, we come to know our own being in a non-contentious way. We discover ourselves not only in what we express, explore and experience, but also in the freedom and spontaneity of the speaking and listening process. We involve ourselves completely in the process and it is the process itself that reveals to us the being that we essentially are - a being that was previously hidden from us, but was, nonetheless, there all the time.

This is how don Juan put it: "If a warrior needs solace, he simply chooses anyone and expresses to that person every detail of his turmoil. After all, the warrior is not seeking to be understood or helped: by talking he is merely relieving himself of his pressure. That is, if the warrior is given to talking. If he is not, he tells no-one."[4]

In our embodiment of our essential being, we enable others to enter into the essential Process that is the Source from which all our particular discernments, selves and worlds simultaneously emerge. Hence we talk about ourselves not only to forget about our limited selves, but also to discover ourselves in the larger Process of our being.

THE PARADOXES OF CREATIVE FREEDOM

There is a straightforwardness in speaking and listening that reflects our having given up all preconceived ideas and subjective opinions. We just explore and express our experiences as they come to us. We explore them as they are and as we are. And this is how we listen to others also. We observe the way they are, with open-hearted acceptance and we help them to flow with their experiences. This we do, firstly, by just being there and listening in an accepting way. Secondly, we help them to flow with their experience by flowing with its expression until it seems to come to an edge - a block - and then we help them to go beyond this block.

To be free of all defensiveness and all judgement - no right or wrong, better or worse, sane or sick, wise or stupid - and to be open to the flow itself, is to receive everything as a gift. It is at this time and in this way that we appreciate everything as it really is. At the same time, we experience everything as being suffused with a consciousness of itself, just as we are conscious of ourselves.

When we engage in the speaking and listening process, we have no idea what will happen next. We have no idea what we will say, until it comes to us to be said. Nor do we have any idea about how we will feel about what we say. We just let it develop and unfold. All we know is that we will be true to the expression that most closely matches the experience that we are focusing upon. When we home in on this expression we continue to develop our awareness of who and how we are and who and how we can be, by continuing to respond to what we express and the effects of so doing.

Because there is complete harmony in what we think and feel and say, we gain an underlying confidence both in the process and in ourselves. In each thing that is accepted and explored, with no holds barred, we experience everything, or, rather, we experience the essential reality - the essential process - in everything that is.

The deep understanding that emerges from the speaking and listening process is something that develops as we represent reality to ourselves in words and symbols. What we both express outwardly and image inwardly enters into our conscious being as a finely tuned awareness of all that is and all that can be. It is not so much the symbols we use that create this fine inner attunement of our awareness so much as the responsiveness that we develop to what is really true in what we are representing to ourselves.

The unfathomable abyss of freedom that we enter in the first phase of speaking and listening, called 'going inside', is the mysterious source of the self and world that we constellate in order to give it expression. It is in the act of giving expression - in spirit and in truth - to what we experience that the reality of self and world 'interdependently arises'. It is to this process that our speaking and listening bears witness.

Through the unconditioned acceptance that we offer one another, in speaking and listening sessions, we find ourselves able to accept and respond to everything, completely. With this freedom comes an ability to respond to the total reality that we express and explore. And this is how our creative freedom develops.

> "Come to the edge, he said,
> They said, We are afraid.
> Come to the edge, he said.
> They came.
> He pushed them . . .
> . . . and they flew."[5]

The creative freedom that we experience, in speaking and listening practice, involves a finely attuned concentration of our energies and their continuous refinement in our expression of them. This fine balance and concentration of our energies is an exercise in letting go to an open-ness that we use to develop our capacity for creative freedom. Our open-ness itself is deeply rooted in humility. This humility, in turn, far from being servile, involves a total rejection of everything that can enslave us or dominate us or remove us from our essential humanity. It involves an abandonment of our egocentric defensiveness for the sake of a Logos/Tao/Fire-centred illumination and transformation of our being.

It is, in fact, in this freedom that the meaning and value of our life is tested. What we call the abyss of freedom is not an empty vacuum with no form whatsoever. It has been called 'formless form'. It has also been called 'the Void' and 'emptiness', yet it is something to which we are called to be true. Don Juan puts it like this:

"Genaro and I have to act the same way that you do, within certain limits. Power sets up those limits and a warrior is, let's say, a prisoner of power; a prisoner who has one free choice: the choice to act either as an impeccable warrior or to act like an ass. In the final analysis, perhaps the warrior is not a prisoner but a slave of power, because that choice is no longer a choice for him. Genaro cannot act any other way but impeccably. To act like an ass would drain him and cause his demise."[6]

Once we have found our true home in the Logos of our being, our way of life can no longer be what it was before. It become our destiny - our duty, our Dharma - not only to live out that value-realising creative freedom that we have found, but also to lead others to it, so that they too may find in it the meaning and the purpose of life itself.

14   *Focused Speaking and Listening Guide*

*"We are never fully ourselves until we realise that those we
truly love become our 'other selves'."*

Thomas Merton[1]

Focused speaking and listening is an integral part of
Fire-centred training. It enables us to consolidate our
thinking within certain vital perspectives. It stimulates a
special kind of responsiveness in us. It enables us to
scan, select and put into words whatever is pertinent to
the focus being adopted. It also facilitates the kind of
listening that enables us to deepen our awareness of
what we think and feel and value. Each perspective
enables us to see and feel dynamic possibilities of
personal being and becoming. We see and feel our
potential to respond to various life situations in creative,
self-transforming ways.

It is within the chalice of interested non-
judgemental listening that we feel the impact of our
circumstances: an awareness of who we are, where we
have come from, what we are doing, where we are
going, where we intend to go. Through looking at
ourselves and our circumstances from different points of
view, we develop our awareness further, eventually
becoming able to clarify to ourselves the values that we
wish to serve and live by. Such values then crystallise
into a standard that we use not only to govern our
thinking and acting, but also our relations with others,
whose way of life and intentionality we recognise to be

both similar to our own and different from it, in certain respects.[2]

RECOVERING OUR PERSONAL REALITY

As human beings, we exist not only in our circumstances, but also in the inwardness of our consciousness. Awareness of 'me' and 'mine' creates an inner world.

This inner world of ours is not a static and unchanging thing, but rather something that is dynamic and responsive, a continuing process, in fact, that enables us to relate to ourselves and our circumstances in creative and flexible ways. It is through our awareness and reasoning that we are able to use our inner world actively and reflectively to situate ourselves in our circumstances. By choosing our intended being and becoming, we play our part in creating ourselves and our circumstances.

When our personal boundaries become blurred, we are apt to find ourselves trapped in the present, with no meaningful connection to the past that we have lived through or the future that lies ahead of us. Loss of personal boundaries very often signifies loss of purpose and direction, more often than not resulting from a failure, for one reason or another, to reflect upon what we have come through, from different perspectives, with different aims in view.[3]

When the future that we anticipate is filled either with vague and uncertain misgivings or with feelings of dread, it is likely that we are failing to sustain a value-realising perspective that could replace such fears and misgivings with a sense of personal destiny and a creative vision of the future. A self-integrating consciousness of our personal history and destiny only emerges when we cease to be passive victims of whatever is happening to us and seek, instead, to take active responsibility for what we really intend.[4]

To be open to the present moment in our lives, in an active self-integrating way, it is good - indeed necessary - to review our experiences from perspectives that draw into focus possibilities, whose meaning and value we see and feel, as we reflect upon them and explore them. Speaking and listening groups generate such perspectives and facilitate the kind of review that helps us to grasp and shape the very substance of our being, intending and becoming. By enabling us to see and feel new possibilities for influencing those events whose meaning is intimately tied up with our own value-realising aims and identity, they enable us to take stock of the historical meaning of our existence in terms of our present aims, values and aspirations.

THE SPEAKING LISTENING GROUP

The group itself is supportive and non-competitive. It belongs to all its members, without any sense of rivalry or one-upmanship. It upholds the view that the door to creative freedom can only be passed through by each person, individually, on their own account and by their own choice. It also upholds the view that such a door cannot be passed through by anyone whose path to it is blocked by security, sensation and power addiction. In speaking and listening groups, we work together to release ourselves from these addictions. This we do by transforming our experiences in and through the way we think and speak about them. By so doing, we make them into bridges that enable us to cross over from a passively reactive or addictively pre-programmed existence to a freely creative, value-realising one. In the group, we also come to view our personal pain as an experience that can help us to enter into a deeper and wider awareness of the human situation as such, a situation that we all share. This situation is one whose personal meaning is re-evaluated as we review all that we have individually and collectively lived through.

As our experience in the speaking and listening group enriches its members' lives, so we find ourselves better able to accept our pain and to work through it in a fearless self-abandoning way. This, in turn, enables others to do the same, thereby realising their freedom and creative intelligence. By exploring and re-experiencing our experiences from different perspectives, we discover not only their deepest meaning and value but also our God-given human potential to understand and live out what constitutes a worthwhile human life.

Because all members of the group speak about their own experiences from similar yet slightly different perspectives, we not only see our own experience from the point of view that we adopt, but we also vicariously experience and become able to see our own experiences from the slightly different point of view that others adopt. This adds to the richness and variety of our way of thinking about our own and other people's lives. It also adds quality of discernment to the way we think about ourselves and others, the way we treat ourselves and others and the way we choose to live our lives.[5]

Each person's life becomes, for the group, both a gift and a bridge. We become free not only individually but also as a group. This, in turn, extends our personal freedom in a way that enables us to discover and serve the spirit in which we wish to live and outside of which we do not wish to live.

We do not, in such a group, attempt to take away one another's pain, anguish, suffering and distress, but rather we aim to deepen these feelings to a level where they can be shared. In this way, we help one another to stop suffering for the wrong reasons. Instead, we mobilise the experiences of our individual lives into a search for the kind of life whose goodness we are prepared to work for - and even suffer for, if need be.

THE WIDER COMMUNITY OF OUR BEING AND BECOMING

Our life is a lie if, at its deepest level, it constitutes a refusal to share in true relationships with others. In addition to being spiritual, value-realising beings, we are also social beings. As a Xhosa proverb expresses it, "Umntu ngumntu ngabantu" - "A person becomes a person through people." It is thanks to other people that each of us becomes who we can be.

Releasing ourselves from defensive postures and pretences, we become able to share our soul's Fire with one another, so creating a true community of being. As we learn to pass from impression-management, mutual manipulation and superficial communication to an honestly appreciative view of the life we are living, we enter into a sharing of that self-transforming creative power that it is our human destiny to realise.[6,7]

FOCUSED SPEAKING LISTENING THEMES

Focused speaking listening sessions can profitably be engaged in through the invocation of such themes and perspectives as are presented below. These serve as an illustration of the kind of speaking listening sessions that you yourself can devise, create and develop.

(A) Alcohol Dependence
1. A successfully recovering alcoholic that I admire and why.
2. The thing I most regret about being alcohol dependent.
3. Something useful I have learned from being alcohol dependent.

4. How I hurt myself and others through my alcoholism.
5. How I accepted I was alcohol dependent and what I gained.
6. What I would most like to teach others about alcohol.
7. What I would most like to achieve with my sobriety.
8. When I am most tempted to go back on the booze.
9. What I do that helps me to stay sober.
10. What I would like my friends and family to know about me.

(B) Anger
1. A time when I was not in control of my anger and it hurt me or it hurt others.
2. A time when I was in control of my anger and did something I am pleased about.
3. How I react when another person expresses anger towards me.
4. When I find it hard to deal with another person's anger.
5. When I find it easy to deal with another person's anger.
6. When I used humour or some other skill to defuse or transform another person's angry feelings towards me.
7. How I express anger without hurting myself or others.
8. A time when I was able to work successfully with my own anger.

(C) Confidence
1. Someone whose confidence I admire.
2. When I feel confident.
3. What I would do if I had the confidence.
4. When I experience loss of confidence.
5. When I helped someone to have confidence.
6. Someone who gives me confidence in myself.

7. What I am doing that needs confidence and/or gives me confidence.

(D) Death

1. The thing about death that scares me.
2. How I would like to die.
3. A close encounter that I had with death.
4. Something I would die for.
5. A person whose death gave me hope.
6. Something I would die to prevent.
7. Why, as God, I created death.

(E) Energy

1. A person whose energy I admire.
2. Something that gives me powerful energy.
3. Something that takes my energy away.
4. The kind of energy that I like to share with others.
5. Something I wasted valuable energy on.
6. Something to which I am prepared to devote a lot of energy.
7. A way that I use to build or restore my energy.

(F) Fear

1. A time when I was not in control of my fear and what I did.
2. A time when I was not in control of my fear and did something that I feel sorry about or ashamed of.
3. How I react when others are anxious or afraid.
4. When I find it hard to accept another person's anxiety or fear.
5. When I find it easy to work with another person's anxiety.
6. How I helped someone who was afraid or anxious.
7. A way I have of overcoming my fear and anxiety.
8. A time when I overcame my fear and did something I am proud of.

(G) God

1. A person whose faith in God I admire.
2. What God means to me.
3. What I would like others to understand about God.
4. A time when my faith in God was tested.
5. The issue concerning God that most concerns me.
6. How I am like God.
7. How I celebrate God.
8. How God celebrates me.

(H) Hang-Ups

1. A hang-up that keeps me going.
2. How I keep my hang-up going.
3. When I find it difficult to tolerate another person's hang-up.
4. A hang-up that I was able to overcome.
5. A hang-up I once had that I now find amusing.
6. When someone else's hang-up scares me.
7. A hang-up that I am working to overcome.
8. How I helped someone to deal with their hang-up.

(I) Messages and Inner Scripts

1. The message my parents gave me that most affected me.
2. Negative messages that I have overcome.
3. Messages that I would like to contradict.
4. A life script that I would like to write for myself.
5. A message I would like my children to receive from me.
6. A life script I have been living out without realising it.
7. The values that I want to promote in myself and others.

(J) Forgiveness

1. A time when I felt hurt and let down by someone I trusted.
2. How I deal with hurts.
3. An experience in which I felt forgiven.
4. Something for which I find it hard to forgive myself.
5. The thing that I fear most in myself or in others.
6. Something that I have been able to let go.
7. Something that I feel defensive about and try to hide.
8. Something for which I have forgiven myself.
9. What needs to happen before I can forgive.
10. What I need to do before I can forgive.

(K) Creative Risk Taking

1. Someone I admire for the risk that they took.
2. A risk that I am pleased I took.
3. A risk that I am afraid to take.
4. A risk that I intend to take.
5. How I helped someone to take a creative risk.
6. A creative risk that I would like someone to help me take.

(L) Love

1. A person who lives a life of love.
2. When I experienced being loved.
3. The kind of person that I love.
4. When love helped me to conquer fear.
5. What I love to do.
6. What I love about myself.
7. What I do that expresses love.
8. A person to whom I would like to show love.
9. What love requires of me.

(M) Man - Woman

1. A man-woman relationship that I admire and why.
2. The kind of man or woman that I always wanted to become.

3. The thing about growing up that I feared the most.
4. A time when I was picked on for being the kind of boy or girl that I was.
5. A time when I used aggression or manipulation to get what I wanted from a person of the opposite sex.
6. The attitude or treatment that I most dislike from a person of the opposite sex.
7. The attitude or treatment that I most like or appreciate from a person of the opposite sex.
8. How I overcame a problem with a person of the opposite sex.

(N) Nature

1. When I feel most natural.
2. When I feel most out of touch with nature.
3. What I love most about nature.
4. The thing about nature that frightens me.
5. What I would like to share with others about nature.
6. How I take on board my share of responsibility for the world of nature.
7. How I show reverence for Nature.

(O) Ordinariness

1. A person whose good ordinary life I admire.
2. A good ordinary thing that I would like to be able to do.
3. When I feel unique and freaky rather than ordinary.
4. Someone I was able to put at ease about being a good ordinary person.
5. A person whose un-ordinariness I find it hard to handle.
6. A person whose un-ordinariness I can take in my stride.
7. The thing I like best about being a good ordinary person.

(P) Peace

1. When I feel most at peace with myself.
2. Something that robs me of my peace.
3. Someone who seems to radiate peace.
4. What I would need to happen before I could be at peace.
5. What I need to do or stop doing to achieve inner peace.
6. How I was able to offer inner peace to someone.
7. What I mostly feel when I am not at peace.
8. What brings me inner peace.

(Q) Skills and Qualities

1. A person whose skills I admire.
2. A quality that I would like to acquire.
3. A habit that I would like to overcome and why.
4. A problem that I would like to face well.
5. A quality I have that I would like appreciated more.
6. Something I did really well.
7. A time when I felt truly appreciated.
8. Someone to whom I would like to show my appreciation.

(R) Responsibility

1. My greatest responsibility.
2. A person that I admire for the way he or she handles their responsibility.
3. Something I find it difficult to respond to.
4. Something I respond to well.
5. A responsibility that I would like to take on board.
6. What stops me being as responsible as I would like to be.
7. A responsibility that others have appreciated in me.
8. A responsibility that I would like to share.
9. A time when I did not act responsibly.
10. A time when someone helped me to be more responsible.

(S) Self-Esteem

1. A person I really respect and admire, and why.
2. Some way that I show respect for myself.
3. A time when I did the right thing even though I was afraid.
4. A way that I care for myself.
5. Something I have learned in my life that has been important for me.
6. Something I have done that I am proud of.
7. Something I plan to do that I will be proud of.
8. A goal that I have set myself and what I am doing to realise it.

(T) Time

1. A person who organises his or her time well.
2. Time that I call my own.
3. Time that does not belong to me.
4. Time that I share willingly with others.
5. Time that I have wasted.
6. Time that I wished would never end.
7. My time that others have wasted.
8. My time that others have used well.
9. Time when I relax.
10. Time that I intend to use well.

(U) Understanding

1. A person whose understanding I admire.
2. A time when I got my life together.
3. A time when I doubted my understanding.
4. What I find most difficult to understand.
5. Something I would like others to understand about me.
6. Something that I would like to understand better.
7. When I felt misunderstood.
8. What I really understand and would like to help others to understand.

(V) Power

1. A powerful person whom I admire, and why.
2. A time when I felt powerless.
3. A time when I felt crushed by someone else's power.
4. A time when I discovered that I had more power than I realised.
5. A time when I used power destructively.
6. A time when I used power creatively.
7. A time when I shared power with a group to achieve something that I could not achieve alone.
8. A time when power just seemed to come to me when I needed it.

(W) Work

1. Work that I love doing.
2. Work that I hate doing.
3. Work that I believe everyone ought to do.
4. When I work well.
5. When I work badly.
6. Work that I avoid.
7. Work that I intend to do.

(X) Acceptance

1. The thing I will not accept about myself.
2. When acceptance helped me.
3. What I find hard to accept in another person.
4. A failure to accept that harmed me.
5. When I felt unconditionally accepted.
6. When I felt conditionally accepting.
7. When I was able unconditionally to accept another person.

(Y) Shame

1. A time when I felt humiliated and ashamed.
2. A time when I realised I had no reason to feel ashamed.
3. A time when I humiliated myself.

4. A time when I helped someone to stop feeling ashamed and believe in themselves instead.
5. People I feel tempted to humiliate.
6. How I deal with my own feelings of shame and humiliation.
7. A time when I was able to contradict my feelings of shame and inferiority and what I did.

(Z) Gifts

1. The nicest gift anyone ever gave me.
2. A gift that I would like to give to someone.
3. Someone's gift or talent that I admire.
4. My greatest gift or talent.
5. A gift that I would like to develop.
6. A gift that I would like to help someone else to develop.
7. A gift that someone discovered in me that I did not know I possessed.

TIPS FOR CONDUCTING A SPEAKING LISTENING SESSION

- When the group has gathered, a time is set for beginning and ending the session.
- A variety of themes may be suggested as possible areas to explore and discover oneself in.
- Through discussion, one particular theme is chosen.
- A point of entry into this theme is selected by the group facilitator, for example, the first focusing statement on the list for this theme.
- Once this statement has been read, the group goes silent as each person in it 'goes inside' and reflects on their own experience from the perspective that is offered by this statement. Elements of experience are scanned so as to select those that best fit the criteria for which a match is required. It is in relation to these criteria that the elements selected come to constitute a

standard against which other experiences can be compared and contrasted. This, in turn, creates a certain ordering of one's inner world, while at the same time generating definite tendencies to move and be moved. Such tendencies are commonly called 'attitudes'.

- When the selected experience and corresponding attitudes are put into words, a flow of feelings generally accompanies this expression. This flow of words and feelings is allowed to continue until all that the speaker needs to say has been said. In no way must this flow be interrupted, side-tracked, interpreted, criticised, or judged.

- The speaker is encouraged to continue, if he or she expresses any misgivings about the process, for example, that they might be continuing for too long, or that they might have strayed too far from the original topic, or that the group may be tired of listening to them; anything, in fact, that seems to indicate that the speaker is feeling socially uncomfortable, isolated or rejected.

- The speaker's attention may be directed along a certain line of exploration, suggested by their own words, if a group member feels this to be appropriate, but no interpersonal dialogue or exchange of experiences is to take place during speaking listening time.

- It is a good idea for all members of the group to gaze at the speaker with relaxed interested attention, so long as he or she is speaking.

- The speaker is thanked by all members of the group whenever he or she has said all that they wish to say. Expression of thanks may be accompanied by hugs. Applause may not be inappropriate. Express appreciation and closeness in the best way you can. Each person in the group is precious and worthy of your deepest respect, appreciation and affection.

- Speaking and listening creates an inner resonance that continues long after the session has ended. At best, this resonance takes place between experiences that have been put into words and experiences that have not been put into words, using criteria of discernment achieved and standards of value realised. Re-evaluation of self and circumstances is not something that the group should expect to take place during a session. It is part of a continuing process of personal growth. For this reason it should not be considered appropriate to ask group members for any immediate feedback on the effects of having taken part in a session.

- Through taking part in speaking listening groups, a new quality of consciousness develops in group members. This new quality of consciousness is characterised by a fine-tuning of inner responsiveness, together with a resolve to think, speak and act in a changed manner regarding issues and choices that speaking and listening has brought to the fore. Such fine-tuning and inner resolve give new value-realising definition to one's self and circumstances. After a number of sessions it is therefore not inappropriate to ask how participation in speaking and listening is influencing each group member's life.

- It can generally be anticipated that participation in speaking listening groups will also render each person in the group better able to take account of the inner world and value-realising potential of other people.

PROGRESS REVIEW SEVEN

Speaking and listening.

CENTRAL IDEA: Trying to hold on to and secure ourselves in certain states of mind has diminishing returns. The more we try to hold on to our experiences, the less easily they flow. The aim of being and loving rather than having and owning frees our consciousness from possessiveness and permits a self-organising flow to develop. This flow is also open to the being and becoming of others, in the freedom that love is.

Illness begins with 'I' and wellness begins with 'we'. Who and how we are always relates us to who and how others are. There is always a 'we' that precedes 'I' and relates it to itself. This is why, above and beyond all else, love is the ultimate challenge and the ultimate fulfilment. Love itself calls for understanding and forgiveness. Letting go of grievances, resentment, guilt and shame allows us to go further, grow more and be more.

Criteria of Attainment

1. You recognise that you have a personal perspective that enables you to translate your experiences into information, which, in turn, lets you interpret what is happening and what is possible. You recognise that this perspective derives both from your past experiences and from your present aims and values.
2. You are aware, as a result of looking at your experiences from different points of view, that other ways of processing your experiences are possible. Some of these have yielded valuable insights into different ways of thinking, feeling and acting. You see their benefits and drawbacks. You have a deeper understanding of where you are coming from, where

you are going and where you would, ideally, like to be.

3. You recognise that breaking through blocks to awareness has a price - namely, the owning, flowing with and processing of disturbing emotions. You accept this price and are gladly willing to pay it.

4. You are prepared to express and explore all the experiences, pleasant and painful, that come to you. You see where they are coming from and where they are leading you. You are able to re-evaluate their worth and decide what to do with the way they make you feel, rather than simply reacting to them, as if you had no choice in the matter. Thus you explore how your experiences function in you. You take an attitude towards them. And you use their energy to act as you intend, in circumstances that give rise to them.

5. You see beyond your merely practical, personal goals into the deeper essence of your being, realising not only that you have a certain freedom of choice in how you are and how you can be, but also that the source of this freedom lies in a pool of uncommitted energy that becomes accessible to you when you let go of your striving, your desire to impress others, and your personal defensiveness. Because you are able to let go of these self-limiting dynamics, both in the speaking and listening process and outside of it, you are able to make free access to your self-transforming creative potential.

6. You become able, as a listener, to recognise the help that other speakers require from you, in order to be able to let go of their defensiveness and flow with their feelings. You are able to encourage them to do so, and thereby you are able to facilitate, in them, a fuller appreciation of your potential.

7. You set personal goals for yourself, your relationships, your understanding, your personal

development, your health and physical wellbeing, your career, your leisure, your environment, your local community, and for the whole world, with different time-tables for each goal. You see how your goals relate to one another or interfere with one another. Seeing this, you are able to reformulate them, so that they become mutually inclusive of one another.

8. You recognise the universal essence of balance and order, within you, as the foundation of all that you are and all that you can be. You therefore continue to use the discipline of inner silence to listen to yourself in new ways. As a result, you are constantly involved in an inner dialogue between the means, goals and values that constitute the order of your becoming, and the deeper order of your being, whose spirit you acknowledge to have a higher claim over your becoming.

9. You are able to choose what experiences you wish to attend to and are able to articulate the way your experience becomes value-realising or value-degrading information.

10. You understand the meanings and values that are central to the spirit in which you wish to live and outside of which you do not wish to live.

11. You understand your responsibility to use this spirit to enable others to confront their own meanings and values, together with the meanings and values of the society in which you live.

12. You take an interest in the visions that enliven other peoples' lives and you encourage them to explore these visions, express them and wherever possible to realise them, for the greater good of all humankind.

Section Seven

Fire-Centred Living

15   *Continuing the Fire-Centred Journey*

"As kingfishers catch fire, dragonflies draw flame;
As tumbled over rim in roundy wells
Stones ring; like each tucked string tells, each hung bell's
Bow swung find tongue to fling out broad its name;
Each mortal thing does one thing and the same;
Deals out that being indoors each one dwells;
Selves - goes itself; MYSELF it speaks and spells;
Crying WHAT I DO IS ME; FOR THAT I CAME."

G.M. Hopkins[1]

The Fire of our being is an intelligence that steers us through all things. It is the wisdom of life itself. To make contact with this wisdom is to make contact with an inner principle of being that is unconditioned and self-regulating. We can rely on this principle to keep us balanced and value-realising in all our undertakings, or, when we lose our sense of togetherness and direction, we can find in it the source of our psychological re-integration.

THE RE-INTEGRATING PROCESS

To take a Fire-centred journey means reorganising our life around the source of our essential being, using its inherent balance and harmony as an inner standard to guide and steer us in our growth and development. Although this source - this essence of our being - can be understood to be 'pre-personal', yet it is also the very

291

core of our personhood, and it remains so, for as long as we live.

The Fire/Tao/Logos of our being is not altered by the conditions of our existence. Its functioning does not depend on our experiences, yet it regulates itself within the context of our experiences. The nature of this self-regulation is not determined by our experiences, but rather our experiences themselves are, in large measure, determined by the nature of its functioning. The way our essential being functions is predetermined and unconditioned. The very best we can do, therefore, is to learn how to respond to it and to work with it, as the core of our creative freedom, rather than allowing it to be, at the opposite extreme, the core of our reactive bondage.

When we become lost in the maze of our personal conditioning, we can take heart from the fact that recourse to our self-regulating essence is always possible. If we can find a way to stay in continuous conscious contact with it, we can not only discover a way out of our reactive bondage, but we can also realise the highest good of our human potential, in a life of value-realising creative freedom.

Our need to make contact with the inner essence of our being translates into religious language in the counsel "Seek ye first the Kingdom of Heaven and all else will be added to you."[2] Because the source of our personal stability cannot be imposed upon us from outside, the Kingdom of Heaven is correctly understood to lie 'within' us.[3] It can only be sought and responded to within an experience of our own being.

The converse side of the 'Seek ye first' counsel is that all external conditions that we might otherwise be tempted to rely upon - and all externally imposed conditioning that others might be tempted to impose upon us - cannot ultimately replace the source of our personal renewal within. This source is able to take account of itself in us only if the boundaries, that we develop to understand and control the way we are, turn around our essential being, as their centre.

The poem by Hopkins, quoted at the start of this chapter, continues as follows:

> "I say more: the just man justices;
> Keeps grace: that keeps all his goings graces;
> Acts in God's eye what in God's eye he is -
> Christ - for Christ plays in ten thousand places,
> Lovely in limbs, and lovely in eyes not his
> To the Father through the features of men's faces."

We are 'more' than dragonflies and kingfishers. The just man justices. He is what he is because he 'keeps grace' - in a receptive and responsive way - and, by so doing, 'keeps all his goings graces', in the justice that he actively embodies. His living out the highest value-realising goodness of his human potential, in this way, is what makes him 'Christ', the person who 'in ten thousand places' realises his or her potential by being 'what in God's eye' he or she already 'is'.

"Before ever Abraham was, I AM," Jesus told his disciples, referring to himself not so much in personal-historical terms, but rather as the Logos, which, through his embodying it, he was able to present to us as the ultimate truth of both his own being and ours.[4] Out of this love emerges the fully alive, conscious, value-realising person.

Our essential being has its own laws. Only if we match these laws in our own 'way of being' can we discover what the Kingdom of Heaven - the Fire of our being - is really like. It needs to reveal itself to us, of its own accord. Nothing can ultimately substitute for this experience.

Over and against the kind of training that leads us to realise the further reaches of our human potential, we find misguided teachings that lead us nowhere, because they seek to convince us, in one way or another, that we are ultimately nothing more than our 'conditioning'.

When our own light is darkness, how great is that darkness! Such teaching is not only greatly deluded, it is also greatly deluding. It leads us away from the truth of the *intentionality* of our personal becoming. It therefore inadvertently traps us in the maze of our reactive bondage.

Only if the false, limited and self-limiting beliefs, expectations and attitudes inherent in this kind of teaching are replaced by a true recognition of our human condition can we properly begin to re-integrate our lives, in a meaningful, value-realising way.

Fortunately for us all, the practice of becoming receptive to the pre-personal essence of our being is able to bring us to a realisation of our potential to be other than who and how we already are. This potential cannot ultimately be hi-jacked. It is the very life of life itself. This is why, as Jesus Christ tells us, it is "Good news for the poor".[4] No matter how little we have, it is something that can never be taken from us. Nor is this essence of our being - this Fire - something merely passive. It is, in fact, an inherent reality of being that actively seeks us out and requires of us that we take account of it, respond to it and take our bearings from it.

And yet, as we are, we may not be able to respond to it. We may need to train ourselves to become so able. And this, to many, constitutes an intellectual stumbling block. Understanding that the right inner condition needs to be created for the 'unconditioned' essence of our being to reveal itself is paradoxical. If we were to rely on our logic alone to realise the truth of this paradox, we would not get very far.

The Zen Buddhists put it this way:

"You cannot get it by taking thought;
You cannot seek it without taking thought."[5]

In soul-on-Fire training, we use mind-body attunement and meditation to make access to that potential within us whose condition of being realised is already established, not depending on our personal preferences, our whims, our wishes or our efforts. The training involved is aimed at realising an unconditional requirement of being-consciousness that we need to fulfil before we can properly understand our need for it.

The first step in soul-on-Fire training involves letting go of everything that stands in the way of our realising the balance and harmony that enables our essential being to reveal itself to us. "Be still, and know that I am God."(6) This capacity to let go is developed through practice, yet what we realise when we do let go is something that is already there. Our work merely enables us to be receptive to it. It does the rest.

Through becoming receptive to the inherent Fire of our being, we learn so to let go of the effects of our past conditioning that the state we enter fits what is already there, like a key fits the lock that was made for it. Our starting point is the essence of being itself, that which, one way or another, prompts our search for it. Having undertaken this search, we discover what we were looking for. This state of unconditioned being, in turn, opens us up to the God-given wonders of our human potential.

The initial 'seeking' and 'finding' that we undertake is only a start. Let us proceed further.

THE JOURNEY HOME

When, through the practice of mind-body attunement and meditation, we realise that the source of our essential balance is also the source of our creative freedom, this, in turn, delivers us to our potential to be more and/or other than we presently know ourselves to be. We now learn how to use the pre-personal essence that we discover, to engage in work that is personal and value-realising. This work is self-defining. We undertake it not only through establishing - and maintaining - contact with the organic depths of our being, but also through self-reflective development of this same contact, in our relationship with others, in situations that we share with them, in the context of the all-encompassing world which everyone shares with everyone else.

While the practices of mind-body attunement and meditation involve detaching ourselves from others - from our relationship with them and our commitment to them - the practices of personal life journalling and focused speaking-and-listening involve reflecting on who and how we are, in these relationships and commitments.

The totality of our personal life involves living with who and how we are, in ourselves and in our circumstances. Soul-on-Fire training enables us to accept who and how we are, so that we can explore who and how we can be, according to our value-realising intent. Through the processes of attending, comparing, contrasting, understanding, evaluating and deciding, we reflect on what is and what can be, preparing ourselves to take action to realise what is ultimately good, for all concerned. Such training thus enables us to live a full life as a person among people. It enables us to live more freely, fully and creatively. It enables us to fine-tune our awareness and our understanding. It also enables us to continue our Fire-centred journey as far as the ultimate acceptance of our journey's end, beyond all personal boundaries.

To engage effectively in soul-on-Fire training, we need to recognise the goodness of rising above the self-defining process of being a person in a world that we share with other people, while at the same time using this capacity for transcendence fully to embrace our personal existence, without, at the same time, becoming totally trapped in it.

The decision to integrate our personal life within the essence of our being involves us in a process of inner purification. While the practices of mind-body attunement and meditation enable us to have no other aim but to be, these practices also ground us in a basic form of authentic self-experience. They enable us to experience a form of being-consciousness that is purified of all distortions, blocks and compromises. When, however, we proceed from this starting point to the task of deciding what to make of ourselves, as self-reflective persons, in the time and circumstances of our life, we discover that our capacity for unconditional surrender to the essence of our being sustains us, in moments of existential choice that might otherwise disorient us and lead us astray. Indeed, such disorientation may lead us to soul-on-Fire training, in the first place. It is through the inner purification that it effects in us that we are able to develop personal power and the courage to be.

Although our personal becoming is necessarily related to something other than our pure potential to be, this ground of possibility, within us, resonates 'more' or 'less' with possible avenues of value-realising growth and development. The direction in which we choose to grow and develop is, therefore, at best, co-determined by resonances of deeply felt personal integrity that spring from - and relate us back to - the self-regulating organic-spiritual unity of our being.

Becoming a person among people, in a world that is mediated by different kinds of meaning and is ordered by different sets of values, is a process that becomes ever more self-correcting and self-governing the more we observe and monitor the relationship between our being and our becoming, our essence and our existence, our potential to be many things and our actualisation of certain definite aims and values. This process involves our correcting and qualifying, from moment to moment, whatever in our thinking, evaluating, decision-making, acting and understanding shows itself to be inadequate to sustain the totality of our alive, value-realising being-in-the-world.

Our journey home - our journey of continuous personal transformation in the Fire of being - is not something that we need to undertake entirely unaided and alone. There are traditions of personal transformation that we can share with others, in our common quest to realise the highest good of our human potential. Others, like ourselves, asking similar questions to those that we are asking, evoke our hope, inspire us to understand what they understand, and stimulate us to follow a path that is similar to theirs. Such shared paths can be of inestimable value to us.

In the process of journeying within such a path, the unconditioned essence of our being (that cannot be intended by us) relates not only to our own awareness, choices and values, but also to the choices that others have made and the values that they embody. At best, this path - perhaps a living tradition - will offer us some overall understanding of the meaning and purpose of our personal journey, giving us a meaningful way to represent to ourselves the ultimate mystery within which we all participate.

We understand ourselves best in the process of change. Hence, the path that we choose to travel needs to teach us how to place both the intended and the unintended elements of our existence within a framework that draws them all together, from moment to moment.

This means that experiences made available to us, through the work undertaken by others, are able to lead us, through imaginative reconstruction of their experiences, to a meaningful understanding of our own. Thus we become able to realise a 'metacommunicative basis' for our reflections and actions. In line with the training and transformation that our chosen path involves, we become able to commit ourselves to spiritual-personal ideas that our shared path inspires us to embrace. We understand the pitfalls that could prevent us from realising these ideals and we resolve to avoid these pitfalls or to overcome them. This, too, we come to recognise as an integral part of our spiritual-personal destiny.

In the soul-on-Fire training and transformation outlined in this book, we have explored certain themes and issues. These relate to experiences generally shared by people in a similar condition. We have sought to understand the meaning and value of these themes and issues, in our own life experience. Now, in this final chapter, our experience and our understanding of ourselves have come full circle. And so, we turn, finally, to reflect upon the nature of the processes that we use to transform our understanding itself.

LIVING AT THE EDGE

To make contact with the essential self-regulating processes of our being is to gain a foothold in value-realising creative freedom. In focused speaking-and-listening, as in personal life journalling, we express what we experience, in an awareness-generating way, and by so doing we become able to explore deeper meanings and value dimensions within the particular focus that we select. It is not only the nature of our practice, but also the nature of our focus that make these dimensions accessible to us. In all this, we validate both the reality of our experience, and the reality of our commitment to the goals that inform our perceptions with value-realising intent. As we amplify and observe the processes that turn our experiences into value-bearing information, we discover our personal reality in the beliefs, expectations, attitudes and aims that both generated these experiences in the first place, and are now able to be expanded, deepened or transformed by our observing and re-evaluating the way that they function in us.

This is how we understand the way that soul-on-Fire training enables us to transform our psychological states. This transformation takes place both in relation to universal-essential dimensions and in relation to value-realising personal-historical dimensions. When we integrate these, one with the other, this places us within a universal-personal dimension that is, in effect, a new level of Self-understanding.

In seemingly negative phases of our life, we are forced to question deeply the meaning and value of what we are doing and what is happening to us. We are thus forced to become alive to new possibilities, or to suffer the almost unbearable consequences of continuing as we are. Taking the problems that we encounter in our life and converting them into the language of imagery, makes it possible for us to move our consciousness beyond the edge of a purely rational mind-set to a deeper pre-logical level of being-awareness. At this level, the inner movement of our being is able to become more clearly apparent to us.

At first, this inner movement seems to take us into a separate reality, yet, as we work with it, we come to realise that this reality had, in fact, been influencing our thoughts, feelings and actions, all the time, in an unconscious way. The problem of how to perceive and relate to this process - whose dynamics have been hidden from us - is solved by our using an indirect method to get in contact with it and work with it. As we engage with this process, our awareness of its true significance deepens, until, at last, we come to recognise it as the underlying reality of our personal existence. The Fire of our being is the Kingdom of Heaven within us. At this stage, it becomes, for us, the centre around which all else is destined to turn. In effect, being able to contact, follow and work with the processes of our soul on Fire changes our whole life.

In personal life journalling, as in focused speaking-and-listening, we find that we are not only able to bring the contents of our experience into a new perspective, but that we are also able to develop a new kind of interior relationship with these contents and with this perspective.

Going hand-in-hand with this development, participants in soul-on-Fire training are able to use criteria of attainment to assess their progress on the Fire-centred journey that they have embarked upon. These criteria constitute markers of growing understanding, control, personal development, Fire-centred transformation and value-realising creative freedom.

All the various practices that we undertake thus enable us consciously to work with processes that enable us to be who we are and become who we can be. We are also able to cross-reference these processes, relate them to one another, and allow them to feed into one another, like streams flowing into a river, uniting them all into a single mighty flow.

Because we are able to identify various kinds of inner movement occurring within us, in different perceptual channels, we are able to learn how to process these inner movements by identifying them, giving them expression in symbolic form, amplifying them, experimenting with them, seeing how they function in us, controlling them and/or allowing ourselves to be transformed by them.

The impact of soul-on-Fire training and transformation is cumulative. It enables us to pass through the critical impasse that stimulated the deeper questioning that brought us into this training, in the first place. It also enables us to journey beyond this impasse into a process of continuous psychological re-integration, which process brings us personal fulfilment, for as long as we live.

A purely intellectual appreciation of what this training is about leaves us existentially outside the process. Only entry into the training itself can bring us the results that we long for. By working with others who are on the same journey as ourselves, we are able to keep going, despite all obstacles, to the destiny that awaits us all, individually and collectively.

Notes, References and Suggested Reading

Chapter 1   *The Fire/Tao/Logos of Our Being*

1. "Just as operations by their intentionality make objects present to the subject, so also by consciousness they make the operating subject present to himself . . . . The object is present as what is gazed upon, attended to, intended. But the presence of a subject resides in the gazing, the attending, the intending." Lonergan, B.F. *Method in Theology*, Dartman, Longman & Todd, London 1971, p.8.

2. "If men are unable to perceive critically the *themes* of their time, and thus to intervene actively in reality, they are carried along in the wake of change. They see that the times are changing, but they are submerged in that change and so cannot discern its dramatic significance." Freire, P. *Education: the practice of freedom*, Writers & Readers Co-operative, London 1976, p.7.

3. "Symbols focus experience, meanings organise knowledge, guiding the surface perceptions of an instant no less than the aspirations of a life time." Mills, C.W. *Power, Politics and People*, Oxford University Press, 1967, pp.105-406.

4. "The bodies we perceive are, so to speak, cut out of the stuff of nature by our perception . . . marking lines along which action may be taken." Bergson, H. *Creative Evolution*, MacMillan, London 1928, p.31.

5. "Horizontal liberty is the exercise of liberty within a determinate horizon and from the basis of a corresponding existential stance. Vertical liberty is the exercise of liberty that selects that stance and the corresponding horizon." Lonergan, B.F. op.cit. p.31.

6. "The act of knowing involves a dialectical movement that goes from action to reflection and from reflection upon action to new action." Freire, P. *Cultural Action for Freedom*, Penguin, 1977, p.31.

7. In a different context, Paulo Freire expressed the following observation: "Illiterates know that they are concrete men. They know that they do things. What they do not know in the culture of silence - in which they are ambiguous, dual beings - is that men's actions as such are transforming, creative and recreative." Freire, P. ibid. p.30.

8. "The TAO, the course of nature, flows of itself. You can get the feel of it by breathing without doing anything to help the breath along. Let the breath out and let it come back by itself, when it feels like it. And then out again when it wants to go out. Keep this up until you are completely comfortable with letting it go its own way and you will notice that the rhythm slows down without the least effort - and at the same time becomes a little stronger. This happens because you are now 'with' the breath and no longer 'outside' it as controller. Something similar happens when you let thoughts, feelings and any other experiences follow their own course." Watts, A. *Cloud Hidden, Whereabouts Unknown*, Jonathan Cape, London 1974, p.29

9. Galatians 2:20

10. Mindell, A. *Working on Yourself Alone: Inner Dreambody Work*. Penguin Arkana, 1990, p.123.

11. "Spiritual symbolism is itself directed towards a true understanding of experience, given that human life itself achieves its highest meaning and fulfilment because of our work to unify it and to live within the unity that we have created." Berdyaev, N. *Freedom and the Spirit*, Centenary Press, London 1935, p.57.

12. The Gospel according to Thomas. Coptic text established and translated by A. Guillaumont, Henri-Charles Puech, Gilles Quispel, Walter Till and Yassah Abd Al Masih, Harper & Row, 1984, p.41

13. Finlay, J. *Merton's Palace of Nowhere*, Ave Maria Press, Indiana, USA 1978, p.31.

14. Castaneda, C. The *Power of Silence: Further Lessons of Don Juan.* Black Swan, 1989.
15. Suzuki, S. *Zen Mind, Beginner's Mind.* Weatherill, New York and Tokyo 1981.
16. Galatians 2:20.
17. "Consciousness seems proportionate to the living being's power of choice. It lights up the zone of potentialities that surrounds the act. It fills the gap between what is done and what might be done." Bergson, H. op.cit, p.189.
18. "The eye of the intellect can only evaluate the logic of one's reasoning on the basis of perceived feeling." Lowen, A. *Pleasure: A Creative Approach to Life.* Penguin, 1977, p.137.
19. "The being who is the object of his own reflection, in consequence of that very doubling back on himself becomes . . . able to raise himself to a new sphere. In reality, a new world is born." Teilhard de Chardin, P. *Let Me Explain.* Fontana, 1974, p.35.
20. Castaneda, C. *Journey Into Ixtlan: the Lessons of Don Juan.* Penguin, 1972, p.32.
21. Castaneda, C. *Tales of Power.* Penguin 1974, p.57.
22. Ibid, p.230.
23. Castaneda, C. *The Second Ring of Power.* Penguin, 1977, p.200.

Chapter 2   Being, Knowing, Loving the Fire

1. The Gospel according to Thomas. Coptic text established and translated by A. Guillaumont, Henri-Charles Puech, Gilles Quiepel, Walter Till and Yassah Abd Al Masih. Harper & Row, 1984, p.3.
2. "The spirit is neither the subject nor the object of the mind. It is the axis of experience, through which mentation and behaviour are mutually reflected." Campbell, R. *Fisherman's Guide: a system's approach to creativity and organisation.* Shambala, London 1985, p.154.

3. Mindell, A. *The Year I*. Penguin Arkana, 1989, p.65. "Psychological development begins with the development of a detached meta-communicator."

4. Miguel de Unamuno. *The Tragic Sense of Life*. Fontana, 1965, p.252.

5. For further understanding of this process Mindell, A. *City Shadows: psychological interventions in psychiatry*. Penguin Arkana, 1991, p.167.

6. "Creativity is . . . an ordering process, integrating towards unity." Hillman, J. *The myth of analysis: three essays in archetypal psychology*. Harper & Row, 1972, p.43.

7. Laing, R.D. "The Obvious" in *The Dialectics of Liberation* edited by David Cooper. Penguin, 1969.

8. Sogyal Rimpoche. *The Tibetan Book of Living and Dying*. Harper Collins, 1992.

9. See Mindell, A. *Dreambody; Dreambody in Relationship;* and *Working with the Dreaming Body*. Penguin Arkana, 1982, 1987 and 1989 respectively.

10. Ephesians 4:23.

11. Acts 17:24.

12. Chuang Tzu. Translated by Herbert Giles, Unwin, 1980.

13. Merton, T. *The Way of Chuang Tzu*. Burns & Oats, 1995.

14. John 1:5.

15. Mindell, A. *River's Way: the process science of the dreambody*. Penguin Arkana, 1985, p.140.

16. Weinberg, G. *Self Creation*. MacDonald & Janes, London 1978.

Chapter 3   Stalking and Mastering the Ways of Anxiety

1. "The Taoist view of life assumes that the way things are unfolding contains the basic elements necessary for solving basic human problems." Mindell, A. *Sitting in the Fire: large group transformation using*

conflict and diversity, Lao Tse Press, Portland, Oregon 1995, p.22.

2. "All through my therapy with patients, I alternate between expanding consciousness on a bodily level and heightening consciousness on a verbal level." Lowen, A. *Bioenergetics*, Coventure, London 1976, p.327.

3. "When a body is filled with stresses, the nervous system is so busy handling them that its potential for attaining higher states of consciousness is extremely limited. There is too much noise in the system, which prevents the nervous system from rising to a higher level." Bentov, I. *Stalking the Wild Pendulum: on the mechanics of consciousness*, Bantam, London, p.210.

4. Watts, A. *Cloud Hidden, Whereabouts Unknown*. Jonathan Cape, London 1974.

5. "Reality is made up of two components: one, an immutable reference line or background; and the other, a dynamic vibrating aspect of the same thing." Bentov, I. op.cit, p.106.

6. "Each of us possesses an innate protective mechanism against 'overstress', which allows us to turn off the harmful bodily effects of the fight or flight response. This response against overstress brings on bodily changes that decrease heart-rate, lower metabolism, decrease the rate of breathing, and bring the body back into what is probably a healthier balance. This is the Relaxation Response." Benson, H. Fountain, London 1976, p.18.

7. "The fully open system is capable of changing its goals and these changes are reproducible." Wilden, A. *Structure and System: essays in communication and exchange*. Tavistock Publications, 1977, p.148.

8. "The body-oriented practitioner uses information to organise the matter-energy of his own body so that he can get on with the business of living in it and with it." Wilden, A. op.cit, p.346.

9. "The essential feature of our intellect is to be a light for our conduct, to make us ready for action . . . to foresee for a given situation the events, favourable or unfavourable that may follow thereupon. Intellect, therefore . . . selects in a given situation whatever is like something already known." Bergson, H. *Creative Evolution*. MacMillan, London 1928, p.31.

Chapter 4   *Letting Go*
1. Lonergan, B.J.F. *Method in Theology*, Dartman, Longman & Todd 1975.
2. Weekes, C. *Agoraphobia: simple and effective treatment*, Angus & Robertson, London 1977.

Chapter 5   *We, Ourselves*
1. Lonergan, B.J.F. *Method of Theology*. Dartman, Longman & Todd, 1975.
2. Lonergan, B.J.F. *Insight: a study of human understanding*. Dartman, Longman & Todd, London 1983.
3. Volkart, E.H. *Social Behaviour & Personality: contribution of W.I. Thomas to theory and social research*. Social Science Research Council, New York 1951.
4. Bandler, R. and Grinder, J. *Frogs into Princes: neuro-linguistic programming*. Real People Press, Utah, USA 1979. "We claim that every piece of behaviour has a positive function. It is the best choice a person has in context . . . If you do systematic de-sensitisation, and you don't replace the 'negative' behavioural pattern with something positive, it takes a long time because the person will fight. It is their only defence. That's why it takes six months, because a person has to randomly put something else in its place." p.122.
5. Weekes, C. *Agoraphobia: simple effective treatment*. Op.cit.
6. See Maltz, M. *Psychocybernetics*. Prentice-Hall, New Jersey 1960. "Emile Coue, the little French pharmacist

who astonished the world around 1929 with the results he obtained with 'the power of suggestion', insisted that effort was the one big reason that most people failed to utilise their inner powers. 'Your suggestive [ideal goals] must be made without effort if they are to be effective,' he said. Another famous Coue saying was his Law of Reversed Effort: 'When the will and the imagination are in conflict, the imagination invariably wins the day'." p.55.

7. Segal, J. (ed.) *Mental Health Program Reports - 5.* National Institute of Mental Health, Rockville, Md. 1971.

8. Mills, C.W. 'The Cultural Apparatus' in *Power, Politics & People: the collected essays of C. Wright Mills.* Ed. I.L. Horowitz, Oxford University Press, 1963.

9. Barker, S. *The Alexander Technique: the revolutionary way to use your body for total energy.* Bantam Books, New York 1979.

10. See Fox, E. 'The Seven-day Mental Diet' from *Power Through Constructive Thinking.* Harper & Row, New York 1940.

11. See O'Brien, T. *Growth to maturity of person and love, the fullness of Christ and the fatherhood of God.* Guild Publications, London 1982.

12. See Kenton, L. and Kenton, S. *Raw Energy.* Century Publishing Co., London 1985.

13. Ashby, W.R. *An Introduction to Cybernetics.* University Paperbacks, Methuen, London 1964.

MY RARE DISEASE

I'm very, very, very 'sick',
How bad, is not quite clear.
I suffer from a rare disease,
An awful thing called fear.
I suffer from it all the time,
No one as bad as me.
It's so distressing that I am
Depressed as I can be.
It saps my strength,
And makes me feel

That I am going 'queer'.
It's worse that anything to have
This nasty thing called fear.
It makes me scared to be alone,
Yet folks fill me with dread.
I don't know which I fear the most,
Getting up, or going to bed.

I quake and tremble, shake and sweat,
Each day I worry more.
I've some new symptom every hour
With muscles always sore.
Inside the house I'm all on edge,
I'm terrified going out,
And I can never understand
What it is all about.
To supermarket I can't go
Nor can I go to Mass.
I have to wait for hours and hours
For my panic spell to pass.
And pass it does with God's good help.
But I'd be a millionaire,
To have a pound for every time,
I've given in to fear.

Sometimes my hands won't move for me,
Most times, it is my feet.
I find it hard to get my breath,
To swallow, or to eat.
My ears start buzzing, eyes go blurred,
I'm sure that I will fall.
I find it hard to concentrate,
Most days, can't think at all.
I cannot ride on bus or train,
I 'panic' going by car,
And not for me an aeroplane,
Nor can I walk too far.
I cannot ride inside a lift,
I gasp and gulp for air,
And I get such palpitations
When climbing up a stair.

My 'loved ones' they had sympathy,
When first my pains began.
I say 'loved ones' with tongue in cheek,
Now, they don't give a damn.
I've taken multi-coloured pills,
And capsules round and square.
I've been on highs, I've been on lows,
I've been most everywhere.
So if anyone has this disease,
And thinks he's going queer,
Don't ever worry, all you've got
Is a nasty thing called fear.
And though you tremble, shake and sweat,
Feel panic, faint, the lot,
Don't worry, friend, for I've been there,
And it's only fear you've got.

And fear can never harm you,
And you won't faint or fall.,
Don't let the panic bother you
It's only fear, that's all.
And pass it will in God's good time.
Hold out your hand, He's there.
And one by one, get off those pills,
The round ones and the square.

Anonymous

Chapter 6   *Love's Body*

1. Brown, N.O. *Life Against Death*. Sphere Publications, 1970, p.278.
2. *The Bhagavad Gita*, translated by Juan Mascaro. Penguin, 1972.
3. *Bhagavad Gita*, text and commentary by Swami Sivananda. Sivananda Press, Durban, 1968.

Chapter 7   *Hatha Yoga - The Practice of Mind-Body Attunement*

1. The concept of homeostasis as it is usually used, excludes self-differentiating and self-organising open systems (such as minds) which import energy from the environment to fuel the changing orders of

organisation in the system. . . . The mind has an essential feature that goes beyond the power of a self-establishing system: the power to create new structures." Wilden, A. *System and Structure: essays in communication and exchange*. Tavistock Publications, 1977, p.140.

2. "By individuation of the self in the depths of the self, the living element, which heretofore has been spread out over a diffuse circle of perceptions and activities, is constituted . . . as a centre in the form of a point at which all impressions knit themselves together and fuse into a unity that is conscious of its own organisation." Teilhard de Chardin, P. *Let Me Explain*. Fontana, 1974, p.35.

3. "To know your mind is really to know what you want or what you feel. . . . To lose your mind . . . is not to know what you feel. This happens when the mind is overwhelmed with feelings it cannot accept and dare not focus upon." Lowen, A. *Bioenergetics*. Coventure, London 1976, p.64.

4. "Spiritual life is life in truth, goodness and beauty that overcomes tensions that exist between mind and body, between thinking and emotional forces, between awareness and inner stress, or between unconsciousness and external pressures." Bertyaev, N. *Freedom and the Spirit*. The Centenary Press, London 1935, pp.46-7.

5. Quoted by Venkatessananda in *The Undivided Self*. Chiltern Publications, Elgin, Cape, South Africa 1971.

6. Psalm 46.

7. Lonergan, B.J. *Method in Theology*. Dartman, Longman & Todd, London 1971.

8. "Inadequate respiration produces anxiety, irritability and tension." Lowen, A. *Pleasure: a creative approach to life*. Penguin, 1977, p.39.

9. "Why do so many people have difficulty breathing fully and easily? The answer is that breathing creates feelings and people are afraid to feel." Ibid., p.39.
10. "The depth of breathing reflects the emotional health of the person." Ibid., p.43.
11. "The diaphragm is the main respiratory muscle and its action is very much subject to emotional stress. It reacts to situations of stress by contracting. If the reaction becomes chronic, a predisposition to anxiety is created." Lowen, A. Ibid., p.244
12. "Because the voice is so closely tied to feeling, freeing it involves the mobilisation of suppressed feelings and their expression in sound." Lowen, A. Ibid., p.273.
13. "We convulse with laughter, cry with pain or sorrow, tremble with anger, leap for joy and smile with pleasure. Because these are spontaneous, unwilled or involuntary actions, they move us in a deep, meaningful way." Lowen, A. Ibid., p.244.

Chapter 8   Use-Perception and Creative Freedom
1. "The aim of education on a general basis is to bring about at all times and for all purposes, not a series of correct positions or postures, but a co-ordinated Use of the mechanisms in general." Alexander, F.M. *The Resurrection of the Body*. Delta, New York 1978, p.15
2. Barlow, W. *The Alexander Principle*. Arrow Books, London 1979, p.37.

Chapter 9   The Living Flame of Love
1. St John of the Cross. 'The Dark Night' in *The Collected Works of St John of the Cross*, translated by Kieran Cavanagh and Otillio Rodriguez, Institute of Carmelite Studies, Washington D.C., 1979, p.711.
2. Galatians 2:20.
3. Gita 2:29.
4. 2 Peter 1:4.
5. Paul in Acts 17:28.

6. Keyes, K. *Handbook to Higher Consciousness.* Living Love Publications, 1979.
7. St John of the Cross. 'The Living Flame' in *The Collected Works* op.cit., p.717.
8. Mindell, A. *Working on Yourself Alone: inner dreambody work.* Arkana, 1990.
9. St Francis of Assisi quoted by Louis Lavelle in *The Meaning of Holiness.* Catholic Book Club, London 1991.
10. Ram Dass. *Be Here Now.*
11. Mindell, A. op.cit.
12. Philippians 2:5-8.
13. Mindell, A. op.cit., p.44.

Chapter 10 Meditation, Choiceless Awareness and Creative Freedom

1. Venkatessananda, Swami. *The Undivided Self.* Chiltern Publications, Elgin, Cape, South Africa 1972.
2. Mears, A. *Strange Places, Simple Truths.* Fontana, 1973. (Mears refers to the unconditioned state realised in meditation as an 'undifferentiated state' of awareness, p.32.)
3. "No rational explanation can account for our centredness in meditation, for reason divides and creates diversity out of unity while meditation replaces diversity with unity." Finlay, J. *The Awakening Call.* Ave Maria Press, Notre Dame, Indiana 1984, p.111.
4. St John of The Cross. "Stanzas concerning an ecstasy experienced in high exaltation" in *The Collected Works of St John of The Cross*, translated by Kieran Kavanough and Ottilio Rodriguez. ICS Publications, Washington D.C., 1979.
5. Tennyson. "Crossing the Bar" in *Tennyson: a selection by W.E. Williams.* Penguin, 1953.
6. St John of The Cross. "Commentary applied to spiritual things" in *The Collected Works*, c.f.(4).

7. St John of The Cross. "The Dark Night" in *The Collected Works*, c.f. (4).

8. "In order to achieve a new balance and direction we need to be able to make available an adequate supply of 'free energy', that is to say, we need to discover within ourselves an uncommitted potential for change." Wilden, A. *Structure and System: essays in communication and exchange*. Tavistock Publications, 1977, p.219.

9. "In meditation something happens deep inside. An undoing takes place, moving us irrevocably away from our attachments and defences and our clinging to any security that is not rooted in deep spiritual meaning and value." Finlay, J. op.cit., p.45.

10. Robert Duncan. "Often I am permitted to return to a meadow" in *Opening of the Field*. McClelland & Stewart, Toronto 1960.

11. St John of The Cross. "Commentary applied to spiritual things" in *The Collected Works*, c.f.(4).

12. "The mystical function is to awaken and maintain in the individual a sense of awe and gratitude in relation to the mystery dimension of the universe, not so he lives in fear of it, but so that he recognises that he participates in it, since the mystery of being is the mystery of this own deep being as well." Campbell, J. *Myths to Live By*. Bantam, 1988, c.f.(10).

13. St John at Ephesus, quoted by Duncan, c.f.(10).

14. St John of The Cross. "Songs of the soul in rapture at the height of perfection, which is union with God by the road of spiritual negation", translated by Roy Campbell in *The Poems of St John of The Cross*. Penguin, 1968.

15. Benson, H. *The Relaxation Response*. Fountain Books, 1976.

16. St John of The Cross. "Songs between the soul and the bridegroom", translated by Roy Campbell in *Poems*, c.f.(10).

17. See Jackins, H. *The Human Side of Human Beings*. Rational Island Publications, 1978.
18. St John of The Cross. "Stanzas concerning an ecstasy experienced in high contemplation", translated by Kavanough & Rodriguez, c.f.(4).
19. See Trungpa, C. *Cutting Through Spiritual Materialism*. Shambala, London 1973.
20. St John of The Cross. "Commentary applied to spiritual things" in *The Collected Works*, c.f.(14).
21. Johnston, W. *Being in Love: the practice of Christian prayer*. Fontana, 1988.
22. St John of The Cross. "Commentary applied to spiritual things" in *The Collected Works*, c.f.(14).
23. St John of The Cross. "Song of the soul that is glad to know God by faith", translated by Roy Campbell in *Poems*, c.f.(14).
24. A poem quoted in Watts, A. *The Way of Zen*. Penguin, 1965.
25. St John of The Cross. "Song of the soul that is glad to know God by faith", translated by Roy Campbell in *Poems*, c.f.(14).
26. St John of The Cross. "Verses written after an ecstasy in high exaltation" translated by Roy Campbell in *Poems*, c.f.(14).
27. St John of The Cross, "Stanzas concerning an ecstasy experienced in high contemplation", translated by Cavanaugh & Rodriguez, c.f.(4).
28. St John of The Cross, "Verses about the soul which suffers with impatience to see God", translated by Roy Campbell in *Poems*, c.f.(14).
29. Jackins, H. op.cit.
30. Brenan, G. *St John of The Cross: his life in poetry*. Cambridge University Press, 1973.
31. Naranjo, C. and Ornstein, R.E. *On the Psychology of Meditation*. Penguin, 1977.
32. Le Shan, L. *Alternative Realities*. Ballantine Books, Toronto 1976.

33. Johnston, W. *Silent Music: the science of meditation.* Fontana, 1977.
34. Johnston, W. *Selected Poems.* Faber, 1961. In which he has a couple of lines that express the way I feel about Juan de la Cruz:
"He is the transparence of the place in which
He is and in His presence we find peace."

Chapter 11   *The Inner Eye of Love*
1. Reich, W. *Listen, Little Man!* Penguin, 1979, p.35.
2. Trungpa, C. *The Myth of Freedom and the Way of Meditation.* Shambala, London 1976.
3. Patanjali. *How to Know God: the yoga aphorisms of Patanjali.* Translated by Swami Prabhavananda and Christopher Isherwood, Mentor. 1969.
4. Merton, T. *The Way of Chuang Tzu.* Burns & Oats, 1995, p.133.
6. Matthew 13:24-30.

Chapter 12   *Keeping a Personal Life Book*
1. Lonergan, B.J. *Method in Theology.* Dartman, Longman & Todd, 1971.
2. O'Brien, T. *Growth to maturity of person and love: the fullness of Christ and the fatherhood of God.* Guild Publications, London 1982.
3. "Maturity in thinking does not mean reaching the end of one's thinking, but rather the state in which the human power of thought is at one's disposal." Tillich, P. *The Boundaries of Our Being.* Fontana, 1973, p.127.
4. "Symbols develop precisely because there are two worlds and two orders of being, and the symbol itself functions to reveal to us that the meaning of the one world and order of being is to be found in the other. Symbols relate these two worlds to one another and unite them." Berdyaev, N. *Freedom and the Spirit.* The Centenary Press, London 1935, p.52.

5. "The orientation of spirit determines the character of consciousness which, in turn, decides the nature of knowledge." Berdyaev, N. op.cit., p.4.

6. "Every insight is both a priori and synthetic. It is a priori, for it goes beyond what is merely given to sense of empirical consciousness. It is synthetic for it adds to the merely given an explanatory unification or organisation." Lonergan, B. *Insight: a study of human understanding*. Dartman, Longman & Todd, 1971, p.xi.

7. In a similar way, Jung spoke of the archetypes having 'their own initiative and their own specific energy'. C.G. Jung, *Man and His Symbols*. Aldus Books, London 1964, p.79.

8. "One cannot apprehend a symbol unless one is able to awaken, in one's own being, the spiritual resonances which respond to the symbol, not only as sign but as 'sacrament' and 'presence'. The symbol is an object pointing to a subject. We are summoned to a deeper spiritual awareness . . . beyond the level of subject and object." Merton, T. 'Symbolism: Communication or Communion' in *New Directions*, 20, pp.11-12, New York 1968.

9. Freud, in a different context, wrote: "The patient does not remember anything of what he has forgotten or repressed, but acts it out. He reproduces it not as memory but as action; he repeats it without, of course, knowing that he is repeating it." Freud, S., 'Remembering, Repeating and Working Through' in *The Complete Works of Sigmund Freud*, Vol.XII, p.151, edited by James Starkey, Hogarth, London 1953.

10. "The past is always remembered, represented, just as the Other is remembered, represented. Time is lost and regained, it is subject, object and relationship in itself. Montaigne speaks to his past, and the past replies with advice about the future, for human time is not chronological but dialectic." Wilden, A.,

Structure and System: essays in communication and exchange. Tavistock Publications, 1977, p.100.
11. O'Brien, T. op.cit.

Chapter 13   Here Comes Everyone
1. Merton, Thomas, quoted by Finlay, J. in *Merton's Palace of Nowhere*, Ave Maria Press, 1978, p.109.
2. Kurtz, R. *Hakomi*, Hakomi Institute, 1984.
3. Suzuki, S. *Zen Mind, Beginner's Mind*. Weatherhill, 1981, p.84.
4. Castaneda, C. *Tales of Power*. Penguin, 1975, p.56.
5. Guillaume Apollinaire, quoted by Edwards, G. in *Living Magically*, Piatkus, London 1991, p.223.
6. Castaneda C. *Tales of Power*. Op cit. p.190.

Chapter 14   Focused Speaking and Listening Guide
1. Merton, T. *The New Man*, Bantam Books, London 1981, p.53.
2. "To be able to go out to the other, you must have a starting place, you must have been, must be, with yourself." Buber, M. *Between Man and Man*, Fontana, 1969, p.39.
3. "It is socially fashionable to ask 'Who am I?'. There is no little 'real self' inside of me. I am who I am committed to be." Powell, J. *Why am I afraid to tell you who I really am?* Fontana, 1978, p.106.
4. "Human beings are active beings, capable of reflection on themselves and on the activity in which they are engaged. They are able to detach themselves from the world in order to find their place in it and with it. Only people are capable of this act of 'separation' in order to find their place in the world and enter in a critical way into their own reality." Freire, P. *Education: the practice of freedom*. Readers' & Writers' Publishing Co-operative, London 1976, p.103.
5. "The capacity for speech seems to be the basis of one's selfhood. Only a man turns and speaks to

another as a being existing for himself as well as in independent otherness and therefore capable of genuine conversation, of personal correspondence. Speech is a journey to the dwelling of other men." Pfuetze, P.E. *Self, Society, Existence*. Harper, New York 1961, p.301.

6. "Whatever cuts a man off from himself cuts him off from other people." Versveld, M. *Persons*. Buren Publishers, Cape Town 1972, p.141.

7. "Simplicity is no more than being ourself, knowing that we are loved." Vanier, J. *Community and Growth*. Dartman, Longman & Todd, 1979, p.19.

8. "What are some of the attitudes that we can extend to another person that we are listening to that will generally contradict their distresses? One of them is approval. I now look approvingly at you . . . Another is delight. I shall be delighted with you . . . Take an attitude of respect. Listen as if the person's words and what they have to say and how they are feeling are worthy of full consideration." Jackins, H. *Fundamentals of co-counselling manual*. Rational Island Publications, Seattle 1982, p.52.

Chapter 15   Continuing the Fire-Centred Journey

1. "As kingfishers catch fire" in *Selected Poems of J.M. Hopkins*, ed. James Reeves, Heinemann, London 1970, p.52.
2. Luke 12:31.
3. Luke 17:21.
4. Luke 4:18.
5. Zenrin poem quoted by Alan Watts in *The Way of Zen*. Penguin, 1965, p.156.
6. Psalm 46.